OPERATION DRAGOON

THE ALLIED LIBERATION OF THE SOUTH OF FRANCE: 1944

ROBIN CROSS

PEGASUS BOOKS
NEW YORK LONDON

OPERATION DRAGOON

Pegasus Books Ltd.
148 W 37th Street, 13th Floor
New York, NY 10018

First Pegasus Books edition March 2019

Interior design by Maria Fernandez

Library of Congress Cataloging-in-Publication Data is available.

ISBN: 978-1-68177-860-0

10 9 8 7 6 5 4 3 2 1

Printed in the United States of America
Distributed by W. W. Norton & Company, Inc.
www.pegasusbooks.us

To the men of 36th Division

CONTENTS

Paris
MARNE
MEUSE
BAS-RHIN
SEINE-ET-MARNE
MEURTHE-ET-MOSELLE
GERMANY
AUBE
VOSGES
HAUTE-MARNE
LOIRET
YONNE
HAUT-RHIN
HAUTE-SAÔNE
CÔTE-D'OR
DOUBS
CHER
NIEVRE
Demarcation Line
SWITZERLAND
SAONE-ET-LOIRE
JURA
Lake Geneva
Montluçon
ALLIER
Geneva
Vichy
AIN
CREUSE
HAUTES-SAVOIE
RHÔNE
PUY-DE-DÔME
LOIRE
Lyon
R-1
Clermont-Ferrand
CORRÈZE
SAVOIE
R-6
ISÈRE
Grenoble
CANTAL
HAUTE-LOIRE
ITALY
R. Rhône
Valence
ARDÈCHE
DRÔME
HAUTES-ALPES
Gap
LOZÈRE
AVEYRON
Digne
R-3
VAUCLUSE
BASSES-ALPES
GARD
Avignon
ALPES-MARITIMES
Apt
TARN
R-2
Nice
BOUCHES-DU-RHÔNE
Cannes
HÉRAULT
VAR
Montpellier
AUDE
Sète
Marseille
Carcassonne
Toulon
Narbonne
ANVIL Landings
SOUTH-EAST FRANCE
The Resistance areas south of the Demarcation Line which divided Occupied from Unoccupied France, 1940–42. R-1 and R-2 are the Dragoon invasion area.
0 20 40 60 80 miles
Paris
FRANCE

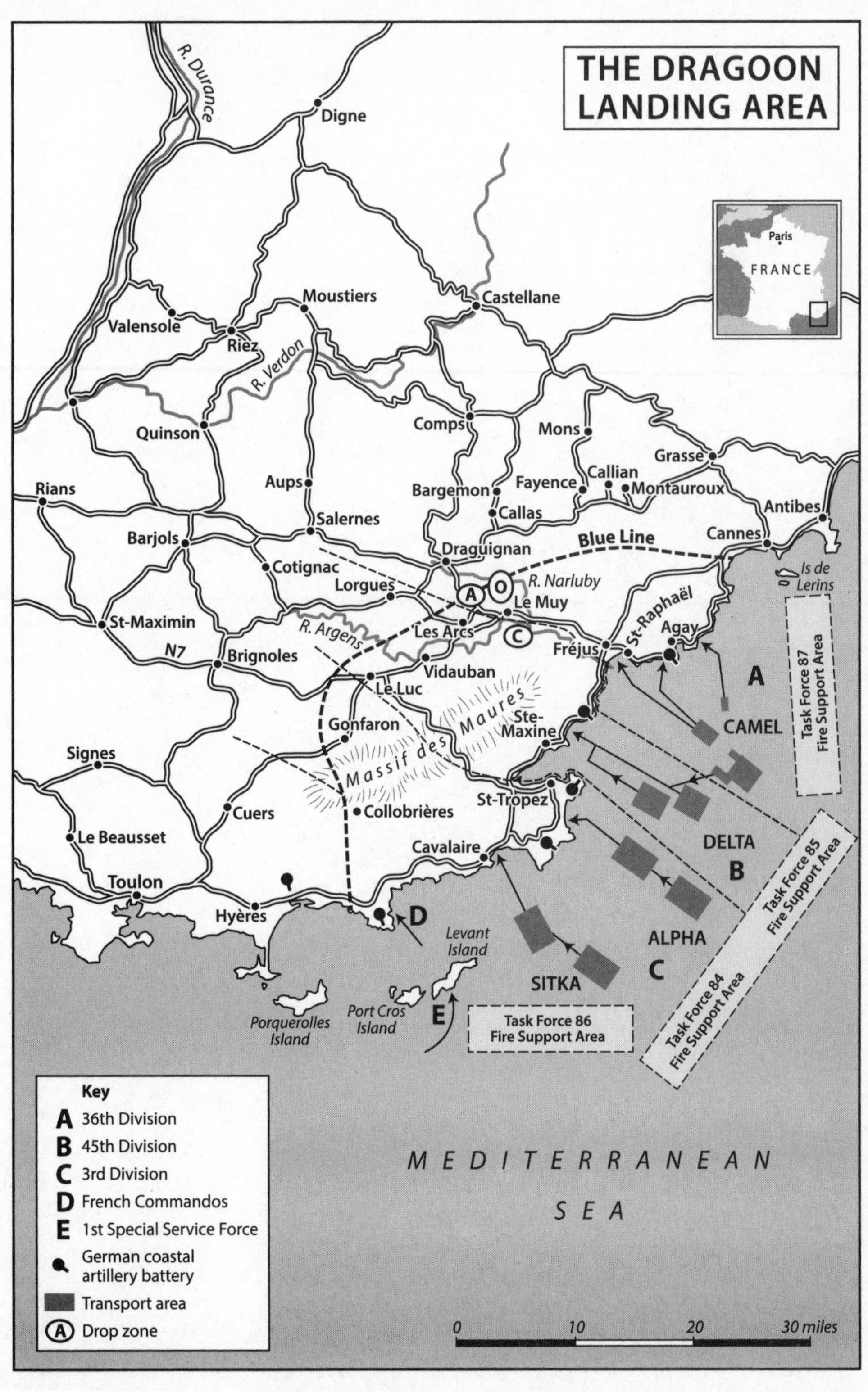
THE DRAGOON LANDING AREA
R. Durance
Digne
Paris
FRANCE
Moustiers
Castellane
Valensole
Riez
R. Verdon
Quinson
Comps
Mons
Grasse
Rians
Aups
Bargemon
Fayence
Callian
Montauroux
Callas
Antibes
Salernes
Barjols
Draguignan
Blue Line
Cannes
Cotignac
R. Narluby
Is de Lerins
Lorgues
Le Muy
St-Raphaël
St-Maximin
R. Argens
Les Arcs
Agay
N7
Brignoles
Fréjus
Vidauban
Le Luc
A
CAMEL
Massif des Maures
Ste-Maxine
Gonfaron
Task Force 87 Fire Support Area
Signes
Cuers
St-Tropez
Collobrières
Le Beausset
DELTA
Cavalaire
B
Toulon
Task Force 85 Fire Support Area
Hyères
D
ALPHA
Levant Island
C
SITKA
Port Cros Island
Porquerolles Island
E
Task Force 86 Fire Support Area
Task Force 84 Fire Support Area
Key
A 36th Division
B 45th Division
C 3rd Division
D French Commandos
E 1st Special Service Force
German coastal artillery battery
Transport area
A Drop zone
MEDITERRANEAN SEA
0 10 20 30 miles

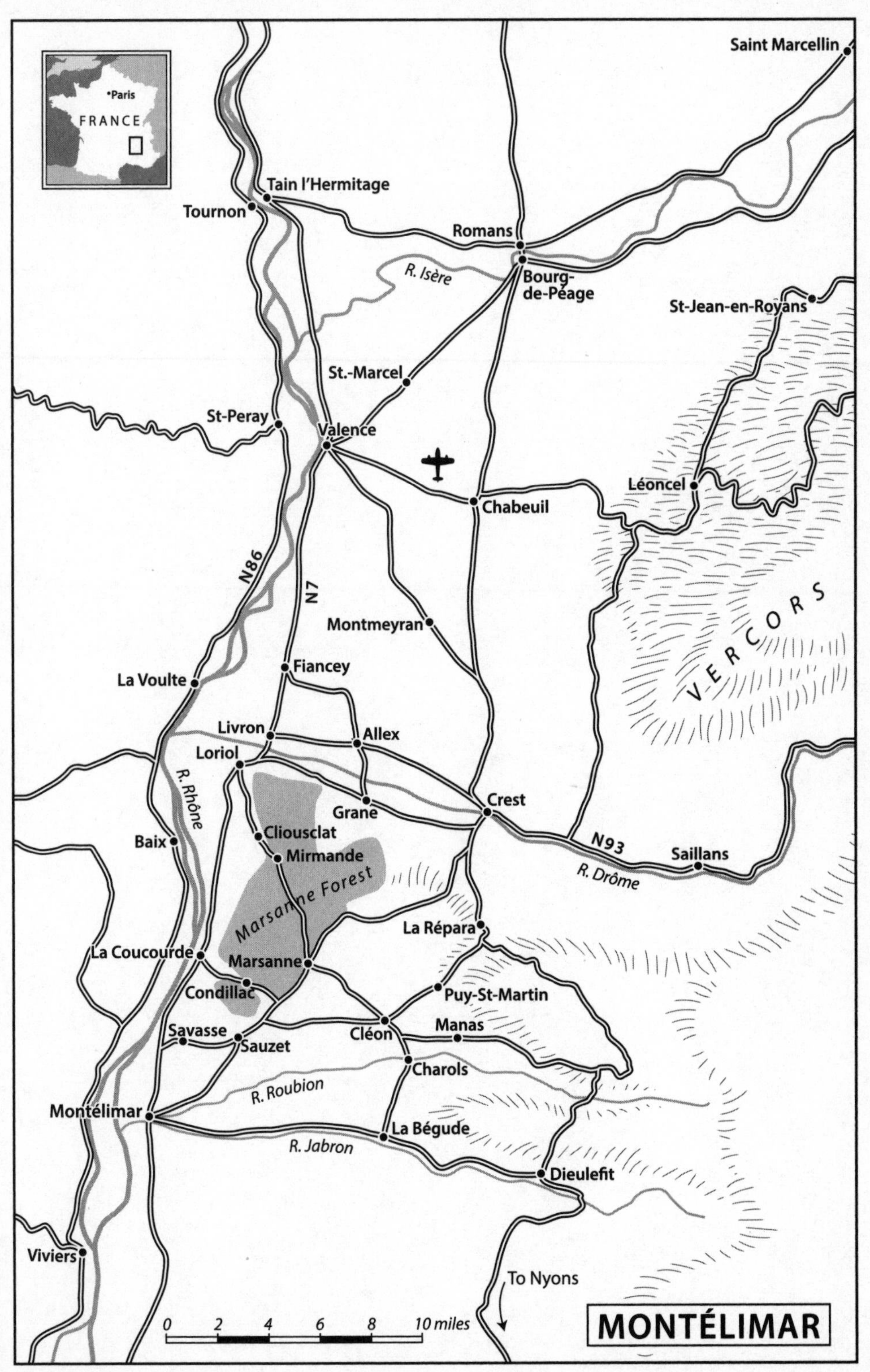

Paris
FRANCE
Saint Marcellin
Tain l'Hermitage
Tournon
Romans
R. Isère
Bourg-de-Péage
St-Jean-en-Royans
St.-Marcel
St-Peray
Valence
Léoncel
Chabeuil
N86
N7
VERCORS
Montmeyran
Fiancey
La Voulte
Livron
Allex
Loriol
R. Rhône
Crest
Grane
Cliousclat
Baix
Mirmande
N93
Saillans
R. Drôme
Marsanne Forest
La Répara
La Coucourde
Marsanne
Condillac
Puy-St-Martin
Savasse
Sauzet
Cléon
Manas
Charols
R. Roubion
Montélimar
La Bégude
R. Jabron
Dieulefit
Viviers
To Nyons
0 2 4 6 8 10 miles
MONTÉLIMAR

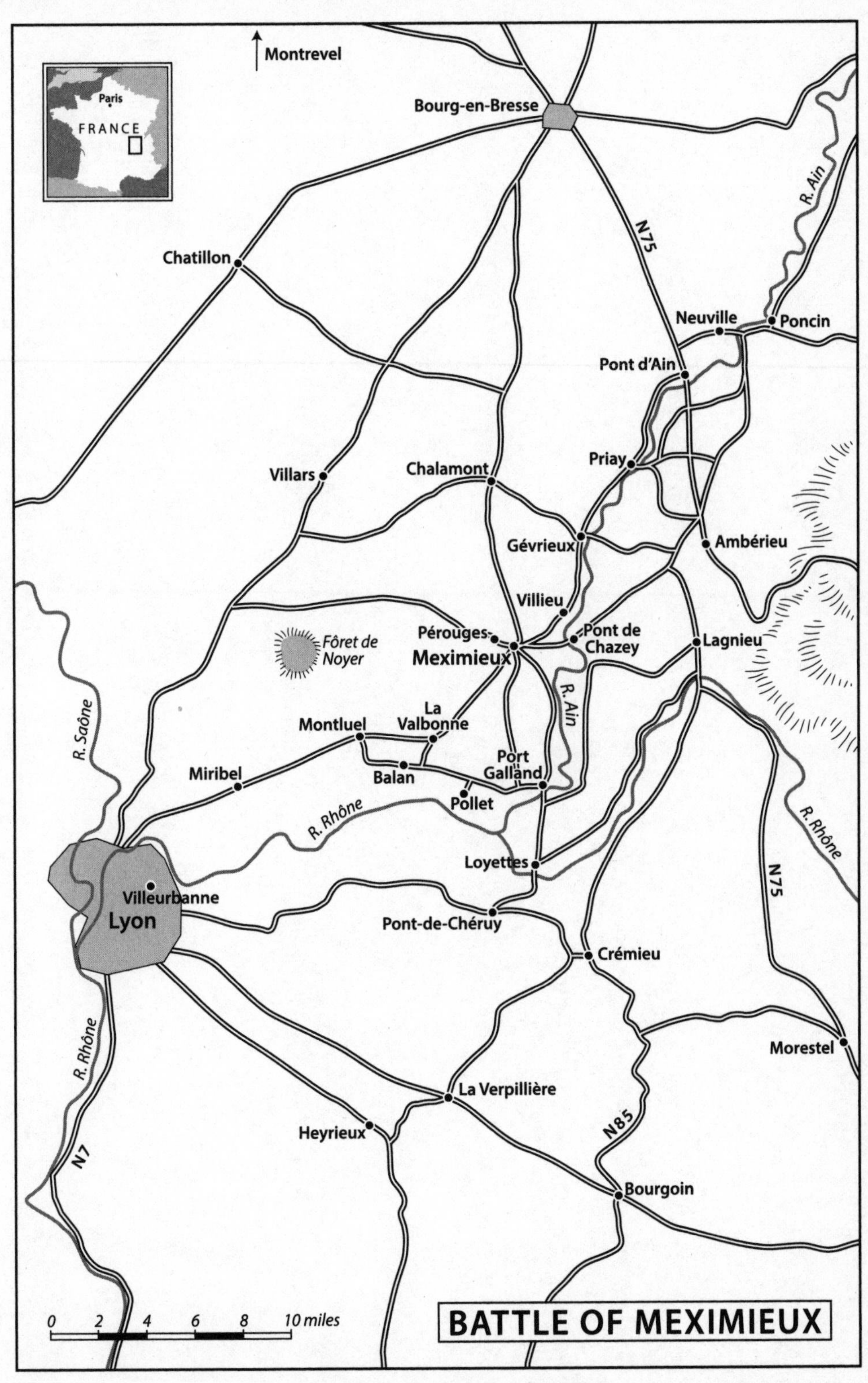
Montrevel
Paris
FRANCE
Bourg-en-Bresse
R. Ain
N75
Chatillon
Neuville
Poncin
Pont d'Ain
Priay
Villars
Chalamont
Gévrieux
Ambérieu
Villieu
Pérouges
Meximieux
Pont de Chazey
Lagnieu
Fôret de Noyer
R. Ain
R. Saône
La Valbonne
Montluel
Miribel
Balan
Port Galland
Pollet
R. Rhône
R. Rhône
Loyettes
Villeurbanne
Lyon
Pont-de-Chéruy
N75
Crémieu
Morestel
R. Rhône
La Verpillière
N85
Heyrieux
N7
Bourgoin
0 2 4 6 8 10 miles
BATTLE OF MEXIMIEUX

INTRODUCTION

Operation "Dragoon," the Allied invasion of the South of France, was for a long time overshadowed by Operation "Overlord," the invasion of Normandy, which preceded Dragoon by over two months. However, in recent years the publication of a number of books has rekindled interest in Dragoon, which in John Keegan's magisterial history of World War II occupies only a few lines. The genesis and gestation of Dragoon nevertheless throws an intriguing light on Anglo-American relations from the autumn of 1943 to the early summer of 1944, and reveals much about the tensions between the two high commands and their political masters during those critical wartime years.

The British contribution to Dragoon, with the exception of the Royal Navy, the Royal Air Force, and a parachute brigade, was relatively slight. French participation, although vital for both military and diplomatic reasons, often proved problematic in the field, and tested the man-management skills of the American high command almost to destruction. The operation's ultimate success depended, in the final analysis, on the flexibility of the U.S. Army's command structure operating in conjunction with its French allies and with the often highly irregular input of British and American special forces—respectively, the Special Operations Executive (SOE) and the Office of Strategic Services (OSS). In a fast-moving campaign, the Allied cause was immeasurably helped by men like the OSS's Geoffrey Jones and SOE's Francis Cammaerts, and the remarkable agent Christine Granville. Their part in the Dragoon story, and that of the French Resistance, will receive the attention they merit. As part of this strand, a spotlight will focus on the significant role played in Allied decision-making by the interception and decryption of encoded German Enigma traffic, the so-called "Ultra" secret.

These elements, singly and severally, played a significant part in Operation Dragoon, alongside the key decisions made by Allied commanders like Generals Patch, Truscott, Devers, and Butler, and their subordinates. Generous space is also given to their German counterparts, among them Generals Blaskowitz, Wiese, and Wietersheim, who strove to prevent a serious reverse from descending into a rout during an epic withdrawal from the French Riviera through the eye of a needle at Montélimar and into the Vosges Mountains. The role of the ordinary soldier—from grizzled German veterans of the Eastern Front to Texas farmboys and African Americans following the fighting on burial details—is a constant theme, taking us from the landings on Riviera vacation beaches to the fogbound autumnal clashes in the Vosges Mountains that closed the curtain on Operation Dragoon.

Above all, Dragoon presents a panoramic picture of the military and industrial might, the greater part of it American, which hastened victory in the West: the logistics that lay behind it; the key decisions that secured it; and the personnel who made it happen. In writing this book I owe a great debt of thanks to the eminent historian Steven Zaloga, who supplied the illustrations and much advice, and Stephen Dew, who drew the maps. I would also like to thank another distinguished historian, Simon Dunstan, for his sound counsel throughout the project. Thanks are also due to the 36th Division's archives in Austin, Texas, which yielded much detail on the course of the campaign from first to last. I am also grateful to Robert Maxham for his invaluable help in the 36th Division archives and to Jean-Loup Gassend for permission to quote material from his his *Operation Dragoon, Autopsy of a Battle, The Allied Liberation of the French Riviera, August–September 1944*.

—Robin Cross
Broxbourne, 2018

ONE
LOST VICTORIES

> "Sir, it is my duty to report that the Tunisian campaign is over. All enemy resistance has ceased. We are the masters of the North African shores."
>
> —Telegram from General Sir Harold Alexander, commander 18th Army Group, to Winston Churchill, May 13, 1943

The period between November 1942 and August 1943 was, for Adolf Hitler's Germany, one of almost unmitigated disaster. It began with the Allied victory in North Africa at El Alamein in November 1942, followed five days later by the Anglo-American "Torch" landings in Morocco and Algeria, and continuing with the destruction of the German 6th Army at Stalingrad in February 1943. In May 1943, German and Italian forces in Tunisia surrendered to the Allies, and Admiral Dönitz's U-boat "wolfpacks" were withdrawn from the North Atlantic after suffering heavy losses. Two months later, in July 1943, the collapse of Operation "Citadel," the summer offensive in the western Soviet Union by the German Army in the East (*Ostheer*), and the Allied invasion of Sicily, delivered a double body blow to the Third Reich. And finally, on the night of August 2 the last of four raids by the RAF Bomber Command concluded the Battle of Hamburg, during which, on the night of July 27, 729 bombers created a firestorm that engulfed four square miles of the eastern part of the city, prompting Hitler's minister of propaganda, Joseph Goebbels, to describe the attack as "a catastrophe, the extent of which staggers the imagination."

On July 19, 1940, flushed with victory in the Battle of France, Adolf Hitler had convened the Reichstag in the Kroll Opera House in Berlin to witness the creation of twelve field marshals. At the end of a long speech he told the assembled puppet deputies: "In this hour I feel it to be my duty to appeal once more to reason and to common sense in Great Britain, as much as elsewhere. I consider myself in a position to make this appeal since I am not the vanquished begging favors, but the victor speaking out in the name of reason. I see no reason why this war should go on."

But it did go on, and in time Hitler acquired enemies vastly more powerful than the British. On January 30, 1943, in circumstances very different from those that accompanied his triumphal gesture of July 1940, Hitler created a single new field marshal, promoting Colonel General Friedrich von Paulus, commander of the German 6th Army encircled on the Volga in the Soviet city of Stalingrad.

No German field marshal had ever surrendered. In effect, Hitler had pressed a suicide pistol into Paulus's unsteady hand. The new field marshal did not pull the trigger. At 0745 on January 31, a young Red Army tank lieutenant, Fyodor Mikhailovich Yelchenko, and fifteen of his men stepped into Paulus's dank and crowded headquarters in the basement of Stalingrad's ruined Univermag department store. Two hours later Major General Ivan Laskin, chief of staff to the Soviet 64th Army, arrived to take Paulus's formal surrender. Fifteen generals went into captivity with him. Two days later the last German troops holding out in the northern part of Stalingrad laid down their arms.

In the Stalingrad pocket the Ostheer lost twenty divisions and over 200,000 men. Of the 108,000 who trudged into captivity, only 5,000 survived the war. Six more divisions—two of them Luftwaffe—had been destroyed outside the Red Army encirclement. Germany's allies on the Stalingrad front, the Italians, Romanians, and Hungarians, lost four armies, 450,000 men, and any desire they once might have had to play an active role in Hitler's war against Bolshevism.

Field Marshal Erich von Manstein, commander of Army Group Don, had failed to relieve Stalingrad but was able to persuade a temporarily unnerved Hitler to allow him to conduct an orderly withdrawal and then launch a successful counterattack (against odds of approximately eight to one) to reestablish a defensive line by March 1943. However, this textbook operation, which demonstrated the Ostheer's continued tactical superiority in mobile operations, acted merely as the prelude to the debacle at Kursk in the summer of 1943.

Half a world away, in December 1941, in the aftermath of the Japanese attack on Pearl Harbor, the British prime minister Winston Churchill visited Washington for the "Arcadia" conference. There for the first time the British and Americans, both of whom were yet to experience the humbling onslaught of the Japanese in the Far East and the Pacific, met as joint combatants to agree on strategic war aims. For the moment, the two allies met as equal partners. At Arcadia the British and American Chiefs of Staff established a Combined Chiefs of Staff (CCS)* and jointly agreed on a memorandum that set out the principal aims of Allied grand strategy.

These aims included: the support of the war industries in the United States, the United Kingdom, and the Soviet Union, the latter by extending to the Soviets the terms of Lend-Lease; and closing and tightening the ring around Germany by sustaining the Russian front and supporting Turkey. (It was an abiding ambition of Churchill to draw Turkey into the war as an ally or base for operations.) Their aims were also to build up strength in the Middle East and secure the entire coast of North Africa; undermine German morale by air bombardment, blockade, propaganda, and a campaign of subversion in Occupied Europe. (The last was the work of the SOE and later its US equivalent, the OSS; see Chapter 4.) They would develop offensive action against Germany, with the proviso that "it does not seem likely that in 1942 any large-scale offensive against Germany will be

* The CCS consisted of army, navy, and air force chiefs of the United States and the United Kingdom meeting regularly in Washington and exercising control over the US/UK war efforts around the world. In the Pacific theater, where the U.S. predominated, the final decisions lay in the hands of the U.S. Joint Chiefs of Staff (JCS). In the European theater, the war was prosecuted as a matter of Anglo-American strategy and debated accordingly.

possible . . . In 1943 the way may be made clear for a return to the Continent, across the Mediterranean, from Turkey into the Balkans, or by landings in Western Europe." In the Far East, at this stage in the war it was deemed sufficient to "safeguard vital interests and to deny to Japan access to raw materials vital to her continuous war effort while we are concentrating on the defeat of Germany."

This last point in the memorandum confirms the decision made by the U.S. Joint Chiefs of Staff in February 1941, at the Anglo-American ABC-1 conference, nine months before Pearl Harbor, that in the event of the United States becoming involved in a simultaneous war against Germany and Japan, priority should be given to the war against Germany, the so-called "Germany First" policy and the constant background noise to the Allied conferences that followed America's entry into the war. Inevitably, six months of Allied reverses in the Far East and Pacific, public outrage in America in the wake of Pearl Harbor, and the clear Pacific priorities favored by the U.S. Navy were to place a considerable strain on the "Germany First" policy.

Churchill was understandably buoyed up by the Arcadia agreement. On the outward voyage to America, in the battleship HMS *Duke of York*, he had ebulliently declared of his new allies, "Previously we were trying to seduce them. Now they are securely in the harem." He put it more tactfully to King George VI on his return at one of their weekly luncheons: "Britain and America are now married after many months of walking out." The Americans, however, harbored serious reservations about Arcadia. Their philosophy of war differed radically from that of the British. At this stage in the conflict the American forces were mobilizing and their high command was poorly organized institutionally and lacking in coherence, realism, and effective leadership. Nevertheless, the unerring view of the US high command was that the defeat of Germany could only be achieved by beating its armed forces in the field by large-scale land operations, the application of mass and concentration in the manner of Ulysses S. Grant in the American Civil War. On January 22, 1942, General Dwight D. Eisenhower, then the chief of the U.S. Army Operations and Planning Staff, wrote: "We've got to go to Europe and fight—and we've got to quit wasting resources all over the world—and still worse—wasting time. If we're to keep Russia in, save the Middle East, India, and Burma, we've got to begin slugging with air at West Europe; to be followed by a land attack as soon as possible."

The British, however, had been unceremoniously bundled out of Europe at the end of May 1940, and thereafter had been preoccupied with nibbling away at the periphery of the Axis empire, in East and North Africa and Greece. In East Africa, Benito Mussolini's tawdry new Roman empire had been destroyed. In the Western Desert of North Africa the Italian forces had also been routed, only for the British 8th Army to encounter a more formidable opponent, from February 1941, in Rommel's Afrika Korps. In Greece the British intervention had been decisively defeated and its expeditionary force had been obliged to repeat the experience of Dunkirk with a double evacuation, first from Greece to the island of Crete and then from Crete to Egypt in May 1941, after a German airborne invasion.

When contemplating the mixed fortunes of the British Army, Churchill reached the gloomy conclusion that, perhaps, the British soldier lacked something of the spirit of his German opposite number. On February 11, 1942, four days before the fall of Singapore to the Japanese, the biggest British military disaster of the war, he told his old friend Violet Bonham Carter that ". . . our soldiers are not as good fighters as their fathers were. In 1915 our men fought on even when they had only one shell left and were under a fierce barrage. Now they cannot resist dive bombers. We have so many in Singapore, so many men—they should have done better." General Sir Alan Brooke, the chief of the Imperial General Staff (CIGS), was of the same opinion, confiding to his diary three days after the surrender at Singapore, "If the Army cannot fight better than it is doing at present we shall deserve to lose our Empire!"

British caution informed a national reluctance to embark on a fresh and premature adventure in Europe, tempered by memories of the slaughter of the Great War on the Western Front where Churchill had briefly served as a colonel commanding 6th Battalion, Royal Scots Greys in 1915–16, and where Brooke also served as a major in the artillery of 18th Division. It was clear to the British that they could not win the war against Germany without the help of allies who would bear the brunt of much of the land fighting. Meanwhile, they were obliged to maneuver and probe and exploit their superior sea power to wrong-foot the enemy and pull him off balance. Only when the enemy was sufficiently worn down and exhausted could the British turn their attention to major land operations. Brigadier General Albert Wedemeyer, the officer who headed the Policy and Strategy Group of the U.S. War Department General Staff, and who observed Churchill at close quarters, recalled that as early as 1942 the prime minister was "constantly looking for places to employ his limited forces in some wasteful periphery picking that he imagined would weaken the enemy without calling upon Britain to go all out for decisive blow."

In contrast to the Americans, the British were unwilling to entertain the idea of opening a Second Front, Operation "Sledgehammer," the invasion of France's Cherbourg Peninsula, proposed by their US ally to be launched as early as the autumn 1942.* The buildup to Sledgehammer was code-named Operation "Bolero" and the landings Operation "Round-up." Sledgehammer would commit the whole of the British and American expeditionary forces, not easily replaced if lost, to an assault on the fortified frontier of a continent containing an army of three hundred divisions and a war-making machine of unparalleled effectiveness. British apprehensiveness about Sledgehammer was to cast a cloud over relations with the Americans through the opening months of their alliance.

In early April 1942, General George Catlett Marshall, Chairman of the U.S. Joint Chiefs of Staff, arrived in London to discuss the US military buildup in the United Kingdom, Operation Bolero, and to hammer out with the British a timetable for the opening of the Second Front. Marshall, who believed that the Second Front should be mounted on the shortest route into Germany at the earliest possible date, was a formidable figure who deliberately and successfully unsettled his commander in chief, Franklin Delano Roosevelt, by declining to laugh at any of the president's jokes and not allowing FDR to address him by his first name. This outstanding soldier and "careful demon of integrity"** was equally stern with the British prime minister, remaining resolutely

* In its original form, code-named Operation "Wet Bob," the peninsula was to have been held to the spring of 1943 before a breakout was attempted.

** From an unpublished poem about Marshall written by a fellow U.S. Army officer, Thomas Hawkins Johnson.

unenthusiastic about Churchill's urging of an invasion of French North Africa, originally code-named Operation "Gymnast" and subsequently Operation "Torch," and insisting on and obtaining from the British a commitment to a Second Front in Europe in 1943. General Brooke noted in his diary that while the British Chiefs of Staff had reiterated their reservations about Sledgehammer in 1942, it remained a remote possibility contingent on the unlikely event of a sudden German collapse. However, at this stage in the war they accepted, albeit unwillingly, the likelihood of offensive action on continental Europe in 1943.

Doubt was thrown over this scenario by Eisenhower, who had been dispatched to England in June 1942 as commanding general, European Theater of Operations (ETO). Eisenhower quickly grasped that the time was not ripe for Sledgehammer. The U-boat menace was still at its height; British ground forces were too thinly spread; the Royal Air Force (RAF) was ill equipped to support an amphibious operation; and the Royal Navy, fearful of a foray by the German fleet (*Kriegsmarine*), was unable to provide sufficient gunfire support for the landings. Moreover, unless all US and British war production was concentrated on Sledgehammer alone, a cross-Channel operation could not be launched until 1944. In addition, Eisenhower detected a distinct reluctance among the British high command, haunted by memories of the Western Front, to contemplate another costly adventure on the continent of Europe.

To this was added a palpable measure of condescension accorded by the British to their American allies. Brigadier General Wedemeyer,* a highly experienced staff officer and a shrewd observer of Anglo-US relations, noted: "This attitude was a trifle odd, not to say presumptuous, for in 1941 the British themselves had very little experience in offensive strategical maneuver. After all, they had been rapidly driven off the continent in 1940, and from then on they had little opportunity except in the air and on the sea, to gain the experience Sir Alan Brooke talked about. . . . The

* Wedemeyer, a deeply conservative officer, had been the driving force behind the Victory Program, the mobilization of manpower in the US armed forces, and was an advocate of the "Germany First" doctrine.

British Army, aside from the small forces engaged in North Africa, was surely no more combat effective than our own."

In June 1942, Churchill returned to Washington, where he encouraged Roosevelt's interest in Torch, arguing that as the US troops gathering in the United Kingdom for Operation Bolero could not be used in 1942 in a cross-Channel operation, they might be gainfully employed in an interim operation in French North Africa (Torch), to precede the invasion of northwest Europe. This would also have the additional advantage of partially satisfying the Soviet leader Joseph Stalin's persistent demands for the opening of a Second Front. It was during this visit, on June 21, in the middle of a long afternoon conference with President Roosevelt, that Marshall walked into the Oval Office bearing a piece of pink paper containing the message that the Libyan port of Tobruk had fallen to the Afrika Korps. This shattering piece of news, subsequently described by Churchill as "one of the heaviest blows I can recall during the war," was in part softened by Marshall's offer of three hundred tanks and one hundred self-propelled guns for the hard-pressed British 8th Army in North Africa.

In July, Marshall was back in Britain, accompanied by Admiral Ernest J. King, the U.S. Navy's chief of operations, an Anglophobe and single-minded supporter of the primacy of the Pacific strategy. Their visit sparked a heated strategic debate in which the Americans renewed their demands for an opening of a Second Front that year while the British Chiefs of Staff and War Cabinet understandably dug in their heels. An appeal was made to Roosevelt, who normally did not directly concern himself with purely military matters, in which he allowed himself to be guided by Marshall. In this instance, however, Roosevelt took Churchill's side, having been convinced by the latter's arguments in the previous June. Help for Churchill came from another unexpected source, Harry Hopkins, Roosevelt's court favorite and "special envoy" to the United Kingdom.

Hopkins was remarkable man, in fragile health from stomach cancer, with no official position at the White House, who nevertheless played a highly influential role in the war as Roosevelt's right-hand man. Like Marshall and Wedemeyer, Hopkins had originally harbored doubts about the wholeheartedness of Britain's grand strategy. In his view, it was based on the overriding importance of maintaining the integrity of the British Empire above all other considerations. However, Hopkins had mellowed under concerted political wooing by Churchill, the Chiefs of Staff, and the War Cabinet. Lobbied by Hopkins and Churchill, Roosevelt decided to present the American Joint Chiefs of Staff with a range of options that excluded a Second Front and among which Torch was the most attractive. Marshall chose Torch, which was enthusiastically endorsed by Roosevelt and launched on November 9, 1942, with landings in Morocco and Algeria.

Churchill had gained a temporary respite but was still flapping on the hook of the British promise of a cross-Channel invasion in 1943. Moreover, his freedom to deploy delaying tactics was being steadily undermined by the fact that the tide of events was turning in the Allies' favor. In the Soviet Union, Hitler had returned to business left unfinished in front of Moscow in December 1941. Once again the panzers rolled: Army Group A struck through the Donets corridor to Stalingrad, the industrial city on the Volga with which Hitler was soon to develop a fatal obsession, while Army Group C drove through the Soviet Union's southernmost oilfields at Baku on the Caspian Sea. In the Pacific, however, the Japanese had been checked at the Battle of the Coral Sea (May 4–8), the first large-scale aircraft carrier encounter that was fought without either surface fleet sighting the enemy. At Coral Sea the Japanese sank one of Admiral Frank Fletcher's two carriers, the USS *Lexington*, and damaged the other, the USS *Yorktown*. Believing that both carriers had been sunk, the Japanese fleet pressed on with its plan to capture the island of Midway. The Americans, who had cracked the Japanese naval code, positioned their fleet to defeat the much stronger enemy task force that the Japanese had assembled to take Midway. In the ensuing carrier battle—one of the most decisive of the war—U.S. Navy dive-bombers destroyed four Japanese carriers for the loss of *Yorktown* and reversed the balance of power in the Pacific. The all-conquering Japanese were now forced to defend a vast ocean empire that might be attacked at any point by the gathering might of the American war machine. The point the Americans chose was the Solomons chain of islands east of New Guinea. On August 7, 1942, U.S. Marines stormed ashore at Guadalcanal, the first move in an epic battle that marked the beginning of the Allied reconquest of the Pacific. In the Battle of the Atlantic the U-boats' so-called "Happy

Time" off the American east coast had been brought to an end. The British 8th Army had held Rommel at the border of Egypt, and Allied victory lay around the corner at El Alamein, followed by the landings in North Africa and the destruction of the German 6th Army at Stalingrad. The strategic initiative was passing to the Allies.

Allied success made it all the more important to secure agreement on common strategy. When in January 1943 Roosevelt and Churchill met at a conference code-named "Symbol" in the Moroccan city of Casablanca on ground recently liberated by General Eisenhower, who had led the Torch landings, the prime minister was keenly aware that the contending arguments among the Americans between the Germany First and Pacific factions were yet to be resolved. The number of troops deployed in the Pacific under General Douglas MacArthur was, at some 350,000, approximately the same as those commanded by Eisenhower in Europe and North Africa.

To clinch the argument with Marshall, Churchill knew that he would have to persuade the U.S. Army chief of staff that a follow-up operation to Torch, preferably the invasion of Sicily, would not disrupt the schedule agreed in the summer of 1942 for the Second Front. For his part, Marshall believed that the American incursion into the Mediterranean had been justified by the clearing of French North Africa, completed in May 1943, and the securing of the Suez Canal, Britain's imperial artery at the eastern end of the Mediterranean. However, Churchill still harbored grave misgivings about the risks attached to the opening of the Second Front, were it to be launched later in 1943. After eleven days of discussion, agreement at Casablanca was reached and deftly summarized by Air Chief Marshal Sir Charles Portal, the British chief of air staff, who happily enjoyed a constructive relationship with both Churchill and his American opposite numbers.

The most significant result of Symbol was the emergence of the so-called "Mediterranean Strategy." The successful conclusion of Torch, the clearing of the North African coast, was to be followed by the invasion of Sicily (Operation "Husky"), another peripheral move but vital for Churchill, as its prosecution would rule out the opening of a Second Front in northern Europe until 1944. Marshall acquiesced as the operation posed fewer shipping problems than the alternative targets, Sardinia and Corsica, which were also beyond the range of US fighter aircraft, a fact that had escaped the attention of German military intelligence, which was still second-guessing the next Allied move.

For the Americans, Husky was only one of a number of available options. Nor at this stage did they commit themselves beyond Husky to the invasion of peninsular Italy. Nevertheless, the Sicily decision, having been made, was one the Americans found increasingly difficult to modify. Wedemeyer later reflected on the superior military diplomacy deployed by the British at Casablanca: "They swarmed down upon us like locusts with a plentiful supply of planners and various other assistants with prepared plans to insure [sic] that they not only accomplished their purpose but did so in stride and with fair promise of continuing in their role of directing strategically the course of this war." Wedemeyer failed to mention that the British had arrived with their own floating communication center, a fully equipped signals ship, which functioned as an extension of the government machine in London.

Symbol yielded a number of important decisions: the acceleration of Bolero; the mounting of a joint bombing offensive against German fighter production (Operation "Pointblank"); and the demand for the "unconditional surrender" of Germany, Italy, and Japan, largely on the insistence of Roosevelt. As far as the Americans were concerned, the Mediterranean remained a secondary theater in which the Allied threat, posed or delivered, would drain German resources away from northwest Europe, where the Anglo-American *schwerpunkt* (decisive blow) would eventually fall, on the coast of northern France. Nevertheless, in the back of the Americans' mind was the lingering anxiety that a campaign beyond Sicily, on the Italian peninsula itself, would act as a greater drain on Allied resources than those deployed in the theater by the Germans and could thus derail the plans for the Second Front.

At Casablanca, another new problem arose in the form of dealing with the French now that their colonies in northwest Africa were in the process of being liberated. At the conference there was a great deal of behind-the-scenes maneuvering between Churchill's protégé, General Charles de Gaulle, who had arrived in England after the fall of France and had assumed command of the Free French movement, and Roosevelt's candidate, General Giraud, commander of the French 9th Army in 1940, who had been taken prisoner by the Germans and imprisoned in Konigstein Castle. He had escaped in 1942 and had made his way to Algeria to rally opposition to Vichy France and had been adopted by the Americans, who were extremely distrustful of the imperious de Gaulle. However the Americans were discomfited when Giraud appeared to be even more imperious than de Gaulle, and wholly divorced from the world of war and politics as they were in the beginning of 1943. After his five minutes of icy fame alongside de Gaulle, Giraud was unceremoniously shunted into the background and dropped by the Americans. De Gaulle, a great but extremely difficult man, remained a hot potato to be passed back and forth by the Allies for the rest of the war.

The "Trident" conference, held in Washington in May 1943, came in the immediate aftermath of General Alexander's defeat of the Axis forces in Tunisia. Over 230,000 prisoners, nearly half of them German, had tramped into Allied captivity. Once again Hitler had been unable to liquidate a front and, as result, presided over another Stalingrad on the southern shores of the Mediterranean. The Mediterranean was now for all intents and purposes open, and Italy was teetering on the edge of collapse. The British urged that, following the invasion of Sicily, landings should be made in Calabria in the toe of southern Italy with a view to expanding eastward into the southern Balkans. In the event of a sudden Italian capitulation, Italy should be occupied as far north as Rome, a bridgehead established on the Yugoslavian coast, and the Dodecanese islands lying off the southwest coast of Turkey should be seized and pressure exerted on Turkey to enter the war on the Allied side. In turn this would force the Germans to dispatch more troops either to the Balkans or to Italy, in all likelihood the former, abandoning Italy to the Allies, who could the use its airfields to raid central and southeastern Europe, particularly the Axis's Romanian oilfields at Ploesti.

It was at Trident that the first formal discussions between the American and British staffs were held about the invasion of southern France. The major topic under discussion was the cross-Channel invasion of northwest France, which was to become Operation Overlord, now envisaged by the Americans for the spring of 1944. Following the successful conclusion of the campaign in Sicily, they planned to begin transferring all their military resources to the United Kingdom to support the cross-Channel invasion. However, this left them with the problem of postponing any engagement on land with the Germans until 1944, a gap of possibly more than nine months. Thus the Joint Chiefs of Staff cast around for other potential targets in the Mediterranean theater that would divert German attention from northern France without impeding the Allied buildup.

Potential target areas included southern Italy, Sardinia, and Corsica, the Balkans, the Iberian peninsula, and southern France. The Americans were reluctant to plunge into the political minefield of the Balkans, were less than eager to launch a drive up peninsular Italy, and saw Spain as a strategic dead end. The last option, the invasion of southern France, was also regarded with some suspicion by the American planners: sufficient forces for its successful accomplishment were not available and the operation would also demand the preliminary occupation of Sardinia and Corsica. Their principal concern was that each of these options ran the risk of developing into a major campaign that would divert resources from the all-important objective of the invasion of northwest Europe.

Now code-named Overlord, the cross-Channel invasion of France was to be reinforced by seven divisions from the Mediterranean theater and launched on May 1, 1944. At meetings in Algiers at the end of May 1943, Churchill weighed into the strategic debate on his return from Trident. The meetings were held at General Eisenhower's villa and attended by, among others, Eisenhower, Churchill, Generals Brooke and Alexander, Churchill's chief of staff General Sir Hastings Ismay, the naval commander in the Torch landings Admiral Sir Andrew Cunningham, commander in chief of Mediterranean Air Command Air Chief Marshal Sir Arthur Tedder, General Marshall, and Lieutenant General Walter Bedell Smith, Eisenhower's highly able chief of staff.

Churchill was always more of an inspired opportunist than a convincing strategist. At Algiers he once more seized the opportunity to take up the cudgels for an attack on mainland Italy. On May 31, the prime minister elaborated on a series of "Background Notes" he had prepared, stating that ". . . compelling or inducing Italy to quit the war is the only objective in the Mediterranean worthy of the famous campaign already begun and adequate to the Allied forces available and already in the Mediterranean basin. For this purpose the taking of Sicily is an indispensable preliminary, and the invasion of mainland Italy and the capture of Rome are the evident steps. In this way the greatest service can be rendered to the Allied cause and the general progress of the war, both here and in the Channel theater [a reference to the cross-Channel invasion]."

General Marshall kept his powder dry, replying that he only wished to emphasize that the Allies should exercise general discretion in choosing what to do after the conquest of Sicily. The outcome of the Algiers meetings was that Eisenhower established two planning groups: one to prepare for an attack on Sardinia and the other for an invasion of southern Italy. Thus when the Allies landed in Sicily on July 10, 1943, nobody had decided what to do next.

However, one man who who had decided to go to peninsular Italy was Adolf Hitler. Since July 5, he had been following from his East Prussian headquarters the progress of Operation Citadel, the attempt by the Ostheer to punch out the huge fist-shaped salient in the heart of the Ukraine, jutting into the German line, at the center of which was the city of Kursk. The buildup for Citadel, aimed at clawing back the initiative after the surrender of the 6th Army at Stalingrad, had taken three months. The Red Army, reorganized and reequipped after the disasters of 1941–42, was well informed of German intentions and, under the overall direction of Marshal Georgy Zhukov, Stalin's deputy commissar for defense, had prepared to defend the salient's shoulders in massive strength and depth. A week after the German offensive had opened, on July 12, the Red Army launched a counteroffensive in the Orel salient immediately to the north of the Kursk bulge.

On July 13, as the German advance was being slowed to a crawl, Field Marshals Kluge and Manstein, respectively commanders of the northern and southern pincers of Citadel, were summoned to Hitler's headquarters, the *Wolfsschanze* ("Wolf's Lair") near Rastenburg in the gloomy, mosquito-ridden Gorlitz Forest in East Prussia. According to Manstein's subsequent account, Hitler "opened the conference by announcing that the Western Allies had landed in Sicily . . . and the situation there had taken an extremely serious turn. The Italians were not even attempting to fight, and the island was likely to be lost. Since the next step might well be a landing in the Balkans or Lower Italy, it was necessary to form new armies in Italy and the western Balkans. These forces must be found from the Eastern Front, so Citadel would have to be discontinued."

In fact Citadel was to continue for several more days before it was finally called off. What was undeniable, however, was that the landings in Sicily had ushered in a new phase in the war in which Germany would have to fight on two fronts rather than stand guard over one and fight on the other. Hitler hoped to contain the situation in Sicily while continuing to prepare for the main blow to the west in Northern Europe. His immediate fear was the overthrow of his fellow dictator, the Italian *Duce*, Benito Mussolini. On July 15, he was informed by General Alfred Jodl, head of operations in all theaters except Russia,* that "as far as can be foreseen, Sicily cannot be held." Hitler deemed that a meeting with Mussolini was essential. On July 19, he flew from East Prussia to meet Mussolini in Feltre, near Belluno, in northern Italy. It was to be the last time he set foot on Italian soil. In sweltering heat the two dictators met in a villa chosen for the occasion. Mussolini, drawn and unwell, a shadow of his former strutting, posturing self, sat silent and listless as Hitler raved uninterrupted for two hours about the Third Reich's new generation of wonder weapons. The Duce's entourage looked on helplessly. Mussolini's silence was in large part due to the fact that he had already been given an ultimatum by his high command to open peace negotiations with the Allies. Hitler doubtless derived some comfort from the sound of his own voice, but on his return to his headquarters in East Prussia he was shown an intelligence report by Heinrich Himmler, his SS chief, that a coup d'état was being planned to replace Mussolini with Marshal Pietro Badoglio, the Duce's former chief of staff. On July 25 Mussolini was arrested after an audience with the Italian king, Vittorio Emanuele III,

---

* Jodl was head of the Operations Section of OKW (*Oberkommando der Wehrmacht*) nominally Germany's supreme joint services command. Fatally, OKW had no control over the German Army high command in the Soviet Union, *Oberkommando das Heeres* (OKH). Nor did it control the Navy (Kriegsmarine) or Air Force (Luftwaffe) high commands, OKM and OKL, an example of Hitler's method of divide and rule.

bundled into a waiting ambulance, and driven under police guard into house arrest on the Mediterranean island of Ponza. Mussolini was subsequently interned at La Maddelena, off the coast of Sardinia. At the end of August he was moved to a mountain resort high in the Abruzzi in central Italy. On September 12, the fallen dictator was rescued by German parachutists and borne off in a light aircraft to another meeting, in Munich, with Hitler.

The Allied campaign in Sicily was short but hard fought since the island was garrisoned by two highly efficient German formations, the 15th *Panzergrenadier* Division and the Hermann Goering Division, but it was all over by August 17. By then over 100,000 German and Italian troops had escaped to the Italian mainland. On September 3, a new anti-fascist Italian government signed a secret armistice with the Allies. On the same day the British landed in the toe of Italy.

On both the Axis and Allied sides, there remained uncertainty about the next move. The German high command had not been surprised by the fall of Mussolini and had for the previous two months been making plans to deal with this eventuality. The result was Operation "*Achse*" ("Axe") entrusted to Field Marshal Erwin Rommel, commander of *Heeresgruppe B* (Army Group B) who after his return from North Africa in March 1943 had been made responsible for the defense of northern Italy.* During August, German divisions were quietly transferred to Italy from eastern and northwestern Europe. By September 9, when the Italian government announced its surrender and the U.S. Fifth Army landed in Salerno, some forty miles southeast of Naples, their number had risen to fourteen and a month later had reached twenty-five, sufficient not only to pacify the Italian countryside but also to compel the Allies to fight for every foot of ground in their advance on Rome.

However, Hitler had more wide-ranging concerns. He was confident that, if necessary, the Italian peninsula could be sealed off. Among his principal preoccupations were the mineral resources of

---

* Another one of Hitler's mistakes. Command in Italy was divided between Rommel and Field Marshal Albert Kesselring, responsible for German forces in the south. Hitler refused to combine the two commands under Kesselring, until November 1943 when it was clear that a line south of Rome could be held. However, Kesselring's freedom of action was still hampered by Hitler's constant interference.

the Balkans—oil, copper, bauxite, and chrome—where the Italians had provided the largest single occupation force and which had to be safeguarded if there was a collapse in Italy. Hitler's high command took a different view, arguing that the deployment of twenty divisions in Yugoslavia, Greece, and the islands of the Aegean was an impossible task, given the pressure that was being exerted on every point on the Third Reich's perimeter. Acknowledging the truth in Frederick the Great's dictum that "he who defends everything defends nothing," General Jodl suggested a shortening of the line in the Mediterranean and the abandoning of the Italian peninsula south of the readily defensible mountain line between Pisa and Rimini at the top of the Italian boot. In Greece and the Aegean, nothing should be held south of the line running east and west through Salonika, positions that in World War I the Central Powers had defended with great success.

Hitler was more inclined to listen to a dissenting voice, that of Field Marshal Albert Kesselring, commander of Heeresgruppe C (Army Group C), the German forces in southern Italy. Kesselring, an immensely able professional soldier, pointed out that a withdrawal to the Apennines would render the Balkans vulnerable to an Allied thrust across the Adriatic. Kesselring, who had commanded Air Fleet (*Luftflotte*) 2 in the Battle of Britain, also saw with an airman's eye that yielding tracts of territory in southeast Italy would gift the Allies with a network of airfields, notably those around Foggia, from which they could deploy bombers over the Balkans and the southern Reich. Thus Italy should be defended as far forward as possible. After a characteristic period of delay, Hitler decided during the first week in November that Italy should be defended south of Rome.

Allied progress up the Italian peninsula was a long, hard slog, made all the more grueling by difficult terrain, missed opportunities, and stiff German resistance in a series of well-fortified positions, notably the Gustav Line running from the mouth of the River Garigliano through Cassino and across the Apennines to a point south of Ortona. Now the Americans found themselves caught on a hook of their own devising. Their commitment to fighting their way up the Italian peninsula had outrun their original plans, although throughout the summer and autumn of 1943 this was the only theater in Western Europe where the Germans could be effectively engaged and in which, by the end of the year, the Allies had achieved their principal objectives. The overall Mediterranean Strategy had been a success. The Mediterranean had been cleared for shipping; nearly fifty German divisions had been sucked into the Italian peninsula and the Balkans; and the important airfields around Foggia were now operating against targets in central and southeastern Europe. Moreover, communications across the Adriatic had been opened and were accelerating the supply of materiel to Marshal Josip Tito's guerrillas in Yugoslavia.

Nevertheless, by the autumn of 1943, the Americans, while still deeming the Mediterranean a secondary theater, were determined that the agreement reached with the British at Trident, that seven Allied divisions should be drawn from Italy for Operation Overlord, should be honored. In the course of another Allied conference, "Quadrant," held in Quebec in August 1943, there were acrimonious exchanges between the two allies as the Americans strove to secure an unequivocal commitment from the British to Overlord that would confirm the Mediterranean's secondary status. In addition they urged a landing in southern France to coincide with Overlord in the north.

This was an idea that had been discussed with the British at Trident, and subsequently at Quadrant, but had now been adopted by the Americans as their own and, in a distant echo of Sledgehammer, been given the code name "Anvil." At this stage the principal aims of Anvil, now seen by the Americans as a three-division operation, was the capture of the ports of Toulon and Marseille, to divert German troops from northwest France, and to provide vital new ports of entry for the Allies. This was seen as the logical culmination of the Mediterranean Strategy, securing Italy as a base for air operations against central Europe and seaborne operations in support of the campaign in southern France which, in conjunction with the Red Army's advance on the Eastern Front, would bring a rapid end to the war. The Combined Chiefs of Staff directed Eisenhower to prepare a plan for Anvil, linked to Overlord, by November 1943. However, the directive was vague and made no distinction between the British view that Anvil should be reduced to a diversionary threat and the American support for a three-division operation, which carried the concomitant risk of weakening Overlord.

❖

At the end of October 1943, Eisenhower submitted his report. By then the Germans were disarming their former Italian allies and had moved twenty-five divisions into the Italian peninsula, while the Allied buildup in the theater was frustratingly slow, creeping toward eighteen divisions. The Allies were facing a stalemate in Italy and there was little hope of reaching Rome before the end of the year. Judging that the Allies would not be able to mount an overland invasion of southern France in the spring of 1944, Eisenhower recommended the seizure of a small bridgehead in the South of France provided that the Germans obligingly abandoned the region to the Allies. Meanwhile the Allies should persevere with the Italian offensive. The British unsurprisingly supported Eisenhower's conclusions and the linking of Overlord and Anvil was, for the moment, shelved.

Shortly before the next Allied conference, in Tehran in November 1943, British and American officials met in Cairo to map out a coherent set of proposals to present to the Soviet delegation. This preliminary conference was code-named "Sextant." En route to Cairo, Roosevelt and his staff discussed topics ranging from the postwar occupation of Germany to operations in the Pacific and the possibility of a Balkan campaign in the European Theater of Operations (ETO). It was nevertheless agreed that the overriding importance of Overlord should ensure a cautious approach to any new operations in the Mediterranean.

Churchill was also in Cairo for discussions with Harold Macmillan, the British minister resident in Algiers. Uppermost in the prime minister's mind was what he saw as the Allies' lack of focus in the Mediterranean and the Americans' failure to grasp the theater's potential, demonstrated in particular by their insistence on withdrawing landing craft and personnel for Overlord. Roosevelt arrived in Cairo on November 22, and two days later Churchill returned to the familiar theme of the Mediterranean. The president had voiced his concern that the development of Overlord could not be sustained while the Allies "kept the Mediterranean ablaze."

Churchill, in a somber mood, observed that all the achievements made in the Mediterranean might be put at risk if Allied progress in the theater stalled. The islands of Kos and Leros, in the Dodecanese, which had been taken by the British after the Italian surrender, had been reoccupied by the Germans on October 3 and November 12, respectively, after amphibious landings supported by airborne drops. The island of Samos had been evacuated by the British on the night of November 19. Churchill hoped that the recapture of these islands by the Allies might bring Turkey into the war. Hitting his stride, Churchill once again urged a drive up the Italian peninsula to capture Rome. Whoever held Rome, the prime minister declared, held "the title deeds of Italy." As far as Overlord was concerned, Churchill maintained that his support for the operation was undimmed but warned that "it should not be such a tyrant to rule out every other activity in the Mediterranean . . . a little flexibility in the employment of landing craft ought to be conceded."

The Tehran conference, code-named "Eureka," began on November 28, 1943. It marked the first occasion on which Roosevelt met Stalin, whom Churchill had met in Moscow in August 1942. Stalin and Roosevelt had two preliminary meetings without Churchill, which left the prime minister childishly anxious that they were ganging up on him. At the plenary meetings, however, Stalin spoke in favor of the plan for the capture of Toulon and Marseille, which bound Britain into a commitment to Anvil, although Churchill's support for both Overlord and Anvil was soon to waver, to the alarm of his American ally. Stalin's enthusiasm for Anvil stemmed from his own military experience with so-called "pincer" operations; his desire to establish the long-delayed Second Front in northwest Europe; and last but not least his keenness to steer the Western Allies away from any involvement in southeastern Europe, particularly the Balkans, which the Soviet leader considered a vital sphere of Russian influence.

Stalin dominated the Tehran conference. He was still basking in the Red Army's victory at Kursk, which had tripped a series of convulsions on the Eastern Front that in two and a half months had thrown the Ostheer back over 150 miles on a front of 650 miles toward the east bank of the River Dnieper. In contrast, Churchill cut a gloomy figure, now clearly the junior partner in the Allied triumverate, and increasingly troubled with misgivings about the role of the Soviet Union not as a wartime ally but as a potential threat in the postwar world. Nor could the prime minister count on unqualified American support in the wider objectives he envisaged flowing from the Mediterranean Strategy.

Churchill was understandably irked by the Americans' lack of interest in the eastern Mediterranean. The prime minister's deep and romantic knowledge of British history was informed by many events in this theater, from Nelson's victory in the Battle of the Nile, to the deaths of the poets Byron at Missolonghi and Rupert Brooke in a hospital ship off the island of Skyros. On a more urgent contemporary note, the ancient city of Alexandria was the base of the British Mediterranean fleet and departure point for the westbound Malta relief convoys. And the Suez Canal was Britain's imperial lifeline, briefly threatened by Rommel in the autumn of 1942.

Churchill also fretted about the Balkans. In a somewhat disingenuous letter to Roosevelt written on October 7, 1943, he had pointed out that operations in this theater would have an impact on Greece, Yugoslavia, the long-hoped-for ally Turkey, and Hitler's increasingly restive allies, Hungary, Bulgaria, and Romania: "I have never wished to send an army into the Balkans, but only agents, supplies, and commandos to stimulate the intense guerrilla [sic] prevailing there . . . What I ask for is the capture of Rhodes and the other islands of the Dodecanese. The movement northward of our Middle East Air Forces and their establishments in these islands, and possibly on to the Turkish shore, which last might well be obtained, would force a diversion of the enemy far greater than required of us."

The Americans regarded the Balkans much as medieval mapmakers saw the terra incognita beyond the boundaries of the known world—"Here Be Dragons." The U.S. Army Planning Staff entertained a particular dread of the region, associating it with the lingering imperialism with which they believed British grand strategy was infected. Little good could come from venturing into this minefield. This was by no means unfair to Churchill, whose freewheeling strategic forays had on occasion to be restrained by calm interventions from the likes of General Brooke. Now acutely conscious of the ebbing away of British power and influence, Churchill was, in Brooke's words, "inclined at times to put up strategic proposals which, in his heart, he knew were unsound, purely to spite the Americans . . . It was usually fairly easy to swing him back on the right line. There lay, however, in the back of his mind the desire to form a purely British theater where the laurels would be all ours."

In the case of the Balkans, Churchill's strategic opportunism had gotten the better of him, as well he should have known. When discussing Marshal Tito's communism with Fitzroy Maclean, the prime minister's representative to the Yugoslavian partisan leader, Churchill asked Maclean, "Are you going to live in Yugoslavia after the war? No? Neither am I. And that being so, the less you and I worry what sort of government they set up, the better. That is for them to decide." As far as Eastern Europe was concerned, both Churchill and the British Foreign Office realized that the tide of war would place it within the Soviet sphere of influence at the end of the conflict. In October 1943, when peace feelers were extended to the Western Allies by King Michael of Romania, Britain's foreign secretary, Anthony Eden, and the U.S. secretary of state, Cordell Hull, agreed that "the Soviet Union was entitled to decide any such questions concerning Romania and Hungary, and Finland as well—since only its forces were engaged in active warfare against these countries." The exception to this rule was Greece, where the British had the kind of long-term interest that the American planners found so sinister and which was also an integral part of Britain's current and postwar plans for the Eastern Mediterranean.

The Americans had long been wary of what they saw as devious British diplomatic skills, a sphere in which the latter were infinitely more experienced than their allies. General Wedemeyer, when reflecting on the outcome of Symbol, admitted, "We lost our shirts . . . we came, we listened and we were conquered." At Trident the British had, it seemed, also outmaneuvered Eisenhower's originally modest plans for an intervention in southern Italy, winning the argument for pushing on to Rome and beyond. Here the Americans should have set stricter limits on the Italian campaign, which, it could be argued, ultimately came to serve Germany's purpose better than that of the Allies. Quadrant had provided Churchill with a final, fleeting opportunity to mount a spoiling operation against the opening of the Second Front. At Tehran, however, his bluff was called by Stalin. The Soviet leader dismissed several of Churchill's pet obsessions—Turkey, Rhodes, Yugoslavia, and the capture of Rome—as unimportant from the Soviet point of view, and then asked the prime minister point-blank whether he believed in Overlord at all or was "only saying so to reassure the Soviet Union?"

Churchill mustered a reply that mixed equivocation and bluster. Provided conditions* were met, he said, "it will be our stern duty to hurl across the Channel against the Germans every sinew of our strength."

In the meetings at Tehran that were devoted purely to military strategy, short shrift was given to the British proposals. At the first, attended among others by Generals Marshall, Brooke, and Stalin's envoy, Marshal Klimenti Voroshilov, an old revolutionary comrade and drinking companion of the Soviet leader, Brooke emphasized the overriding importance of active engagement with the Wehrmacht. This he planned to achieve by launching amphibious attacks up the Italian peninsula with landing craft assigned to the Mediterranean until such time as they were withdrawn to participate in Overlord. From the outset, Brooke stated that he was opposed to a landing in the South of France as ongoing operations in Italy left him little or no room for maneuver. Moreover, simple geography made it impossible for the landings in the north and south of France to be mutually supporting until the two expeditionary forces joined hands.

Marshall, on the other hand, chose to concentrate on the logistical challenges posed by Overlord and the complementary role envisaged for Anvil, which he suggested should be launched no more than two or three weeks before Overlord. He saw the continued emphasis on the Mediterranean as a factor that might delay Overlord, the buildup for which was well underway. Voroshilov, not the sharpest military tool in the box, then asked Brooke if the British considered Overlord to be of "the first importance." Brooke parried with the standard British equivocation that Overlord was crucial but could only be launched in the right conditions when victory was assured. This prompted Voroshilov to observe that, from the Soviet point of view, all operations in the Mediterranean were by their very nature auxiliary. Brooke agreed but added that unless these operations were undertaken, Overlord would fail.

At the conference's second plenary session, on November 29, 1943, Stalin lobbed a large rock into the pool of Allied consensus by asking

* The conditions included a reduction in the strength of the Luftwaffe's fighter defenses, the presence in France and the Low Countries of no more than twelve mobile divisions, and the elimination of the possibility of the Germans transferring more than fifteen divisions from other fronts in the first sixty days of Overlord.

who was to be the commander of Overlord. Churchill and Roosevelt had no answer. Stalin then observed, "Then nothing will come out of these operations," before going on to give his allies a lecture about the importance of having a commander, without whom Overlord would be little more than a map exercise. Roosevelt had originally considered Marshall for the job, but the general's continued presence in Washington was deemed indispensable, and so within days the post of supreme commander of the Allied Forces for Overlord was filled by Marshall's protégé, Eisenhower.

The Tehran conference concluded with agreement among the "Big Three"—Roosevelt, Stalin, and Churchill—that Operation Overlord was to be launched in May 1944 in conjunction with Anvil, the invasion of southern France, the latter a left-handed blow in the Mediterranean. These operations were to be aided by a major offensive launched at the same time on the Eastern Front (this was eventually to be Operation "Bagration," which opened on June 22, 1944). At this point the only question mark hanging over Anvil was the availability of landing craft in the Mediterranean theater, a theme to which the prime minister was to return with some vigor in the spring of 1944.

The other cloud on the Allied horizon was that, in spite of his fine words about "stern duty," Churchill's gaze was still being tugged toward the Balkans by an alternative proposal, advanced by Roosevelt at Tehran, of a right-handed blow, delivered from Italy in the Adriatic on the Istrian peninsula toward the Ljubljana Gap, in Yugoslavia, and on to Vienna. Churchill was unperturbed by the contradictions inherent in this strategy, a revival of the peripheralism that had been forced upon the British from 1940 and which flew in the face of the American high command's conviction that northwest Europe was the crucial place to confront and destroy the German enemy. But, as Churchill airily concluded, "All this lay five or six months ahead. There would be plenty of time to make a final choice as the general war shaped itself, if only the life of our armies in Italy was not paralyzed by depriving them of their modest requirements in landing craft." To the British prime minister all seemed well: "Surveying the whole military scene, as we separated in an atmosphere of friendship and unity of immediate purpose, I was personally well content." In this untroubled vision of the future he was joined by the British Chiefs of Staff, who viewed the South of France and Balkan thrusts as equally viable, the latter seen as merely an extension of the campaign in Italy. What had conveniently been ignored by Churchill was the impossibility of the Allies fighting simultaneously on three separate fronts.

Churchill's satisfaction at the conclusion of Eureka nevertheless masked a shifting in the tectonic plates that underpinned the Anglo-American alliance. For the first twelve months after they joined the war the Americans had, as a rule, deferred to their British allies, relied on their strategic and tactical advice, and raised no major objections to Churchill's peripheralist strategy. By 1943, however, they commanded the largest war economy, truly "the arsenal of democracy," and the military makeup of the Allied forces was becoming more decidedly American. In contrast, from 1943 British strength was in decline as its industrial and manpower resources had started to ebb away. This became clearer at Cairo and Tehran, and the inevitable tensions that arose between the two allies were to play a complicating role in the evolution of the plan to invade southern France.*

The Tehran conference having concluded, the Anglo-American Sextant conference was resumed in Cairo on December 3. Much discussion revolved around the resources available for Overlord and Anvil. Admiral Cunningham, the Royal Navy's chief of staff, pointed out that there were only enough naval vessels in the Mediterranean to support two major amphibious operations, Overlord and Anvil, not the three that Churchill, still eyeing the eastern Mediterranean, had in mind. Cunningham suggested that the gap might be filled by withdrawing vessels from the Bay of Bengal where they were assembling for Operation "Buccaneer," the projected invasion of the Andaman Islands, off the coast of Burma.

---

* Churchill's foot-dragging over Overlord and Anvil can in part be explained by the disastrous landings at Gallipoli in the Dardanelles in 1915, an amphibious operation championed by Churchill, then the First Lord of the Admiralty, which incurred heavy losses and achieved no discernible gain. It was failure at Gallipoli that prompted Churchill to leave politics and fight on the Western Front. At Gallipoli the Turks, as allies of the Central Powers, were the enemy, and this may also explain Churchill's obsession with persuading Turkey to join the alliance against Germany in World War II.

This proposal was blocked by Roosevelt, who insisted that something must be done to help Chiang Kai-shek's Nationalist China. Field Marshal Sir John Dill, the head of the British Joint Services Mission in Washington,* was of the opinion that it was not possible to simultaneously launch Overlord and Anvil at optimum strength as any attempt to do so might adversely affect the strategic balance, with unforeseen political consequences. Roosevelt hauled the debate back on track with his summary. Its principal point was that no action should be taken to hinder Overlord and Anvil, which would remain the two major operations in the European Theater carried forward by the Western Allies and which would be launched during May 1944. The Combined Chiefs were to send Eisenhower a report compiled by their planners on the landings in the South of France. Eisenhower undertook to prepare an outline for the operation, based on the ominous assumption that it would be launched when Allied forces in Italy had reached the Pisa-Rimini line.

* In April 1940 Dill had been appointed vice-chief of the Imperial General Staff, succeeding General Ironside as CIGS a month later. His cautious approach did not appeal to Churchill and he was replaced by General Brooke and dispatched to Washington in December 1941 as the head of the British Joint Services Commission, liaising with the CCS, where his tact and diplomacy greatly eased Anglo-American cooperation.

TWO
THE STRANDED WHALE

"I had hoped we were hurling a wildcat on the shore, but all we got was a stranded whale."

—Winston Churchill
on the Anzio landings

Winston Churchill deemed that the "soft underbelly" of the Axis crocodile was located in the South of France, Italy, and the Balkans. He may have been right in the first assertion but not in the other two. In particular, Italy's topography lent itself well to defense, as Field Marshal Kesselring, one of the ablest fighting generals of World War II, keenly appreciated. The Italian peninsula has a central, mountainous spine, rising up to 10,000 feet in places, which throws numerous spurs east and west toward the Adriatic and the Mediterranean. Between these spurs rivers flow through deep valleys into the sea. Together, these formidable constituent parts of Italy's topography offer a succession of defensible lines made all the more difficult to breach because the spine forces the north-south highways into eastern and western coastal strips, where the bridges that carry them are overlooked by natural strongpoints on the looming spurs above. Add to this the fact that in 1943–44 these lines were for the most part defended by German formations of the highest quality, transferred to the peninsula after the Italian surrender, and one can begin to appreciate the problems facing the Allies as they crawled up the leg of Italy.

The topographical challenges became evident at the Allied landings at Salerno (code-named "Avalanche") on September 8 and 9, 1943. The wide and level coastal strip where U.S. Fifth Army and British 10th Corps came ashore was dominated on all sides by high ground, and its northward exit to the Allies' Avalanche objective, Naples, was blocked by the massif of Mount Vesuvius. En route the invasion force had been informed of the Italian surrender and was expecting little or no resistance. Instead, they encountered fierce opposition from General Heinrich von Vietinghoff's 10th Army, principally 16th Panzer Division and 29th Panzergrenadier Division. On September 12 the 16th Panzer Division threatened to split the US and British landing forces and break the bridgehead in half. The Americans were forced to contemplate re-embarking their assault divisions before halting the Germans by bringing down a colossal weight of firepower, which with air support drove the Panzergrenadiers back. By September 15, the crisis had passed. With General Sir Bernard Montgomery's 8th Army approaching from its landings in Calabria, Kesselring granted Vietinghoff permission to conduct a fighting withdrawal toward the mountain line to his north, the Gustav Line. The next day advanced elements of 8th Army made contact with American forces in the bridgehead south of Salerno.

On the night of September 14, while the outcome of the landings still hung in the balance, the U.S. 3rd Division, commanded by Major General Lucian King Truscott Jr., was dispatched from Palermo to the Salerno bridgehead. Truscott made the journey aboard a British motor torpedo boat, and in his memoir, *Command Missions*, left a vivid account of the approach to the bridgehead: "Our first sight of Avalanche in the gathering dusk was a ring of fire that flamed and glowed and sparkled in the distance with occasional flares streaking through the heavens like great sky rockets, and occasional bursts of flame that mushroomed and fell in showers of fire. It was beautiful, although not a comforting, view."[1]

The gravel-voiced Truscott* was a tough customer, Texas-born in 1895 and raised in Oklahoma, who had joined the U.S. Army in 1917, lying about his educational qualifications to be accepted for officer

---

* Trucott's husky tones were said to be the result of a childhood accident, when he ingested some acid.

training. During the closing months of World War I, he served with the 17th Cavalry Regiment in Arizona. Subsequently he served in various cavalry and staff roles, marrying, in 1919, Sarah "Chick" Nicholas Randolph, a descendant of Thomas Jefferson. In the summer of 1940 Truscott, now a colonel, was appointed as battalion executive and regimental S3 (operations and training officer) in the 13th Armored Regiment in the newly formed Armored Force. In January 1941 he was transferred to the staff of 9th Army Corps at Fort Lewis, Washington, whose chief of staff was by happy accident Colonel Dwight D. Eisenhower. After the outbreak of war, in the spring of 1942, Truscott was asked by General Mark Clark, chief of staff, Army Ground Forces, to develop Commando units similar to those that had been pioneered in the United Kingdom by the British Army. Truscott was to travel to Britain at the head of a group of American officers attached to the staff of Admiral Lord Louis Mountbatten, chief of British Combined Operations. Clark then ordered Truscott to report to Eisenhower, now promoted to the rank of general.

At their first meeting, Eisenhower outlined the "Germany First" policy and the importance of ensuring that the Soviet Union stayed in the war. Eisenhower's briefing ranged over the Allied options discussed in the first chapter of this book, including Marshall's overoptimistic belief that a foothold could be obtained in France in 1942. Eisenhower also made it clear that the chief of staff was concerned that the U.S. Army had little or no battle experience and that every American assault unit should have within its ranks a few men who had met the enemy in battle and could impart their experience to their comrades. This was the reason behind Truscott's mission.

One of the officers who accompanied Truscott to London was the then Colonel Albert Wedemeyer, who had already accompanied Marshall to Britain after Pearl Harbor and who had been Truscott's classmate at the General Staff School in 1934–36. Truscott and his comrades arrived in May 1942, and his memoir vividly recalls his initial reaction to a down-and-out wartime London: "We were surprised at the drab and untidy appearance of the women we saw in the streets and in the shops, for we had just come from an America in which the rough hand of war had not yet swept aside the luxuries, much less the necessities of life. Nor did we appreciate the psychological change that results from continued exposure to danger [the Blitz was not long over], denial of the ordinary amenities of life, and from conditions of existence that could offer only 'blood, sweat and tears.' We were not prepared for the number of women in uniform and in military formations. Women manned most of the clouds of balloons which kept hostile planes far above the streets of London. They drove most of the vehicles we saw in the streets and replaced men in many other positions. While it was new to us, this mobilization of women brought home to us the strain which war had placed on British manpower."[2]

Truscott quickly grasped the organization, aims, and methods under which Commando missions were undertaken, and on May 26 recommended to Marshall that American units should be formed along the same lines and given the name Rangers, after the elite soldiers whose ranks predate the French and Indian Wars. Men of the Rangers were to become the first US ground forces on the continent of Europe to carry the fight to the Germans in World War II. Truscott was an observer of Operation "Jubilee," the raid on the heavily defended, German-held resort and seaport of Dieppe on August 19, 1942, in which a fifty-man Ranger detachment took part. The raid was mounted in large part to soothe Soviet complaints about the lack of a Second Front in Europe and also to provide battle experience for men of the Commandos and the 2nd Canadian Division.

This "reconnaissance in force" proved to be a disastrous operation, which incurred heavy losses and was a salutary warning about the dangers of a premature invasion of northwest Europe. Nevertheless, it taught the Allies many vital lessons in organization and tactics, a point of view that was shared by Truscott, who later wrote, "I am not one of those who consider the Dieppe raid a failure. It was an essential though costly lesson in modern warfare."[3]

In November 1942 Truscott arrived in North Africa at the head of 60th Infantry Regiment (part of 9th Infantry Division) and 66th Armored Regiment (part of 2nd Armored Division) to serve under Major General George S. Patton, commander of the Western Task Force. Truscott, a keen observer of the strengths and weaknesses of his fellow officers, was subsequently highly critical of the leadership of Lieutenant General Lloyd Fredendall, commander of U.S. 2nd Corps, whose tactical grasp was shaky and who, in contrast to his German opponents, led from the rear like a World War I château general. Fredendall's lack of grip led to the rout by 10th and 21st Panzer Divisions of his corps at Kasserine Pass, Tunisia, in February 1943. The situation was swiftly retrieved by General Sir Harold Alexander, the Allied deputy commander in chief in North Africa, whose harsh opinion of the Americans was that "they are ignorant, ill-trained, and rather at a loss, consequently not too happy." Fredendall was relieved by Patton, who was later told to his face by Alexander that he found American troops "mentally and physically soft, and very green."

These words were not lost on Truscott, who in North Africa and later in Sicily initiated a tough training program for the 3rd Infantry Division after assuming command in March 1943. He recalled: "I had long felt that our standards for marching and fighting in the infantry were too low, not up to the standards of the Roman legions nor countless examples from our own frontier history, nor even to those of Stonewall Jackson's 'Foot Cavalry' of Civil War fame. My experiences during the past year had confirmed me in these opinions. I had observed modern war at Dieppe . . . and I had just been closely associated with American troops in the first battle against the veteran Germans. Not least in importance, I had acquired an intimate knowledge of the plans and personalities involved in the conduct of war in Europe that few division commanders could hope to have."[4]

Herein lay the origins of the "Truscott Trot," derived from Rangers and Commando training, when Truscott saw firsthand what could be accomplished in the physical and psychological preparation of men for battle. He was convinced that an average infantry battalion could approach Ranger and Commando standards in "speed marching" when presented with the challenge, such was the natural competitive instinct of most Americans. Truscott's instincts were correct. In Sicily, two battalions of the 3rd Division beat Patton's armor to the city of Palermo on the island's northwest shore. On July 22, the day after the city was taken, Patton greeted Truscott with the words, "Well, the Truscott Trot got us here in a damn hurry."

After Salerno, the 3rd Division fought its way up the Italian peninsula as part of U.S. 6th Corps, commanded by General John P. Lucas, who was an old friend of Truscott. The autumn advance to the River Volturno, north of Naples, was made through particularly difficult terrain that favored the defender and hindered armored advance. Truscott recalled: "Narrow valleys were broken by intensely cultivated plots. Rugged mountains rose to an elevation of more than 5,000 feet. Our road wound its way through defile after defile, crossed over numerous bridges, and clung precariously to precipitous cliffs in many places. Off the roads, occasional cart tracks led to villages nestled among the mountains, and a few mule paths led to the mountain tops, and along the mountain ridges. Off these roads and tracks, the country was passable only for men on foot and for mules. We were to find many places that pack mules could not climb where supplies had to be carried by men."[5]

Then the Italian winter kicked in. On Christmas Day 1943, Fusilier Gus Platts of the British 6th Parachute Battalion, 2nd Independent Brigade Group, 8th Army, was pushing through the mountainous Abruzzi in central Italy, on the Adriatic side to the east of the central spine: "Just before Christmas we had taken a place called Casoli, a village on top of a hill, seemingly a favorite place for villages in that part of Italy. We set up our position on a day when it was snowing. We dug our mortar pits four or five feet down, did one or two shots during the day and then at night the snow really came down. We were just below a ridge about ten feet high. I went into my slit trench, put my groundsheet on top of me and in next to no time I was asleep, sitting on my steel helmet to keep out of the wet trench. I was absolutely snowed under and had to be dug out. If they hadn't found me, I would have still have been there now, frozen solid. My sergeant gave me a tot of rum to thaw out."

While Fusilier Platts was nearly freezing to death in the Abruzzi, decisions of the greatest importance were being made in London about Overlord and Anvil. England was now groaning under the weight of accumulated men and materiel as Generals Eisenhower and Montgomery met in London in January 1944. They were there to review the plans drawn up by General Sir Frederick Morgan, who in January 1943 had been appointed chief of staff to an as-yet-undesignated Supreme Allied Commander (COSSAC) for the Allied return to northwest Europe in Operation Overlord. The landing beaches on which Morgan had settled were in Normandy.

Eisenhower had been picked for the job of supreme allied commander by Roosevelt in December 1943. "Ike" was not a fighting soldier. His skills were essentially diplomatic, oiled by an ability to weld a coordinated team from a collection of powerful individuals with conflicting views and personalities. The land fighting* by the Allied 21st Army Group, once ashore, was to be commanded by General Montgomery, Britain's battle-winner in North Africa, Sicily, and Italy. "Monty" was prim, schoolmasterly, and a teetotaler, but nevertheless a prima donna with a stunning lack of tact, with whom Eisenhower was obliged to exercise monumental patience. Montgomery was less benign. In a letter to Brooke in October 1944, he fulminated, "If you want to end the war within any reasonable period you will have to get Eisenhower's hand taken off the land battle. I regret to say that in my opinion he just doesn't know what he is doing." In the words of Admiral Cunningham, the British commander of naval operations during Husky, Montgomery "seemed to think that everyone would dance to a tune of his piping."

In mid-January 1944, in the cold and fog of a winter-bound London, Montgomery and Eisenhower could at least agree on Overlord. The original COSSAC plan had been based on what was available; the final Overlord plan was based on what was needed. Eisenhower and Montgomery expanded the assault force from three to five divisions on an extended front that included a beach, Quinéville-Pouppeville, at the base of the Cotentin Peninsula. This effort at the western edge of the Allied assault was to be supported by American airborne landings designed to secure the routes inland from the coast and into the peninsula from the rest of Normandy, and speed the capture of the port of Cherbourg, essential to the success of Overlord. At the eastern edge of the Allied landing area another, British, airborne drop was to be made northeast of Caen. The five seaborne divisions were to be supported by a second seaborne wave, consisting of one reinforced armored division, one artillery division, and an understrength infantry division, all landed on the same day as the first wave, with the balance of the understrength formation, plus a full-strength infantry division coming ashore the next day. The numbers involved—men, shipping, and aircraft—were almost double those of the original COSSAC calculations, with a corresponding

* On September 1, 1944, Eisenhower took over operational command of Allied land forces in northwest Europe. Montgomery's consolation prize was promotion to the rank of field marshal.

increase in assault shipping for the first day of Overlord. On D-Day itself, the Allies had to find enough assault shipping to lift a force comprising 174,320 men and 2,018 vehicles.

When Eisenhower, Montgomery, and their staffs made these calculations, the principal problem that confronted them was the amount of assault shipping required for Overlord, which it seemed could only be found by extending the operation's target date to May 31 and simultaneously reducing the scope of Anvil or, as Montgomery preferred, canceling it altogether. Eisenhower, supported by the U.S. Joint Chiefs of Staff, was firmly opposed to the latter solution. Anvil was to be retained as a three-division adjunct to Overlord. Eisenhower reminded Montgomery that this had been promised to the Russians and was also the most effective use of the French divisions in North Africa and the US divisions in Italy earmarked for the operation. Anvil had to be a force multiplier not merely a threat. Eisenhower then began to play a numbers game in which Anvil's landing craft would be exchanged for transports, a ploy that met with Montgomery's objections. On February 22, Eisenhower engineered a temporary compromise in which Overlord remained the top Allied priority but, by the same token, commitments were given to operations in Italy.

The new supreme Allied commander in the Mediterranean, the British general Sir Henry Maitland Wilson, was ordered to prepare plans for operations to complement Overlord, the most important of which was that for Anvil. For the next month there was to be a moratorium on all shipping moving in and out of the Mediterranean. Wilson, however, was at this stage in the war no supporter of Anvil and indeed, like Montgomery, suggested that it should be canceled and that he [Wilson] "should be given a fresh directive to conduct operations with the object of containing the maximum number of German troops in Southern Europe with the forces earmarked to be at my disposal." The hard fighting in Italy, he argued, was by itself diverting more German forces than anyone had expected, rendering Anvil surplus to strategic requirements.

Alexander was of the same opinion, although in retrospect his opinions seem self-serving. He believed that in spite of the Italian campaign's slow progress, it fulfilled its strategic mission: "Our role was subordinate and preparatory. Ten months before the great assault in the west [Overlord] our invasion of Italy, at first in very moderate strength,* drew off to that remote quarter forces that might have been turned against us in France. As the campaign progressed, more and more German troops were drawn in to oppose us . . . when the value of our strategic contribution was at its greatest [in the period running up to Overlord] fifty-five German divisions were tied down in the Mediterranean by the threat, actual or potential, presented by our armies in Italy. The record of comparative casualties tells the story. On the German side they amounted to 536,000. Allied casualties were 312,000."

By mid-January 1944, the Allied advance on Rome had been halted by the imposing obstacle of the heavily fortified town of Cassino, surmounted by a Benedictine monastery and the lynchpin of the Gustav Line, which dominated the Liri Valley carrying Route 6, the only practicable road by which the Allies could reach the Italian capital. The seeds of Operation "Shingle," the Allied attempt to outflank the Gustav Line by a landing on the west coast of Italy behind the formidable German defensive lines, had been germinated by Alexander in November 1943. However, on October 18 Brooke had warned him that "My difficulty all along has been to persuade the Americans that our commitment in Italy would be a heavy one. They seem to have an ineradicable impression that our hearts are not in Overlord, and that we will take any opportunity of diverting to the Mediterranean resources which they consider should be concentrated in Great Britain."[6]

Then Churchill, ambivalent about Overlord, seized hold of the idea in Tunis in December 1943 after falling ill with pneumonia on his return from Tehran. The prime minister's imagination had been fired by the prospect of the liberation of Rome. He chafed at the stagnation of the campaign in Italy and the lack of landing craft that inhibited bold amphibious operations to break the deadlock on the Gustav Line. He eagerly grasped Brooke's suggestion that Shingle might be revived with a landing at Anzio, thirty miles south of Rome, near the mouth of the Tiber, to coincide with a major Allied push along the Garigliano-Cassino Line. Alexander, Cunningham, Wilson, and the American general Jacob Devers, Wilson's deputy in the Mediterranean, were

* This was due to the shortage of landing craft.

among the top brass summoned to Carthage, and discussions about Shingle began on Christmas Eve. A revitalized Churchill greeted his high command in a padded silk dressing gown sporting blue and gold dragons. A few days earlier his physician, Lord Moran, had feared that the prime minister was on the point of death. In an excess of Christmas spirit, perhaps, caution was thrown to the winds. Under the overall command of Lieutenant General Mark Clark, now leading U.S. Fifth Army, an initial assault force of two divisions (British 1st and U.S. 3rd Infantry) were to be landed at Anzio under Major General John P. Lucas, commander of U.S. 6th Corps. The Allied plan made no provision for immediate reinforcement and the assault force was to land with supplies for no more than eight days, the time allowed for the junction of the two Allied fronts, one breaking out of the Anzio bridgehead and the other breaking through the Gustav Line, also known as the Winter Line.

Not everyone in the Allied high command shared Churchill's enthusiasm for Shingle. Alexander's chief administrative officer, Major General Brian Robertson, advised the cancellation of the operation, "unless there is a reasonable prospect of a successful junction between Shingle and the [U.S.] Fifth Army within one week of landing." Mark Clark anticipated that the landings might be opposed by two or three German divisions and considered that two weeks, "or probably longer," should be allowed between the landing and the junction. He urged Lucas "not to stick his neck out."

Over the entire operation, launched on January 22, 1944, hung a confusion about its precise purpose. Was its principal aim to sever German communications and force an evacuation of the Gustav Line, thus enabling the Allies to make a dash for Rome? Or was the major priority to establish and expand a force strong enough to withstand any German counterblow against the bridgehead, and not to move forward until this was achieved? Alexander wanted to follow the first option, referring to "a battle for Rome," but failed to grasp that the accomplishment of this objective depended entirely on the rapid seizure of the Alban Hills surrounding the beachhead. Mark Clark, on the other hand, insisted on the securing of the beachhead, while Lucas, depressed, lethargic, and caught in the middle of competing arguments, compounded the muddle by agreeing to loading arrangements that prevented his main body of armor from landing until D+6. By then, the hapless corps commander was aware that "a strong odor of Gallipoli" had settled over Shingle.

Morale in the beachhead was further weakened from February 5, when continuous bombardment began by two massive K5(E) German railway guns—"Leopold" and "Robert" to their crews but "Anzio Annie" to the Americans—which were concealed in railway tunnels some twenty miles from the Allied lodgement. After firing up to eight rounds, each of which weighed some 700 pounds, the two guns were trundled back into the darkness of the tunnels, although on one memorable day no fewer than seventy-two rounds were fired. Targets included harbor installations, fuel and ammunition dumps, and supply ships riding at anchor. The last were forced some three miles out to sea to avoid the guns' attentions.

Lucas had achieved the worst of all possible worlds by landing large numbers of men and equipment, cramming them into a tiny bridgehead, and exposing them to considerable risk, while failing to impose any on the enemy. Kesselring, rescued from a crisis, assembled "emergency units" (*Alarmeinheiten*) from soldiers returning from leave and rushing them to Anzio while larger units were moved at top speed from the North and quiet sectors on the German front. When Lucas tried to move inland on January 30, his way was barred. Two weeks later the newly formed German 14th Army counterattacked in strength in Operation "*Fischfang*" (Fish-hook) with orders from Hitler to throw the enemy back into the sea,* a warning to the Allies of the fate that awaited an invasion of northwest Europe.

Fischfang failed, but so had the wretched Lucas,** who on February 23 was replaced by his old friend Truscott. After the war, Truscott gave his own candid view of the Allies' failure to take Rome: "I suppose that

---

* The information was revealed in 1970 in an interview with Mark Clark conducted by Nigel Nicolson, author of *Alex: The Life of Field Marshal Earl Alexander of Tunis*. This provided an early indication, albeit unintentional, of the Ultra Secret.

** In the early 1950s, Lucas was introduced to Audie Murphy, who had fought at Anzio with 3rd Division, on the set of one of Murphy's postwar movies. Murphy saluted Lucas and then turned on his heels and walked away. He had lost too many friends at Anzio to banter with the general.

armchair strategists will always labor under the delusion that there was a 'fleeting opportunity' at Anzio during which some Napoleonic figure would have charged over the Alban Hills, played havoc with the German lines of communications, and galloped on into Rome. Any such concept betrays lack of comprehension of the military problem involved. It was necessary to occupy the Corps beachhead line to prevent the enemy from interfering with the beaches. Otherwise, enemy artillery and armored detachments, operating against the flanks, could have cut us off from the beach and prevented the unloading of troops, supplies, and equipment. As it was, the Corps beachhead line was barely distant enough to prevent direct artillery fire on the beaches."[7]

In this Truscott was supported by Major General (later Field Marshal) Sir Gerald Templer, who commanded the British 1st Division at Anzio: "I never understood how Anzio could possibly work. I am absolutely convinced that if Lucas had gone on (which he could have) he could have gotten to Rome, but within a week or a fortnight there wouldn't have been a single British soldier left in the bridgehead. They would all have been killed or wounded or prisoners. We would have had a line of communications forty-five miles long from Anzio to Rome with absolutely open flanks. The Germans produced seven divisions in ten days, with plenty of armor, and we wouldn't have had a chance."

Between February 29 and March 2 successive German counterattacks on the Anzio beachhead, now reinforced by the U.S. 45th Division and the British 56th Division, were contained by ferocious artillery fire, a belated tribute to Lucas's painstaking defensive preparations, and massive air bombardment. Thereafter the beachhead came to resemble a World War I battlefield. At Anzio and Ypres from 1915 the lines were within grenade-throwing distance of each other, and during successive lulls in the fighting men spent their days pressed against the earth walls of their bunkers listening anxiously for the discharge of short-range weapons and bracing themselves for the shock of the explosion. Rest periods were spent no more than four miles to the rear, where they were exposed to the tender mercies of "Anzio Annie."

Finally, on May 23, 6th Corps launched a breakout operation as part of the long-delayed Allied drive on Rome. On June 3, 1944, three days before D-Day, Hitler authorized Kesselring to withdraw from Rome and declare it an open city to spare the destruction of the first Axis capital to fall to the Allies. Troops of the U.S. Fifth Army entered the city on June 4. Eighty years earlier, after seven attempts, Ulysses S. Grant had wired President Lincoln: "Vicksburg is ours, and fairly won." The commander of Fifth Army, Mark Clark, could not say the same as he triumphantly motored in his jeep through an almost deserted Rome. At the end of May his eyes had been fixed on the city, but, egotist that he was, Clark was afraid that Alexander would allow the British 8th Army to beat U.S. Fifth Army to the prize. Truscott, one of the great fighting generals of World War II, was ordered by Clark to disengage from the Anzio breakout, in which he was on the point of encircling ten German divisions, and head straight for Rome. Like the good soldier he was, Truscott changed the axis of his advance but was stalled by the recovering Germans, as agile as ever in adversity, who then escaped northward. Clark's ambition had overridden his primary military objective, the destruction of the German Army in Italy, which lived to fight another day.

Truscott encountered Clark in Rome on June 4, in the latter's moment of glory, shortly to be eclipsed by the Normandy landings. Truscott, as ever the pragmatist, avoided the spotlight and just wanted to move on to the next assignment, of which he was well aware. For some time he had known that he was to command the assault forces in the invasion of southern France that was to take place as soon as the naval vessels and assault craft could be made available from Overlord. For the moment, he pressed on north of Rome. At Civitavecchia he had the pleasure of capturing Leopold and Robert, which had been stranded by Allied interdiction of the Italian rail bridges. On June 10, eighty-five miles north of Rome, Truscott took his leave of the Italian campaign.

The Anzio stalemate and the demands of Overlord had threatened to squeeze the life out of Anvil. In March Eisenhower, seeking to increase the size of Overlord, recommended the postponement of Anvil as the Anzio debacle was beginning to consume forces intended for the invasion of southern France. Churchill went further, urging the immediate abandonment of the operation and, when shipping became available, the transfer to northern France of the French formations allotted to Anvil. In this he was supported by his Chiefs of Staff, who were still convinced that Anvil should be retained merely as a strategic threat. Marshall was also coming around to the view that the implementation of Overlord and Anvil as broadly concurrent operations was no longer feasible if Rome was not liberated before April 1944. Still reluctant to abandon Anvil altogether, he suggested that the Joint Chiefs of Staff would not object to a stabilized front south of Rome if this ensured that Anvil could be executed at around the same time as Overlord.

By the end of the month, however, the Allies' position on Anvil had shifted again. Possibly concerned about Churchill's continuing obsession with the Balkans, the Joint Chiefs of Staff enlarged Anvil to a two-division operation on July 10. They had also been informed by Wilson that he would have the greatest difficulty in deploying more than eight divisions north of Rome, which raised the possibility of a two-division assault in southern France launched with transport shipping that the Americans would make available. The British, however, stuck to their guns, insisting that the priority remained with Wilson in Italy and any available shipping should be allotted to him rather than Anvil.

The deadlock between the Americans and the British was not eased by Marshall, who declined to allocate any more resources to the prosecution of a campaign in Italy that the Americans had expanded beyond their original intentions and in which they no longer had much faith. All options in the Mediterranean were off the table unless the British began to make immediate preparations for an Anvil operation to be launched at the end of July. To this end, formations would have to be released from the Italian theater by the middle of May. Wilson was not prepared to play ball. By the end of the first week in April, he had finalized his plan for the spring campaign in Italy and informed the CCS that its execution depended on the retention of his entire force. He could spare nothing for Anvil before late August. The disagreement over Anvil had opened a new chapter in Anglo-American relations. Previously the British and American Chiefs of Staff rarely disagreed over a major issue. Now they were more often than not on different sides. For the British this now meant the losing side.

The British Chiefs of Staff unilaterally ordered Wilson to press ahead and set about preparing a directive for a general offensive in Italy with all the resources in the Mediterranean. This proposal was then submitted to the CCS. The U.S. Joint Chiefs of Staff, understandably annoyed, approved Wilson's directive but with the proviso that they would withdraw their previous offer of additional amphibious lift. In his diary entry of April 19, 1944, Brooke observed of the American demand, "History will never forgive them for bargaining equipment against strategy and for trying to blackmail us into agreeing with them by holding the pistol of withdrawing craft at our head."[8]

Wilson, however, felt vindicated. It seemed that the divisive arguments over Anvil had been stilled. His spring offensive could go ahead on May 10, 1944. Anvil nevertheless remained extremely difficult to shelve. Within a matter of days, the Joint Chiefs and British Chiefs of Staff, possibly regretting the harsh words exchanged during the last weeks, decided to reconsider options in the Mediterranean. Wilson assured them that when the troops in the Anzio beachhead joined hands with the Allied main force, he could begin to release strength to mount a major operation, although only with a single division assault lift. Wilson then muddied the waters by suggesting a number of options that included landings in southern France or, to the Americans' dismay, the head of the Adriatic. Churchill, ever contrary, urged a landing in the Bay of Biscay, while the British Chiefs of Staff indulged in some elaborate coat-trailing with a proposal for a small-scale landing in the South of France at the end of June.

This encouraged the Joint Chiefs to revive their offer of amphibious lift from the Pacific while placing their weight behind the South of France. The British, in an onrush of diplomacy, dropped the Adriatic option, but still advanced a range of landing sites that included southern France, the Bay of Biscay, the Gulf of Genoa, in northwest Sicily, or the Italian west coast between Rome and Genoa. The Americans, grateful that they had kept Anvil in play, accepted the British proposals as the basis for future planning. The capture of Rome and the D-Day landings lent urgency to the Allies' final decision. Wilson remained in favor of driving to the Po and then forking northeast through the Ljubljana Gap, overlooking the fact that this operation would require most if not all of the divisions in Italy, certainly those that had been provisionally allotted to Anvil.

THREE
THE TUG OF WAR

> "Jake [Devers] who has at last heard a gun go off in anger talked in a big way till [late] . . . He has now become a great strategical expert, but he believes everything he is told [by the British] until someone tells him differently."
>
> —General George S. Patton

The operation originally code-named Anvil, and later Dragoon, had endured a complicated gestation. It was originally discussed at length by the British and American high commands at Quebec in August 1943 and subsequently in Cairo the following November, where it was confirmed. Roosevelt and Churchill approved the proposal in Cairo as did Stalin in Tehran, also in November 1943. General Eisenhower was then directed to prepare for the invasion of southern France with up to ten divisions. These would consist principally of rearmed French troops from North Africa and Italy, and American units when they became available. Furthermore, the availability of shipping and assault craft was crucial to the planning and timing of the operation.

Churchill, however, had to be dragged kicking and screaming into the invasion of southern France. One of the sticking points to which he repeatedly returned was the shortage of LSTs (landing ships, tank), the backbone of amphibious operations in the Mediterranean, European, and Pacific theaters. In a telegram to General Marshall on April 16, 1944, on the vexed subjects of Overlord/Anvil and the tug-of-war over operations in Italy, Churchill confessed: "The whole of this difficult question only arises out of the absurd shortage of the LSTs. How it is that the plans of two great empires like Britain and the United States should be so hamstrung and limited by a hundred or two of these particular vessels will never be understood by history."

With the advantage of hindsight, it would seem that the prime minister was protesting too much. The shortage of landing craft was illusory rather than objective. By 1943 the production of LSTs from British shipyards alone was already sufficient to meet the demands of Overlord. However, the planners at SHAEF, the Supreme Headquarters Allied Expeditionary Force (COSSAC had been renamed after Eisenhower's appointment) had convinced themselves that the U.S. Navy's requirements in the Pacific were depriving the ETO of its just allocation. The reason was more likely to have been misjudgment rather than the machinations of the U.S. Navy's chief of operations, Admiral King, a staunch proponent of the priority of the Pacific theater. Nevertheless, the resulting debate led to the postponement of Overlord by a month, from May to June, and the placing of Anvil on ice, to be resurrected after the fall of Rome. In effect this was self-defeating, as in this changed scenario Anvil could no longer be seen as direct support to Overlord.

The American high command's support for Anvil, however, was undimmed, but the postponement of both operations, Overlord and Anvil, gave the British encouragement. They favored the employment in Italy of the French divisions allocated to Anvil, a cynical maneuver that the Americans found unacceptable. Had the French known it, they would have deemed it wholly unpalatable. The British were nevertheless convinced that their argument was strengthened by "Ultra"* intercepts from November 1943, which indicated that the German attempts to build a strong blocking Apennine position, the Gothic

* Ultra was the British code name indicating the security grading attached to German movements and intentions acquired by intercepting the enemy's Enigma-coded signal traffic. The home of Ultra decryption was a country house in Buckinghamshire, Bletchley Park.

Line,* were far from complete and would take months to finish. This fact had been admitted by Hitler in mid-June 1944, but the intercept revealing this was not decrypted by the code-breakers at Bletchley Park until the end of the month.

By this time the Combined Chiefs of Staff had debated a proposal by Alexander, made on June 17, ten days after D-Day, that he should retain all twenty-seven of the divisions under his command in Italy to break through the Apennines to the Po Valley, reach the River Piave north of Venice with eighteen divisions (the rest held in reserve), and carry on to the Ljubljana Gap, through which the main road and railway line ran from Italy into northern Yugoslavia. Alexander saw the Ljubljana Gap as the gateway to Vienna, whose capture by the Allies would be of immense political and psychological value. He discounted the mountainous terrain that lay in the Allies' path on the grounds that his men had dealt with similar obstacles in Italy, as well as a determined enemy.

This was certainly the view at Alexander's headquarters, where Air Marshal Sir John Slessor, commander of RAF units in the Mediterranean, recalled Alexander's unwonted optimism: ". . . everyone in Italy was still too cock-a-hoop at the capture of Rome, and no one foresaw the skilful and dogged defense that we still had to overcome." The British Chiefs of Staff, while sympathetic to Alexander's proposal, were sceptical of the Vienna option, not least because victory in Italy had yet to be won and that taking the road to Vienna would threaten the buildup in Normandy and doom Anvil, now languishing in a state of suspended animation but awaiting resuscitation by the Combined Chiefs of Staff.

On June 23, the pragmatic Brooke reminded Churchill that even by Alexander's wildly optimistic reckoning, the advance beyond the Pisa-Rimini line could not start until after September 1944, which would condemn Alexander to advance on a single road, battling winter, hostile topography, and fierce resistance, in effect three enemies rather

---

* A heavily fortified defensive line, some ten miles deep, running from the Magra Valley, south of La Spezia, on the west coast, through the Apuan mountains to a chain of strongpoints guarding the Apennine passes and on to a point on the Adriatic between Pesaro and Cattolica. It was to this system that German 10th and 14th Armies retired after the fall of Rome. Originally known as the "Apennine Position," it was renamed the Gothic Line on April 24, 1944.

than one. But, in Churchill, Alexander had a found a willing ally, deeply opposed to Anvil and chafing at the American insistence that the operation must be mounted as a traveling companion to Overlord. Moreover, the prime minister's previous insouciance about the Red Army's drive into Eastern Europe had been seriously undermined. His personal physician, Lord Moran, noted that in the early summer of 1944, "Winston never talks about Hitler these days; he is always harping on the dangers of Communism. He dreams of the Red Army spreading like a cancer from one country to another. It has become an obsession and he thinks of little else."

The Americans were less than impressed by Alexander's scheme, and their views were hardened by the fierce Channel storm of June 19–22 that wrecked the Allied harbor facilities on Omaha Beach in Normandy. This made Eisenhower even more determined to secure the ports of southern France to ensure that the Allied buildup in Normandy was not overtaken by a German counterblow akin to the one that had bottled up the Allied lodgement at Anzio. In these circumstances, Eisenhower demanded a landing in the South of France as soon as possible. The Vienna option was out of the question. Equally whimsical alternatives, also advocated by Churchill, such as a landing around Bordeaux, on France's Atlantic coast, were also ruled out.

Churchill persisted, making personal appeals to Roosevelt on June 28 and July 1, both of which were rejected. The president was facing reelection in November 1944, and ending the war in Europe while satisfying the wishes of Stalin and the French were his main concerns rather than acceding to British priorities in the Balkans. Churchill's advocacy of the Vienna option had, in large part, been an old man's pipe dream, a glorious example of his wall-map approach to strategy and overreaching vision. It was, as military historian H. P. Willmott has observed, an example of de Gaulle syndrome—"a penchant for increasingly divisive and irresponsible actions in response to a declining ability to influence decisions and events to one's own advantage."

Brooke, who had a qualified opinion of Alexander's generalship, had the last word: "His [Alexander's] scheme was fantastic mainly because he had not gotten the data to base it on. I quote this episode because as an example of Alex's lack of appreciation of what he was faced with. He and Harding [Alexander's chief of staff, General Sir John Harding] had been seeing a great deal of Winston during the last few days, and in their pipe dream had repeatedly captured Vienna, and expressed hopes that this could be accomplished by an all-British force. Unfortunately in examining the winning post they were forgetting to devote enough attention to the fences immediately in front of them."[1]

By January 1944 the outlines of Anvil were emerging, albeit slowly. Eisenhower had been assigned to the Allied Expeditionary Force preparing for Overlord and had been succeeded in the Mediterranean by General Sir Henry Maitland Wilson, a burly Colonel Blimp–like figure whose nickname was "Jumbo." He had fought in the Boer War at the turn of the century and in 1940 commanded British troops in Egypt. In March 1941 he was appointed commander of the British and Commonwealth corps dispatched to Greece, conducting the subsequent retreat and evacuation with considerable skill. In 1943 he succeeded Alexander as Commander-in-Chief Middle East and in January 1944 was appointed Supreme Allied Commander in the Mediterranean based in Algiers, where he found himself caught in the middle of Anglo-American wrangling over Anvil.

Wilson's deputy and commanding general of the North African Theater of Operations was the American Lieutenant General Jacob L. Devers, who had been commissioned in the U.S. Army's field artillery in 1909 but had arrived in France after the November 1918 armistice brought an end to the fighting. Between the wars Devers became a champion of mechanization and the "armored idea," and in August 1941, now a major general, was appointed to head the U.S. Army's Armored Force, overseeing its expansion from four to 16 divisions. He was less than impressed with the Army's M3 Grant/Lee Medium Tank, which entered service with the US (as the Lee) and British (as the Grant) Armies in 1941 and carried a sponson-mounted 75mm main gun that had a total traverse of only 30 degrees. Devers threw his weight behind the more heavily armored M4 Sherman, which entered service in 1942, whose main armament was a turret-mounted 75mm gun with full 360 degree traverse. The Sherman proved to be the Allies' best and most numerous medium tank of World War II, a match for the PzKpfw 4 (the *Panzerkampfwagen IV*), but not the equal of the heavy Mk 5 Panthers and Mk 6 Tigers subsequently deployed by the Germans. The cough of a Tiger's engines starting up in the distance was something all Allied tank crews remembered with respect mingled with apprehension. The rule of thumb in the U.S. Army was that it could take at least five well-handled Shermans to finish off a cornered Tiger. But the Americans thought that this was a price worth paying as their military philosophy, stemming from the United States' vast industrial base, favored mass over technology. Just over 49,000 Shermans of all types rolled off the production lines between 1942 and 1945 compared with 1,300 Tigers and some 5,500 Panthers.

Devers swam against the tide in his advocacy of rigorous combined arms training, advocating that anti-tank and antiaircraft battalions should form organic elements within infantry and armored divisions. In this he clashed with General L. J. McNair, commander of the U.S. Army Ground Forces, who believed that separate tank and tank-destroyer battalions should be assigned on a "mission-needs" basis, a fallacy that was repeatedly demonstrated during the fighting in Normandy in the summer of 1944. Nevertheless, in September 1942, after Devers was promoted to the rank of lieutenant general, McNair rated him among the top five of the seventeen men of the same rank in the U.S. Army.

Two other senior US commanders with whom Devers did not always enjoy the easiest of relations were Eisenhower and Patton. The source of Eisenhower's antipathy probably stemmed from the visit Devers made to North Africa in December 1942, at the request of Marshall, to report on the progress of the Allied campaign in Tunisia commanded by Eisenhower. The first six weeks of the campaign had been a wretched time for Eisenhower. He had been out of his depth as a field commander; and was suffering from high blood pressure and a respiratory ailment aggravated by his smoking. Marshall had sharply ordered Eisenhower to avoid the distractions of local French politics and concentrate on the battlefield. As Overlord was to demonstrate, Eisenhower was more a political than a fighting general, albeit one with man-management skills of a very high order. Eisenhower, however, viewed Devers's visit with great suspicion, imagining that he had been sent to replace him, just as he had replaced the ineffectual General James E. Chaney as commander of US troops in Europe in June 1942.

At the end of his visit to North Africa, Devers had another uncomfortable meeting, this time with Patton, a former West Point classmate, in Casablanca. Patton wrote patronisingly in his diary, "Jake [Devers], who has at last heard a gun go off in anger talked in a big way till [late] . . . He has now become a great strategical expert, but he believes everything he is told [by the British] until someone tells him differently." Devers, who was essentially a highly capable rear-area soldier with a tendency to occasional tactlessness, was never going to come out ahead in a sparring match with an egotist like Patton, the epitome, some might say caricature, of the flamboyant all-American fighting man. Patton and Devers also fell out over the tactical employment of tanks, the former favoring lighter tanks, festooned with machine guns, used in an exploitation role in breakthrough operations. Devers, who in the 1930s had, to his credit, studied the groundbreaking works of Heinz Guderian, the prophet of blitzkrieg, was a more cautious advocate of armor. He believed that the best weapon to beat a tank was a better tank. In this battle, at least, Devers emerged the victor.

In April 1944, General Wilson had been ordered to launch an all-out offensive in Italy; to "develop the greatest possible threat to contain German forces in southern France; and to "make plans for the best possible use of the amphibious lift remaining to you, either in support of operations in Italy, or to take advantage of opportunities arising in the South of France or elsewhere for the furtherance of your object." The British still seemed to be hedging their bets over Anvil, relying on a threat rather than an actual operation, but they were being firmly nudged toward activating it by their American allies, even though the overall picture was blurred by the sheer scale of activity in the Mediterranean and northwest Europe.

The US formation chosen for Anvil was the Seventh Army. It had started life as 1st Armored Corps, commanded by Patton, which was the first all-US force to take part in the fighting in North Africa. In early July 1943 it was redesignated the Seventh Army while en route to Sicily as the leading American element in Operation Husky. In Sicily, Patton clashed with his British opposite number Montgomery, another prima donna, commanding the British 8th Army in the race to Messina. It was during this operation that Patton's career nearly came to an abrupt end when, in two separate incidents, on August 3 and 10, 1943, he struck hospitalized soldiers suffering from battle fatigue. The incidents were brought to light by the journalist Drew Pearson, who conflated the two slappings into one, and the resulting row ensured that Patton did not command a force in combat for the next eleven months,* ruling him out of consideration for Anvil.

Lieutenant General Mark Clark assumed command of the Seventh Army after Patton's departure for the United Kingdom in January 1944 while retaining the command of the U.S. Fifth Army, and then briefly came into the frame for the role of Anvil commander. There was little doubt that the charismatic Clark was an excellent staff officer, but doubts hung over his abilities as a commanding general and his considerable personal ambition. On January 4, 1943, Brooke noted in his diary: "[General] Jacob just back from North Africa came to COS [Chiefs of Staff] with most recent news. Apparently Clark has been creating trouble. Very ambitious and unscrupulous, has been egging on [General] Giraud to state that French troops could not fight under British! So as to ensure that he should be given the Tunisian front . . ." Eisenhower quickly became aware of these maneuverings, removed Clark from his post as his deputy commander and dispatched him to command the reserve forces in Morocco, a move heartily welcomed by Brooke. Subsequently, as commander of Fifth Army in Italy, Clark displayed a poor tactical grasp; almost lost his nerve at Salerno; mishandled the attacks by the Fifth Army on Cassino; gave General Lucas ambiguous orders at Anzio; and wasted the opportunities presented by the eventual breakout from the beachhead to make a publicity-driven dash for Rome. It was not surprising, therefore, that Eisenhower chose to overlook Clark, not only for Overlord but also for Anvil.

The man chosen for the job was a friend of Patton, General Alexander M. Patch. Born in Arizona in 1889, Patch was the son of a West Point graduate, stern disciplinarian, and veteran of the prairie wars, who retired from the U.S. Cavalry to become a railroad executive in Pennsylvania. Patch followed his father to West Point in 1909, where

---

* In January 1944 Patton was appointed commander of the U.S. Third Army in the United Kingdom as part of the Fortitude deception plan to convince the German high command that the main Allied blows were aimed at the Pas de Calais, not Normandy. In July 1944, the Third Army led the Normandy breakout.

he balked at Academy traditions like the ritual hazing of "plebs" (first-year cadets) by their "upperclassmen" seniors, and finished near the bottom of his class. He was commissioned in the summer of 1913 and assigned to the 18th Infantry Regiment in Texas. He took part in General Pershing's punitive expedition against Pancho Villa in 1916, where his superiors noted his promise and judgment. In November of that year he married a general's daughter, Julia A. Litell, and in June 1917 deployed to France as an infantry captain with the U.S. 1st Infantry Division. In France, Patch commanded the American Expeditionary Force's machine gun school at Langres and, in spite of suffering from a bad bout of pneumonia, finally saw action with 18th Infantry Regiment at the end of the war.

In the interwar years, Patch served three tours as a military academic before his appointment as the commander of the 47th Infantry Regiment, 9th Infantry Division, at Fort Bragg, Carolina, where the commanding general was Jacob Devers. In January 1942, after the Japanese attack on Pearl Harbor, Patch was promoted to major general and given the command of Task Force 6814, an ad hoc division-sized formation fashioned from two National Guard regiments, dispatched to defend the French colony of New Caledonia in the southwest Pacific, an important Allied base throughout the war.

After securing New Caledonia, and suffering a recurrence of his pneumonia, Patch's next appointment was as the commander of the Americal Division (a combination of America with New Caledonia) dispatched to relieve 1st Marine Division on the bitterly contested island of Guadalcanal on December 9, 1942. In January 1943, at the head of 14th Corps, consisting of Americal, 2nd Marine, and 25th Divisions, Patch drove the exhausted Japanese enemy westward away from Henderson Field, the American airstrip that had become the entire focus of the grueling seven-month land and sea battle for the mosquito-ridden and malarial island. American pilots based at Henderson Field lasted only thirty days before losing the hand and eye coordination required for combat operations. The Japanese were not cleared from Guadalcanal until February 1943. The clash of carriers at Midway (June 4, 1942) and the battle for Guadalcanal had nonetheless demonstrated that the Japanese could be beaten at sea and on land.

Patch's name was rarely associated with the battle for Guadalcanal. In the public mind the great hero of that campaign was General Archibald Vandegrift, commander of 1st Marine Division, but the self-effacing and quietly efficient Patch was never one to hog the limelight. After the conclusion of the Guadalcanal campaign, Marshall recalled Patch to command 4th Corps at Fort Lewis. While he recovered his health, Patch assembled a loyal staff, many of whom had served with him in the southwest Pacific and who remained with him for the duration. In March 1944, he took command of Seventh Army, charged with the planning of Anvil, and was pitched straight into the inter-Allied arguments over the operation.

The capture of Rome and the D-Day landings added urgency to the Allies' final decision. Wilson remained in favor of driving to the Po and then forking northeast through the Ljubljana Gap, the road to Shangri-La, overlooking the fact that this operation would require most if not all of the divisions in Italy, certainly those that had been provisionally allotted to Anvil. However, on July 2, the Combined Chiefs of Staff ordered Wilson to launch a three-division Anvil on August 15, reinforcing the assault force with airborne troops and follow-on French divisions. The objectives were the capture of Toulon and Marseille before exploitation northward up the Rhône Valley. Wilson was to push up the Italian peninsula as best he could with his remaining divisions.

This was almost the last straw for Churchill, still nursing hopes of landings in the Balkans or in Bordeaux. The Normandy breakout at the end of July had prompted him to renew his battle against Anvil and his demands for landings on the French Atlantic coast, where, he argued, reinforcements sailing directly from America could be more easily landed and fed into the northern European battleground. The Joint Chiefs of Staff noted that there was insufficient information on landing areas in this part of France and that they were also beyond the effective range of aircraft flying from Mediterranean bases. There was little point in abandoning a well-prepared operation for the sake of one that rested entirely on hypothesis.

Churchill sulked until almost the last moment, August 11, when the British Chiefs of Staff gave Anvil the go-ahead. The prime minister complained bitterly that he had been "dragooned" into agreeing to Anvil. On August 1 the code name for the operation had been changed to Dragoon, ostensibly because it was feared that Anvil had been compromised. Churchill may not have been pleased but Major General Truscott, preparing to lead the landings, regarded the switching of names as an excellent omen.

FOUR
FROM ANVIL TO DRAGOON

"... a man about my age, with thin hair graying around the temples, a square open face with cold eyes, medium height, trim, neat and very soldierly in appearance."

—General Truscott on his French counterpart General Jean de Lattre de Tassigny

At the highest political level of the Anglo-American alliance, the wrangling over Anvil had swung back and forth since the idea of the invasion of southern France had emerged in embryo in 1943. At the level of theater commander, both Eisenhower and Wilson had finessed their positions according to the changing circumstances that presented themselves as the war progressed, notably the demands of D-Day, deadlock at Anzio, and the prospect of driving through the Balkans to Vienna. Throughout these shifting Allied perspectives, Anvil remained a constant factor, sometimes in the background, sometimes in the foreground, nonetheless a significant element in the grand strategy designed to bring the war in Europe to a close. At a lower level, however, that of army and corps commanders, the planning and preparation for Anvil continued, unaffected for the most part by the often heated strategic debates within the Combined Chiefs of Staff and the American and British Chiefs of Staff.

After the capture of Rome, Truscott's 6th Corps was withdrawn from the campaign in Italy to prepare for the invasion of southern France. Although he knew little more at this stage, Truscott had been informed by Mark Clark at the end of December 1943 that an invasion of southern France, to coincide with Overlord, was being planned for the following May and that Eisenhower had been chosen as supreme commander of the Allied expeditionary force in northwest Europe. Clark told Truscott that Eisenhower wanted him to command the American assault force in southern France. The planning for the operation had been entrusted to Seventh Army headquarters, and Clark was to assume command of the Seventh while retaining command of Fifth Army until after the capture of Rome.

Thereafter, Clark confidently expected to be taken to the United Kingdom to command the Overlord landings. But he had not anticipated Eisenhower's misgivings about him, nor the long-running stalemate at Anzio. In March 1944, Clark was relieved of the responsibility of planning Anvil/Dragoon, and replaced by General Patch, while Truscott was directed to plan the assault and choose the American formations that would undertake it.

Truscott's first two choices, 3rd and 45th Infantry Divisions, were easy. The first had fought in World War I, where it gained the nickname of the "Marne Division" after it had prevented the German Army breaking though to Paris on the River Marne in July 1918. In November 1942, the 3rd Division had landed in French North Africa as part of Patton's Western Task Force. In February 1943, the division gained a new commander, one Major General Lucian Truscott, who led it during Operation Husky, the landings in Sicily, as part of Patton's Seventh Army, marching ninety miles in three days to take Messina. On September 18, 1943, the 3rd Division came ashore at Salerno with the 6th Corps, under Major General John P. Lucas (who had commanded the division between September 1941 and March 1942). In Italy as part of General Clark's Fifth Army, the corps saw some of the most bitter fighting in the European war before being held up by the Gustav Line. Having been pulled out of the line for rest and refurbishment, the 3rd Division was in action again as part of 6th Corps during the Anzio landings (Operation Shingle) and subsequent battle to retain the beachhead. In a two-day battle on February 28 and 29, 1944, the

3rd Division repelled an attack by two German divisions, Hermann Goering and the 362nd, plus elements of several others. By then the division's commander was Brigadier General John E. "Iron Mike" O'Daniel, Truscott having succeeded Lucas as commander of the 6th Corps. In late May 1944, the 3rd Division led the breakout from the Anzio beachhead, Operation "Diadem," but was then diverted by Mark Clark to Rome, allowing the greater part of the German 10th Army to escape destruction. Thereafter the division embarked on training for Dragoon.

The 45th ("Thunderbirds") Division,* commanded by Major General William W. Eagles, was drawn from the Oklahoma National Guard and was one of the first National Guard formations to be mobilized after the Japanese attack on Pearl Harbor. It arrived in French North Africa in June 1943 and first saw action in Sicily when it ran into the Mk 6 Tigers of the Hermann Goering Division. After participating in the drive for Messina, the division was taken out of the line for rest and rearguard duties, before transferring to 6th Corps for the invasion of peninsular Italy. It went ashore at Salerno and at the beginning of November crossed the River Volturno. Thereafter its advance was slowed by rivers swollen with autumn rain and mountainous terrain. The division was halted by the Gustav Line where, as part of Alexander's 15th Army Group, it could only inch forward, reaching a point north of Cassino by the end of the first week in January 1944. For Operation Shingle, the 45th Division was assigned Combat Command A of the 1st Armored Division, and one of its regiments (179th Infantry) was attached to the British 1st Infantry Division, capturing the Aprilia "factory," the focus of much subsequent fighting, which changed hands a number of times during the battle for the beachhead. Along with the rest of the Shingle assault force, 45th Division could not break out of the beachhead and could only hold its ground during repeated German counterattacks while being subjected to daily artillery bombardments. On May 23, 1944, the 45th joined the breakout from the northeast corner of the Allied lodgement, swinging northwest toward the Alban Hills and Rome, entering the Italian capital on June 4. Troops of the 45th were the first Allied troops to reach the Vatican.

---

* Many of 45th's men were Cherokee and Apache native Americans.

Thereafter the division was pulled from the line in preparation for Anvil.

Truscott's third choice was the 36th ("Arrowhead") Division, which was part of the Texas National Guard and had fought in the closing weeks of World War I in the Meuse-Argonne offensive. In World War II, the 36th Division arrived in French North Africa in April 1943 and initially spent much of its time supplying men to guard the 275,000 Axis prisoners of war taken at the conclusion of the Tunisian campaign. It was earmarked for the Husky landings but was passed over by Patton who favored troops with combat experience for the operation. However, Mark Clark, who was familiar with the 36th from his time as chief of staff to the Ground Forces, chose the division to spearhead the Salerno landings alongside two British divisions, the 46th and 56th.

Salerno proved a costly combat debut, in which 36th sustained some 4,000 casualties before being taken out of the line and placed in Fifth Army's reserves. It was back in action in November and saw heavy fighting in harsh winter weather on the Bernhardt Line (also known by the Allies as the Winter Line) stretching from the River Garigliano to Castel di Sangro in the Apennines, which was designed to delay the Allies as they approached the Gustav Line. While attempting to cross the River Gari, the 36th suffered heavy casualties when it ran up against the 15th Panzergrenadier Division.*

Subsequently, Clark came under a barrage of criticism for ordering a frontal attack against an experienced well-dug-in formation. He defended himself by claiming that the attack drew down German reserves from northern Italy that might have been used to counter the Shingle landings at Anzio. What Clark did not know at the time was that the reserves identified by the Allies in northern Italy had already been committed to the front by the British 10th Corps's first assault on Monte Cassino at the end of January 1944, undermining the reason he gave for the attack over the Gari.

* In forty-eight hours the 36th Division sustained 1,681 casualties: 143 killed, 663 wounded, and 875 missing, out of nearly 6,000 men who participated in the action. Many were recently arrived raw troops. In contrast the panzergrenadiers' casualties were 64 killed and 179 wounded.

In the second week of March 1944, the 36th was withdrawn from the line and on May 22 arrived by sea at the Anzio beachhead as part of Truscott's 6th Corps. Here it took part in the breakout from the beachhead, entering Rome on June 5, 1944, the day before the Normandy landings. In July, a new commander was appointed to the division, Major General John E. Dahlquist. Born to Swedish parents in Minnesota, Dahlquist had been commissioned in the U.S. Infantry in 1917 and subsequently served in the Allied occupation of the Rhineland in the aftermath of World War I. In the interwar years he served as an instructor in the Philippines, and in the mid-1930s attended the U.S. Army War College before becoming a staff officer. In early 1942 he was sent to England as a deputy chief of staff to Eisenhower before becoming assistant divisional commander (ADC) of 76th Division. In June 1943, promoted to the rank of major general, he became commander of 70th Division and a year later took command of 36th Division. Dahlquist had as yet gained no combat experience but later in the war he was criticized by his officers over the use of the Japanese-American men of the division's 442nd Regimental Combat Team as expendable, often assigned to near-suicidal missions. In October 1944, during fighting in the Vosges in the aftermath of Dragoon, the losses incurred by the 442nd in France came close to forcing his corps commander, Truscott, to consider relieving Dahlquist of his command.

The responsibility for planning Anvil was initially given to Allied Forces Headquarters (AFHQ) Joint Planning Staff, among whom were representatives of Admiral Cunningham's naval headquarters and the Mediterranean Allied Air Forces (MAAF). However, the demands of the campaign on mainland Italy meant that this task was handed to the staff of the Seventh Army based in Sicily and now consisting of no more than a skeleton headquarters, a move that was formalized, at Eisenhower's request, in December 1943. This was useful as a deception measure, but as the other headquarters planning Anvil were in North Africa the arrangement proved impractical, and the greater part of the planning was eventually moved to Algiers and Oran as Task Force 163.

It was not until March 1944 that the French were brought into the planning process for Anvil in the form of a small contingent headed by Colonel Jean Petit, who was little more than a liaison officer. Two months later, in June, a French team representing the French army, navy, and air force was fully integrated into the planning. This was a sore point with General Charles de Gaulle, president of the French Committee of National Liberation and commander in chief of the Free French Army. De Gaulle was determined to achieve both political and military legitimacy for the organizations that he headed, but in this he was thwarted by President Roosevelt, who persuaded his British ally to reach only military agreements with the French leader.

When the AFHQ brought de Gaulle into the planning of Anvil, the French were informed that almost the entire Free French Army—some eight divisions plus support and service units—would participate in the invasion of southern France. This prompted the French to propose that a senior French general should be appointed to lead the ground operations. They argued that their case was strengthened by the excellent performance in Italy of the French Expeditionary Corps with the U.S. Fifth Army. Moreover, they knew more than their American allies about the topography and the Resistance forces that the Allies would encounter in the southern French theater.

Clearly compromise was called for. De Gaulle, for his part, was able to agree that the French lack of experience in amphibious warfare disqualified them from a command role in the initial phase of the operation, but suggested that thereafter an army group headquarters be established to oversee the northward advance of the American and French armies. Wilson, the Supreme Allied Commander in the Mediterranean, suspected that the French might then demand control of the headquarters, but de Gaulle and his generals declared that they were willing to agree to an independent army command headed by an American. Wilson, his suspicions unallayed, then proposed a period between the assault and the establishment of a group headquarters during which the three corps, one American, two French, would be controlled by an American army headquarters.

De Gaulle was not satisfied with this arrangement, and toward the end of April appointed General Jean de Lattre de Tassigny as the commander of all French ground forces earmarked for Anvil. A cavalryman, de Lattre had been badly wounded in September 1914 in a mounted duel with a German lancer, an episode from a now-vanished form of warfare. In 1916, as a company commander, had fought at Verdun where he was wounded five times, receiving a citation, a

Military Cross, and the Légion d'Honneur. By 1939, he had risen to become chief of staff to the French 5th Army, relinquishing this post to command the 14th Division during the Battle of France, fighting with distinction amid the chaos and confusion of defeat. A nonpolitical soldier, de Lattre declared his loyalty to the French Army after the 1940 capitulation and was sent by the Vichy government to command troops in Tunisia. There he declared some pro-Allied sympathies, was recalled to France, and was sentenced to ten years in prison after the dissolution by the Germans of the Vichy army following the Torch landings in November 1942. He escaped in 1943 and made his way to England where he placed himself under de Gaulle's command and was appointed commander of Army B, a headquarters that the French had established specifically for Anvil.

Wilson went back to the drawing board, informing de Gaulle that de Lattre would temporarily assume command of the first French corps ashore in the South of France but would nevertheless be subject to the orders of the commander of U.S. Seventh Army. On the arrival of the second French corps, de Lattre would assume command of Army B, which was later redesignated the 1st French Army, but would remain subordinate to the commander of the Seventh Army, ensuring that the latter exercised a dual role as an army and army group headquarters. The aim was simple: the retention in American hands of control over civil affairs, troops, and supply priorities; and the easing of coordination with Eisenhower's SHAEF forces to the north.

De Gaulle agreed to the placing of a full French general under the command of an American lieutenant general provided that de Lattre retained all the other privileges of the commander of an army. Nevertheless, de Lattre had to be handled with kid gloves. General Truscott met him for the first time at a lunch to which he had invited the French general some three weeks before the launching of Anvil. He remembered ". . . a man of about my age, with thin hair graying around the temples, a square open face with cold eyes, medium height, trim, neat and very soldierly in appearance. Even his greeting was cold and reserved, wholly lacking in warmth I had found in previous contacts with Frenchmen."[1] He could have been describing Adolphe Menjou's cynical French World War I general in Stanley Kubrick's 1957 movie, *Paths of Glory*.

De Lattre quickly made Truscott aware of the reason for his froideur. He complained that Truscott had previously inspected some of his units without his presence and without permission, violating customary military protocol and, crucially, the honor of France. De Lattre then drew Truscott into a private conversation where he continued to make the strongest objection to the Anvil assault plan, about which he had not been consulted, particularly the loan of an armored combat command allotted to him to serve under an American commander beyond the time limit—D+3—he had agreed with de Gaulle. It subsequently took all of Truscott's tact to defuse the situation and smooth over the potential rupture with de Lattre's more sympathetic subordinates.

The French also proved prickly about more practical matters. By the end of 1943, a number of French divisions were in the process of being raised. The first two, 2nd Armored (*2e blindée*) and 1st Motorized Infantry (*1ere motorisé d'infanterie*) were from the outset aligned with de Gaulle's Free French. The other divisions were raised from the African Army (*Armée d'Afrique*) after Operation Torch in November 1942. Four infantry divisions had fought in Italy under General Alphonse Juin as the French Expeditionary Corps (*Corps expéditionnaire français, CEF*) and had distinguished themselves in the mountain fighting around Cassino in early 1944. De Lattre had also raised three divisions, 1st and 5th Armored (*1ere* and *5e blindée*) and 9th Colonial Infantry (*9e Infanterie Coloniale*) as part of Army B. The plan envisaged by de Gaulle was to extract the CEF from Italy and amalgamate them with Army B for the liberation of southern France, in the process forming the new 1st French Army. However, only four divisions arrived in time to fight in the opening phases of the invasion of southern France: 1st, 3rd, and 9th Infantry, and 1st Armored, plus a number of special forces units.*

---

* The French colonial troops were undoubtedly brave but also prone to outbursts of savagery. The British writer Norman Lewis, who served as a field intelligence officer in Italy, wrote of them in his book *Naples '44*: "The French colonial troops are on the rampage again. Whenever they take a town or village, a wholesale rape of the population takes place. Recently all females in the villages of Patricia, Pofi, Isoletta, and Supino were violated. In Lenola, which fell to the Allies in May, fifty women were raped but—as there were not enough to go round—children and even old men were violated."

The Free French units raised in North Africa in 1943–44 were armed and equipped by the Americans along American lines. By the end of 1944, these divisions split approximately into component parts of two-thirds *Indigènes* (native Africans) and one-third *Européens* (European settlers) approximately 154,000 men in all. The French were eager to make the best possible use of their limited manpower resources in combat units unencumbered by the range of supporting service units that the Americans considered indispensable. Still smarting from the national humiliation of 1940, the French felt deeply that their honor depended on the deployment of the maximum number of troops in combat, at the expense of what they considered the Americans' predilection for over-elaborate service support. There were practical reasons for this. In the invasion of southern France two of Army B's three infantry divisions, the 3rd and the 9th, were composed of Algerian, Senegalese,* and Moroccan troops, many of whom lacked technical skills and were functionally illiterate. Until they were able to draw on the resources of metropolitan France, the French would find it all but impossible to provide comprehensive technical services along American lines. To fill some of the gaps caused by the illiterate draftees, French women were taken into the Army Auxiliary, the AFAT (*Auxiliaire feminin de l'armée de terre*) to serve in technical support roles as radio operators, typists, drivers, and nurses. Of the 250,000 troops eventually deployed by the French 1st Army in the closing stages of the war, some 5,000 were women.

It was also anticipated that the French Resistance would play an important part in Anvil. The rugged topography of much of southern France was more suited to Resistance activity than the milder and more easily patrolled landscapes of the northwest, and the term for those who fought in this role, Maquisards, is derived from the Corsican word for "bush." De Gaulle sought to dignify these guerilla forces as the French Forces of the Interior (*Forces françaises de l'intérieur, FFI*) implying that they were a regular military organization rather than a band of outlaws, and on June 9, 1944, they were recognized as a component of the Free French Army.

* The term "Senegalese" was used by the French to describe sub-Saharan troops from a variety of colonies including Madagascar, the Ivory Coast, and Senegal.

❖

"Now set Europe ablaze!" was the stirring instruction issued in July 1940 by Winston Churchill to Hugh Dalton, the director of the newly formed Special Operations Executive (SOE). Simply stated, the agency's task was to encourage and aid resistance to Nazi rule in Occupied Europe, but all too often the harsh facts of topography and the brutality of the German occupiers militated against the sustained and successful prosecution of irregular warfare. The conflagration envisaged by Churchill never transpired, but from late 1943 the looming prospect of an Allied invasion of mainland Europe energized the Resistance movement that was now supplied and aided by two agencies, SOE and its American equivalent, the Office of Strategic Services (OSS) that had been established in June 1942.

SOE ran several sections that operated in occupied France, the most significant of which were its own independent F Section, the Gaullist Free French RF (*République Français*) Section, and AMF Section that operated from Algiers and latterly collaborated closely with the OSS and DF Section handling escape and evasion. Friction sometimes arose between the OSS and SOE over dealings with the French authorities in North Africa. This prompted Eisenhower to bring the two agencies together under one roof as the Special Forces Headquarters (SFHQ) that formed part of the Operations Division of the Supreme Headquarters Allied Expeditionary Force (SHAEF). Significantly, SOE's F and RF Sections' operational methods were markedly different. F Section maintained small, autonomous cells that remained independent of each other, reducing the risk of enemy penetration and the rolling up of entire networks, while RF Section chose to run larger networks, controlled from the center, a model that by its very nature exposed an infiltrated network to much greater danger of betrayal and penetration by enemy agents.

In France the Resistance had emerged after the humiliating defeat in the summer of 1940, which was followed by the German occupation of three-fifths of the country. The remaining two-fifths and France's overseas colonies were governed by Marshal Philippe Pétain's puppet government based in the spa town of Vichy some seventy-five miles northwest of Lyon. In February 1943, the Vichy government introduced *Service de Travail Obligatoire* (Compulsory Work Service) that dispatched hundreds of thousands of Frenchmen to work in Germany, some of whom were pressed into service in the German armed forces. As the German ambassador in Paris, Otto Abetz, later observed, this measure served as a first-class recruiting drive for the French Resistance.

Many young Frenchmen avoided deportation by becoming active members of the Resistance. Another boost to the Resistance had preceded compulsory work service, in November 1942, following the Allied landings in North Africa in Operation Torch. The Vichy territory of central and southern France was immediately occupied by the Germans, the Vichy government reduced to a cipher, and its token armistice army of some 100,000 men disbanded, prompting many officers and other ranks to join the Resistance, becoming members of the ORA (*Organization de Résistance de l'Armée*). One of them, Henri Zeller, was to command the Resistance in southeast France. The men of the ORA took with them their ranks, customs, sometimes their regimental standards and their continued observance of military discipline, understandable perhaps but a trait that did not always endear them to *Résistants* who came from a civilian background. More welcome were the arms, ammunition, and equipment that the men who had joined the ORA had been smuggling out of army barracks and depots from 1941 onward.

From the outset, the Resistance had many aims and many faces covering a wide and often ungovernable political spectrum, from Communists to members of the old aristocracy and from peasants to university professors. Among its principal aims up to 1944 were monitoring German troop movements and defenses; countering German propaganda with secretly printed pamphlets; exfiltrating downed Allied air crews to the safety of neutral countries; sabotaging strategic installations; executing collaborators; and stockpiling weapons in anticipation of the Allied invasion of France. Resistance cells usually specialized in one or two of these activities. René Lefèvre, an alarming figure with a tattooed face and rictus grin, who operated on the Vercors plateau in southeast France, specialized in the killing of collaborators, customarily after downing a strong drink to steady his revolver hand. He was rumored to have dispatched more than fifty "*collabos*" in this fashion. Lefèvre was one of the more outrageous Resistance activists, a far cry from the so-called "*sedentaires*," Résistants who maintained a civilian front while training at weekends. Needless to say, the Germans made no distinction between the two types of Résistants. By the spring of 1944, Resistance numbers in the South of France were some 3,700 armed activists and some 10,000 unarmed members, all of them covering a wide range of political allegiances.

After Hitler's invasion of the Soviet Union in June 1941, the French Communist Party recognized that the Nazis were, for the duration of the war at least, the real enemy and threw its formidable experience in clandestine operations into supporting the Resistance as the FTP/*Francs-Tireurs et Partisans* (Sharpshooters and Partisans) a name that they appropriated from the term used for irregular infantry in the Franco-Prussian War of 1870–71. Politics inevitably played a big part in the history of the Resistance, and the FTP often found itself at odds with Gaullist FFI, which they regarded as a tool of British intelligence. The FTP's Résistants were equally unsympathetic to the ex-regular officers of the ORA, a body of men unlikely to harbor political views similar to their own. The FTP's exceptionalism also extended to membership of the MUR (*Movements unis de la résistance*) an umbrella organization that it studiously ignored.

The Gaullists in the Resistance maintained their links with SOE in London through a parallel organization established by de Gaulle, the Central Bureau of Intelligence Operations (*Bureau Central de Renseignments D'Action, BCRA*) headed by a dapper, bowler-hatted regular soldier, Colonel André Dewavrin, almost a French parody of an upper-class Englishman, who adopted the nom de guerre "Colonel Passy." In contrast, the FTP looked for military and political leadership first to the French Communist Party and then to the National Council of the Resistance (*Conseil National de Résistance, CNR*) the body established by de Gaulle to unify the disparate Resistance movements in France and coordinate their activities.*

* The Council had been convened for the first time in May 1943 by Jean Moulin, de Gaulle's delegate-general in France. A month later Moulin was captured by the Germans and died at their hands.

The professional and class divides that split the FFI were embodied in men like François Huet (code name "Hervieux") who from May 1944 was the military commander of the Resistance on the Vercors massif in the Drôme department in southeastern France, the northeastern corner of which overlooked the city of Grenoble. Born into an upper-class Grenoble family, Huet passed through Saint-Cyr, the elite academy for French officers, in the mid-1920s before joining a colonial regiment. A highly intelligent man who was keenly aware that he had a role to play in France's society and overseas empire, he joined the Vichy army after the French capitulation, but after its dissolution in 1942 had cast his lot with the Resistance and went underground in 1944. A devout Catholic, humorless, a believer in traditional church and state hierarchies, and wedded to notions of conventional rather than guerrilla warfare, Huet fought gallantly but often unavailingly to steer a way through the maze of competing Resistance factions vying with each other on the Vercors.

Huet's polar opposite on the Vercors was Eugène Chavant, a socialist and mayor of the mountain resort of Villard-de-Lans who had served as an NCO in World War I and in World War II had gone underground with the Resistance. A man who was never afraid to express his views, Chavant nevertheless resisted arguing with his military comrades on the Vercors but could not avoid clashing with the military commander of the southern half of the Vercors plateau, Captain Narcisse Geyer, Huet's subordinate, a cavalryman who had served in an elite regiment and a fervent believer in "*la gloire*" and "*l'honneur*" (not unlike de Lattre). Geyer was seldom seen out of the saddle and regarded the Maquisards as "civilians playing at soldiers." Such were some of the underlying fault lines in the French Resistance in the South of France.

The Maquisards steered clear of open country and garrison towns, preferring to establish bases in forests. In southeast France they favored the Alpine high country, where winding roads, rocky escarpments, and densely wooded plateaux discouraged the constant attention of German patrols. Captain Geoffrey Jones was an OSS agent who had parachuted into the Alpes-Maritimes at the beginning of August 1944. The headquarters of the Maquis he joined was "out there in the middle of nowhere on this mountain. We had a beautiful view because from it you could see all the way from Italy down to Marseille. You could see the whole coast of southern France . . . The Germans had left these people alone because it was so far away from the road. There was nothing, absolutely nothing else up there. The only way the Germans could have gotten to them was by helicopter or by using parachute infantry. And then we would have seen them coming long enough in advance to have melted into any one of the caves that pocked the sides of the mountain. So we had good security there just so long as we didn't harass the Germans too much."[2]

Inaccessibility was also the key to the lengthy survival of the Vercors as a center of Resistance activity. The Vercors is a 3,000-foot massif straddling the departments of the Drôme and Isère and marking the dividing line between northern temperate France and the warmth and abundance of the Mediterranean. Topped by northern and southern plateaux, thickly wooded with birch and pine forests broken by open meadows, drenched in the scent of wild thyme and cut with deep gorges and ravines, this immense bastion—a land of vivid greens and purples, baking in summer and snowbound in winter—commands important lines of communication. To the south, the Drôme; to the west, Valence and the Rhône Valley artery; to the north and northwest, the River Isère; and to the east, the Route Napoléon and the Route des Alpes d'Hiver from Grenoble to Aix, Marseille, and Nice.

By the end of June 1944, there were some 4,000 armed Résistants on the Vercors, many of whom had never fired a shot in anger but were burning to strike a blow at the Wehrmacht. In the spring of 1944, Allied planners had envisaged using the plateau as a springboard for attacks on German lines of communication in the immediate aftermath of D-Day and had considered air landings by glider-borne troops from Algeria on an airstrip at Vassieux, in the heart of the Vercors, improvised by the Resistance. But on June 8 the fighters on the Vercors jumped the gun, declaring its three hundred square miles of wooded and rolling farmland an independent republic. The Allied air landings never came, and the Germans responded at first with probing attacks launched by 157th Division from Grenoble followed on July 21 by air landings of their own at Vassieux. The lightly armed Résistants were drawn into a set-piece battle with a well-equipped enemy in which they suffered some 650 casualties. At least two hundred civilians also lost their lives, many of them murdered by men of the *Ost* (East) battalions, the so-called "Mongols," flown onto the plateau after the initial assault. This major setback served as a warning to the Maquis that they should avoid direct confrontations with the Wehrmacht until the arrival of Allied forces. They returned to the more traditional style of *petite guerre*, harassment and ambush. Nevertheless, in 1975 Alain Le Ray, who from January 1944 headed the FFI in the Isère Department, argued persuasively against the view that the Vercors episode was a complete disaster, suggesting that the battle for the Vercors tied down a significant part of the German Army in France and "induced in the German war machine a kind of paralysis, both moral and material" in the locality targeted by the Allied forces landing in the South of France.

In the months leading up to Anvil, the attention of SOE and OSS had been tugged away from Italy and the Balkans, previously their major preoccupation, to the Mediterranean coast of France. One of the most significant of SOE's networks (or circuits) in the region was code-named "Jockey," established in 1943 and run by Francis Cammaerts, a twenty-seven-year-old Anglo-Belgian graduate of Cambridge University and one of the agency's most cool-headed and resourceful organizers. The tall and imposing Cammaerts (code-named "Roger" and nicknamed "Big Feet" by his Resistance comrades) was responsible for a huge area running up and down the left bank of the Rhône Valley between Vienne and Arles and inland between the Isère and the Riviera hinterland. Cammaerts had been caught up in the fight for the Vercors, which he considered little short of a disaster, but had escaped capture.

A former conscientious objector, Cammaerts had been ordered by SOE to "coordinate sabotage and other subversive activities including the organization of the Resistance, and . . . providing advice and liaison on all matters in connection with the Patriot [Resistance] forces up to the time of their embodiment into the regular forces . . . Sabotage of communications and other targets must be carefully regulated and integrated with operational plans." In other words, Cammaerts was to train and direct the units he armed so that they gave the maximum support to the Allied invasion when it came. Until D-Day and immediately thereafter, he was not to put his weight behind objectives that were purely French. Up till the early spring 1944, the stop-start progress of Anvil had starved the Maquis in Provence of supplies air-dropped by the Allies. Thereafter, in the run-up to the Allied landings in southern France they received delivery of some 5,600 Sten guns, 4,400 rifles, 290 machine guns, 22 mortars, and 30 PIAT* anti-tank launchers.

From May, a stream of SOE and OSS personnel arrived in the region. There were three types of mission: so-called Jedburghs, inter-Allied teams, usually of three men assigned a specific mission; Operational Groups, OSS paratroops in squads of fifteen or thirty, again tasked with specific combat missions; and counter-scorch teams composed of French naval personnel whose specific task was to minimize the effects of German sabotage in the harbors of Toulon and Marseille. The U.S. Seventh Army also established the 4-SFU (Special Forces Unit No. 4) composed of experienced British and American agents to coordinate the movement of Maquis activists with those of those of the U.S. and French military when they arrived. On July 6, a month after D-Day, there was another arrival, that of SOE agent Christine Granville,** a member of "Mission Paquebot" tasked with building an airstrip for Allied aircraft near the village of Vassieux in the heart of the Vercors. Granville was eventually to rendezvous with Francis Cammaerts, and we will hear more of their exploits in Chapter 12.

A month before his disconcerting encounter with de Lattre, on June 16, 1944, Truscott had flown to AFHQ in Algiers, where he learned that Marshall was due to arrive on the following day. At Force 163 headquarters he met Patch for the first time, noting: "I was fully aware of his fine reputation and knew that he was highly esteemed. He was thin and wiry, simple in dress and forthright in manner—obviously keenly intelligent with a dry Scottish humor [Patch was of Scottish-Irish descent]. His quick and almost jerky speech and movement gave

* Projector, Infantry, Anti-Tank, a spigot discharger using a heavy steel rod propelled by a spring. The bomb had a hollow tail shaft containing a propelling cartridge and a shaped-charge warhead. It was laid in a trough at the front of the PIAT; on pulling the trigger the steel spigot was released and flew forward, into the tail of the bomb, to fire the cartridge. The explosion launched the bomb and also recocked the spigot ready for the next shot.

** Christine Granville was the code name for Countess Krystyna Skarbek, a Pole who had established links with British intelligence from the early days of the war and later joined SOE's Massingham station near Algiers.

me the impression that he was nervous and found some difficulty in expressing himself. Our conversation during the evening concerned our war experiences. Patch had served in the Pacific . . . He and his staff were new to the European Theater and this was to their first assault landing operation. This, I think, influenced both of us in our early association."

The next day Truscott met Marshall, with whom he drove into Algiers from the Maison Blanche airfield, the hub for the U.S. Air Force's transport and combat operations. On the drive Marshall informed Truscott that Eisenhower had wanted him to command the American component in the Overlord beachhead* but had decided that he was too valuable an asset in Italy. The rest of the day was devoted to discussion of the plans for Anvil/Dragoon. The details were still sketchy but Patch provided an outline. The plan was for the 6th Corps to make a three-division assault landing on beaches east of Toulon, followed up by seven French divisions, subject to the availability of shipping. Truscott's corps was to hold the beachhead and protect its right flank while the French corps took Toulon. The two corps were then to drive westward to capture Marseilles, the principal objective of the landings. In his discussion with Patch, Truscott laid great emphasis on the importance of undivided command responsibility during the initial phase of the operation. It was vital to assemble army, navy, and air planners to evolve detailed plans as soon as possible, initiate rigorous training, and finally to move the Corps's headquarters to Naples the better to coordinate planning.

* General Omar Bradley, Patton's deputy commander in Sicily, was eventually chosen to lead the Normandy landings as commander of the U.S. First Army.

FIVE
THE OTHER SIDE OF THE HILL

> "When I arrived in France, we received one loaf of bread for two soldiers. After a few weeks we had to share one between four men, then six men, and in the last few weeks we received one loaf for ten men. Everyone got one slice. Imagine what that was like for seventeen- and eighteen-year-olds who were still growing and needed strength."
>
> —Karl Cyron, 164th Reserve Grenadier Battalion, 148th Division

A collaboration has been envisaged between our two countries. I have accepted it in principle." With these words the eighty-four-year-old Marshal Philippe Pétain, the hero of Verdun and now the president of a defeated France, announced the agreement he had reached with Adolf Hitler at Montoire in October 1940. France had been humiliated on the battlefield but did not join the war on the German side. For the Germans, French neutrality in the conflict continued to serve their interests, ensuring the delivery of goods, labor, and stability within metropolitan France while Hitler turned his attention to the East. The French prisoners of war in German hands guaranteed Pétain's good behavior, and his drive to create an authoritarian state, administered by a compliant civil service, made the German occupation of his country all the more easy.

In the years 1940–41, when the German high command believed that the war was all but over, Pétain's collaborationist stance gave them good reason not to press his Vichy regime to deliver more than they could give. By the end of 1942, however, events began to turn the Allies' way, swelling the sails of the French Resistance, until then only a minor irritant, and threatening to disrupt the deceptively peaceful continuity promised by the aged Marshal.

Until the onset of winter in 1943, the German high command had been largely preoccupied with the prosecution of the war of the Eastern Front. By November 1943, however, it realized that an Anglo-American invasion of northwest Europe presented as big a potential threat as a Red Army breakthrough in the East. This particularly exercised Hitler's morbid imagination. An invasion on the northern coast of France not only threatened Germany's industrial heartland, the loss of which would end the war, but would also open the path to central Europe. The Führer's answer lay in his concept of "Fortress Europe" (*Festung Europa*) on which work was been progressing since 1942.

Before November 1943, the principal task of the German theater command responsible for the defense of France, *Oberbefehlshaber West* (OB West), under Field Marshal Gerd von Rundstedt, was to provide a reservoir of reinforcements for the Eastern Front, rest and recreation for those formations battered in that brutal theater of war, and, as the occasion arose, which it did more frequently, replenishment for the units in Italy and the Balkans. Now Hitler and his high command, *Oberkommando der Wehrmacht* (OKW), began reinforcing OB West to meet an Allied amphibious invasion on the coast of northwest France. For Hitler, often unwilling to yield an inch of ground,* the coast of France was to be the German main line of resistance. On November 3, 1943, he issued Führer Directive No. 51** that provided the framework for the defense of Fortress Europe: "Everything indicates

* Hitler's stubbornness on this issue was by no means unyielding, but after the war was exaggerated in the recollections of many of his generals. On occasion he could be made to see reason.

** Hitler's Directives of World War II run from the plan to attack Poland (August 31, 1939) to his last orders to troops on the Eastern Front (April 15, 1945) to choke the Red Army in "a bath of blood." They reveal Hitler's state of mind throughout the war, from Germany's initial triumphs to stalemate, retreat, and imminent disaster.

that the enemy will launch an offensive against the Western Front of Europe, at the latest in the spring [of 1944], perhaps even earlier. I can, therefore, no longer take responsibility for further weakening in the west, in favor of other theaters of war. I have therefore decided to reinforce its defenses, particularly those places from which the long-range bombardment [by the V-1 pilotless bombs] of England will begin. For it is here that the enemy must and will attack—unless all indications are misleading—that the decisive battle against the landing forces will be fought." That month he appointed Field Marshal Erwin Rommel commander of Heeresgruppe (Army Group) B with special responsibility for strengthening the coastal defenses of northern France.

The defenses Hitler was proposing to reinforce were those of the Atlantic Wall (*Atlantikwall*) the grandiloquently named defense system stretching 1,700 miles from the North Cape to the Spanish frontier. It was not the impregnable barrier of Hitler's imaginings—in the Normandy area only 18 percent of the planned construction had been completed by June 6, 1944. Hitler had boasted to General Heinz Guderian, "I am the greatest builder of fortifications of all time," prompting the panzer leader to reflect, "Hitler was a man of the 1914–18 trench warfare epoch, and had never understood the principles of mobile operations." The Wall never became a true defensive line but remained a series of semi-isolated strongpoints, many of them possessing a kind of brutalist grandeur. Rundstedt considered that the Wall was "an illusion conjured up by propaganda." OB West had already concluded that it faced a well-nigh impossible task with the means it had at hand, and launched a preliminary examination of a withdrawal of its forces from southern France the better to defend the country's northwest coast.

German intelligence's estimation of Allied intentions in the West was essentially accurate—an invasion in northwest France was expected in the first third of 1944. Intelligence also concluded that the invasion would be timed to coincide with a major Soviet offensive in the East (Operation Bagration, which was eventually launched on June 22, 1944, the third anniversary of Barbarossa) and a series of secondary peripheral attacks aimed at dispersing and pinning down German forces before a cross-Channel assault was attempted.

German intelligence initially thought that the Anzio landing was just such an attack. When it detected the presence of substantial uncommitted forces in North Africa, it drew the conclusion, in February 1944, that a landing in southern France might precede the cross-Channel assault. A closer examination of Allied shipping potential, however, suggested that the South of France option was more likely to be retained by the Allies as a threat, a conclusion that accurately reflected the Anglo-American deliberations of the early spring of 1944.

After June 6, 1944, the Germans kept a wary eye on the South of France, and by early August OKW anticipated that the Riviera was the likeliest candidate for an Allied landing; only OB South-West, in the Italian theater, held out for the Ligurian coast in northern Italy. By August 1944, German commanders in southern France were steeling themselves for an attack, but were still undecided about the precise location of the assault beachhead. Meanwhile, events in northern France were having a significant impact on the German dispositions in the south. By the third week in July, the Allies were poised to break out of their Normandy bridgehead. A month earlier Rundstedt, convinced that the position was already irretrievable, urged that all the OB West forces, including those in southern France, be pulled back to defend Germany's western border. Hitler's response was to replace Rundstedt with Field Marshal Günther von Kluge, the only survivor of the original army commanders with whom he went to war in 1939, with orders to throw the Allies back into the sea.

Kluge, a realist and a veteran of defensive battles on the Eastern Front, could not stem the Allied tide as Patton's U.S. Third Army poured through the bottleneck at Avranches, on the French Atlantic coast, at the beginning of August. Hamstrung by Hitler's no-withdrawal orders, handicapped by his dwindling armored reserves, and harassed during daylight by Allied dominance of the air, Kluge could do little more than preside over the collapse of the German front in France. OKW now faced two options: a general withdrawal from France, both north and south, or an immediate counterattack. Predictably, Hitler chose the latter, aimed at the flank of the Allied breakthrough at Mortain, twenty-five miles southeast of Avranches, and launched on August 7. Simultaneously, the German commanders in the South of France were ordered to hold the Mediterranean coastline at all costs while OKW prepared contingency plans for a general withdrawal to a new line across northeast France.

The counterattack at Mortain was mounted by six Panzer divisions, but the armored losses in Normandy meant that their strength was now the equivalent of little more than three. Hitler wanted to delay until the divisions were reinforced, but Kluge, anxious about steadily mounting Allied pressure on his flank, decided to attack. The preliminaries to the attack had been revealed to the Allies by Ultra intercepts, but it appeared at first that the Mortain blow had succeeded, and an elated Hitler issued orders to roll up the entire Allied position in Normandy. However, further progress was halted by ferocious Allied air attacks after an advance of some ten miles, twenty miles short of Avranches. Within thirty-six hours, the German were back on their start lines.* Within five days, 7th Army, 5th Panzer Army, and Panzer Group Eberbach were themselves threatened with destruction as they tried to wriggle out of the Falaise Gap, a pocket formed by Canadian 1st Army and British 2nd Army to the north and the U.S. First and Third Armies to the south. Only 20,000 of the 80,000 Germans trapped in the pocket escaped, leaving behind them 380 tanks and self-propelled guns, 700 artillery pieces, and 5,000 assorted vehicles. In his report on the debacle, SS General Paul Hausser, commander of the 7th Army, observed of the troops who struggled out of the pocket: "Conditions of clothing are appalling. Many without headgear, without belts, and with worn footwear. Many go barefoot. In so far as they cannot get supplies from the supply centers they live on the country without consideration for property. Hatred and terrorist [Resistance] activity is thus intensified among the population . . . Morale badly shaken. The enemy command of the air has contributed specially to this." On August 17, two days before the Allied jaws snapped shut on the Falaise pocket, Kluge was relieved of his command, and committed suicide by swallowing poison.

---

* A crucial factor in the Allied success at Mortain was the daily intelligence on German strength and intentions at the battle front, including Hitler's order to attack, that Field Marshal Montgomery was receiving via Ultra decrypts of German radio traffic. The Mortain decrypts were the most important supplied to any general in the course of the war.

Before this chain of events began to unfold, the responsibility for the defense of northern France had rested with Field Marshal Erwin Rommel,* commanding Army Group B (Heeresgruppe B), and of southern France with General Johannes Blaskowitz commanding Army Group G (Heeresgruppe G).** The boundary line between the two formations ran along the River Loire to the Alps.

Born in 1885 in East Prussia, Blaskowitz was the son a Lutheran pastor and had served as a staff officer in World War I on both the Eastern and Western Fronts, seeing action in the latter at Verdun. After the armistice in 1918, Blaskowitz remained in the *Reichswehr*, the 100,000-strong postwar German army permitted by the Allies under the terms of the Treaty of Versailles, rising to the rank of general. Unlike many of his fellow officers, he was politically neutral, as the Reichswehr was originally intended to be, and was seemingly untroubled by Hitler's emergence as German chancellor. Nevertheless, as his fellow officer, General Günther Blumentritt,*** later recalled, he was unusually high-minded, nationalistic, and deeply religious. In 1938–39, Blaskowitz led the forces that occupied Austria and Czechoslovakia, and in the invasion of Poland in September 1939 he commanded the German 8th Army in the Battle of the Bzura, the largest single engagement of the campaign, in which elements of two Polish armies were destroyed in an encirclement in the bend of the River Vistula, near Warsaw.

During the Polish campaign, Blaskowitz was awarded the Knight's Cross of the Iron Cross and was subsequently appointed to command the Army of Occupation in Poland. Here he ran into trouble. In a memorandum he sent to Field Marshal Walther von Brauchitsch, the

* Rommel had been badly injured when on July 17, 1944, his car was strafed by a British fighter. While recovering, he came under suspicion of being involved in the July 20 bomb plot to assassinate Hitler. Offered the choice of poison or a show trial with attendant threats to his family, Rommel chose the former. It was publicly announced that he had died of his wounds and he was accorded a state funeral.

** Army Group G headquarters became operational on May 12, but was initially designated as an *Armeegruppe* with an inferior status to Heeresgruppe B. Army Group G was reclassified as a Heeresgruppe on September 11, 1944. Technically command of an army group should have resulted in Blaskowitz's promotion to field marshal, but Hitler would not countenance this.

*** Rundstedt's chief of staff in France, tasked with planning counter-invasion measures.

commander in chief of the German Army, he complained in forceful terms of the treatment of the Poles by their German conquerors, particularly the SS: "It is misguided to slaughter tens of thousands of Jews and Poles as is happening at present; because in view of the huge population neither the concept of a Polish state nor the Jews will be eliminated by doing so . . . If high officials of the SS and police demand acts of violence and brutality and praise them publicly, then, in a very short time, we shall be faced with the rule of the thug . . . The resettlement program is causing especial and growing discontent throughout the country. It is obvious that the starving population, which is fighting for its existence, can only observe with the greatest concern how the masses of those being resettled are left to find refuge with them completely penniless and, so to speak, naked and hungry. It is only too understandable that these feelings reach a pitch of uncontrollable hatred at the number of children dying of starvation on every transport, and the wagons of people frozen to death. The idea that one can intimidate the Polish population by terrorism and rub their noses in the dirt will certainly prove false."[1]

Hitler considered Blaskowitz's protest against the treatment of the Poles by the SS as nothing more than "maudlin sentimentality" and "infantile," and at the end of May 1940 he was relieved of his command in Poland and appointed military governor of northern France, moving five months later to command the 1st Army on the French southwest coast between Brittany and the Spanish border. In May 1944, Blaskowitz became commander of Army Group G, comprising the 1st and 19th Armies, defending the South of France with headquarters at Rouffiac in the Charente.

In the early summer of 1944, the condition of the two army groups under Rundstedt's overall command in France was far from satisfactory. The field marshal had at his disposal over 850,000 men and 1,550 tanks in 59 divisions—48 infantry, one panzergrenadier, and 10 panzer. Two more of his panzer divisions were on the Eastern Front, and on June 12 were ordered back to France. Rommel's Army Group B, 15th and 17th Armies defending the crucial theater from Holland to the Loire, was the more significant of Rundstedt's army groups, and during the Normandy campaign was to absorb a number of Blaskowitz's best formations.

❖

Blaskowitz's Army Group G comprised two subordinate commands, 1st Army on the Atlantic coast from Spain to the Loire estuary, and 19th Army on the Mediterranean coastline. In command of the 19th Army from June 1944 was General Friedrich Wiese. Born in 1892, Wiese had served in World War I, and in the chaos of postwar Germany had been a member of the right-wing paramilitary *Freikorps* before becoming a police officer in Hamburg. In 1935 he was recalled to active duty in the German Army with the rank of major. A zealous Nazi, he fought in France in 1940 and later on the Eastern Front. Cool-headed, imperturbable, and a skilled tactician, he had been told by Hitler on his appointment to command the 19th Army to "fight to the last man and the last bullet." At the beginning of August 1944, Wiese commanded seven infantry divisions controlled by three corps headquarters.

Between January and June 1944, Army Group G had suffered a steady degradation as troops were transferred first to Italy and, after the Allied invasion of France, to Normandy. Three of Blaskowitz's four panzer formations, 2nd SS Panzer Division, 9th Panzer Division, and 17th SS Panzergrenadier Division, were sent to Normandy, leaving only the 11th Panzer Division, which also had to relinquish half its tank strength to northern France.* Before June 6, Blaskowitz disposed of only four battle-ready, full-strength infantry divisions, and three of these were also sent to Normandy. The nine he retained comprised four "static" and five "reserve" divisions. The static (*bodenstandig*) divisions were intended principally for field fortifications and coastal defense, but were thinly stretched with an average defensive frontage of some sixty miles, over five times more than was recommended. These divisions consisted of a high proportion of older men, convalescents, and inexperienced officers. Their ranks were filled by a bewildering range of foreign volunteers and impressed men, among them Russians, Hungarians, Yugoslavs, Volksdeutsche Poles and Czechs who had been incorporated into the Third Reich, Romanians, and Dutchmen. Pay books were issued in eight different languages

* The authorized wartime strength of 11th Panzer was 78 PzKpfw Mk4s, 73 PzKpfw Mk 5s, and 21 assault guns.

just to deal with the various peoples from the Soviet Union, of whom some 60,000 found themselves in France in 1944.

The fighting qualities of these troops were of a low order. Rundstedt considered them "a menace and a nuisance to operations in France." Moreover, these fragile formations were further weakened by the "combing out" of their fittest soldiers to serve on the Eastern Front. They were often replaced by Ost (East) battalions of Russian POWs who had volunteered to serve in the Wehrmacht rather than face a lingering death in prison camps. The men of the static divisions were usually armed with captured or cast-off weapons and had little or no transport. They were even short of the horses and carts that provided the infantry with a large part of its motive power on the Eastern Front. "Mobility" was provided by a bicycle-borne company in each battalion. Most, if not all, of these men realized that Germany was going to lose the war, as did Rundstedt.

Typical of the static divisions was 19th Army's 242nd Infantry Division, one of two divisions in Lieutenant General Ferdinand Neuling's 62nd Corps,* headquartered in Hyères on the Mediterranean coast. The division, commanded by Major General Johannes Baessler and the formation that was to take the brunt of the Allied landings in the South of France, was responsible for approximately one hundred miles of coastline from Cap Dramont near Saint-Raphaël in the east to Cap Sicié west of Toulon. Raised in 1943 from depot troops and originally based in Belgium, the division numbered some 12,000 men, but in April 1944 three of its twelve infantry battalions had been replaced by Armenian and Azerbaijani Ost troops. The division's weapons inventory overwhelmingly came from French, Italian, and Russian sources. Instead of the standard issue of German MG 34s and MG 42s, it boasted no fewer than thirteen types of machine gun, including World War I Maxims. Its small-caliber artillery was augmented with obsolete anti-tank guns, and the majority of its mortars were Italian or French. Similar make-do-and-mend measures meant that French and Italian light field guns were pressed into service as coastal defense artillery. In the event of an Allied landing, the division had to fight

* Neuling's second division, the 148th, was responsible for the Mediterranean coastline running east from Anthéor to the Italian border, taking in Nice and Cannes.

with whatever was to hand with no chance of resupply. Consequently, it was given a higher allocation of mortar and artillery ammunition than its counterparts in northern France—some six units of fire* as opposed to three.

Army Group G's principal reserve was the 11th Panzer Division, a veteran of the war on the Eastern Front, which had been redeployed to France to rest and refit after suffering heavy losses in the Korsun-Cherkassy pocket in February 1944. In the Balkans and Russia, the 11th Panzer had earned the nickname of the *Gespenster* (Ghost) division, from its ability to arrive on the battlefield when least expected. Its emblem was an eerie sword-brandishing specter on a half-track, and its commander from August 1943 was Major General Wend von Wietersheim. Born in 1900, Wietersheim had served in World War I as a hussar. Retained by the Reichswehr after the war, he transferred to the armored branch in 1938 as an adjutant with the 3rd Panzer Division, with which he took part in the invasion of Poland, leading a motorcycle infantry battalion, a role he repeated in France in the summer of 1940. In July 1941 he was appointed commander of a rifle regiment in the 1st Panzer Division, an element of General Erich Hoepner's** 4th Panzer Group, which reached the outskirts of Moscow in December 1941 before being thrown back by a ferocious Red Army counterattack.

At full strength, the 11th Panzer Division numbered some 13,700 officers and men in fifteen battalions and detachments and divisional trains (logistics units). It was organized on a regimental system, with a two-battalion panzer regiment (fielding the long-serving Mk 4 and the powerful Mk 5 Panther),*** two panzergrenadier (armored infantry) regiments, each of two battalions, a three-battalion artillery regiment,

* A unit of fire was the equivalent of a day's usage in combat. A unit of fire for a light howitzer was 900 rounds.

** Hoepner had a long history of opposition to the Führer. He had been involved in the 1938 Army conspiracy which collapsed when the Munich agreement gave Hitler Czechoslovakia without a fight. In July 1944 he was nominated by the anti-Hitler conspirators to assume command of the German Home Army if the bomb plot against the Führer succeeded. The plot failed and Hoepner was arrested and executed on August 8, 1944.

*** An American armored division had three tank battalions equipped with 177 M4 Sherman medium tanks and a reconnaissance battalion equipped with light tanks.

a mechanized reconnaissance battalion equipped with eight-wheeled armored cars (*pakwagens*), and mechanized or motorized support units (engineers, signals, ordnance, quartermaster, etc.). On operations, the Germans mixed panzer and armored infantry companies in improvised *Kampfgruppen* (battle groups) in combined arms teams, a practice that was also adopted by the Allies. In August 1944, the 11th Panzer Division fielded forty-nine Mk 5 Panthers and twenty-six Mk 4s. However, the training of new crews was incomplete and there was a shortage of fuel.

In contrast to American armored divisions, all of whose infantry battalions traveled in M3 half-tracks, only one of the panzer division's four panzergrenadier battalions rode in armored half-tracks, usually the versatile and technically sophisticated Sonderkraftfahrzeug 251s, of which there were no fewer than twenty-two models. Hard schooling on the Eastern Front gave German unit leaders and their vehicles more versatile battlefield reflexes than their US counterparts. The other panzergrenadier battalions traveled in Opel Blitz trucks, which lacked the front-wheel drive of the rugged American GMC 6x6 "deuce and a half" truck. In the last year of the war, the German Army, beset with shortages of all kinds, was forced to use civilian and French vehicles, even wood gas-fueled trucks. The 11th Panzer Division was no exception, and its adjutant, Captain Franz Thelen, had to make frequent trips to Paris to beg, borrow, or steal appropriate equipment.

Only one of the division's artillery (tank destroyer) battalions was self-propelled. The rest were towed. In contrast, all three US artillery battalions were self-propelled on the M10 carriage. Here the Germans possessed an advantage as all the American howitzers were 105mm, with a range of 12,000 yards, while the Germans fielded 150mm pieces with a range of 15,000 yards. Some of the latter, notably the *Hummel* (Bumble Bee), were self-propelled, prompting the Americans to routinely attach or divert from corps assets a 155mm artillery battalion. The Germans also used a 105mm self-propelled howitzer, the *Wespe* (Wasp) originally based on a PzKpfw chassis but later in the war based on captured French chassis. With a higher infantry-to-tank ratio than its US equivalent, and with equipment shortages further sapping its armored strength, the 11th Panzer closely resembled a standard U.S. infantry division of the period with its normal attachment of one tank battalion of sixty tanks, one self-propelled tank destroyer battalion of thirty-six pieces, and motorized support units.

South of the River Loire, the 11th Panzer Division, rebuilding but short of fuel, was Army Group G's only mobile strike force. Wietersheim had to prepare for three possible scenarios if the Allies came ashore in southern France: an Allied landing on the Riviera; a landing near the Rhône River delta; or simultaneous landings near Narbonne, in the Golfe du Lion, and the Biscay coast to isolate France from Spain. The division was stationed in the Toulouse area so that it could intervene westward into the sector controlled by the 1st Army around Bordeaux should the Allies land in the Bay of Biscay; or eastward toward Marseille and Toulon if the Allies targeted the two major ports in the region.

Playing a limited and lackluster role in the defense of southern France was the German Navy (Kriegsmarine). The Admiral, Atlantic Coast controlled naval units from Brittany south to the Spanish border while the Admiral, French South Coast presided over those on the shore of the Mediterranean. Both commands answered to Navy Group West, headquartered in Paris, but the French South Coast was further subdivided into Naval Command Languedoc, west of Toulon, and Naval Command French Riviera, running from Toulon east to the Italian border. Both of these commands consisted of land-based units of coastal defense artillery and antiaircraft batteries. The only significant surface unit in the theater was the 6th Security (*Sicherungs*) Flotilla, whose patrol craft, a motley collection of ex-French torpedo boats, anti-submarine corvettes, minesweepers, artillery barges, and armed trawlers, reported through Security Forces West to Navy Group West.

Blaskowitz's control over naval artillery was limited. Technically, control was to be divided after an Allied landing, with the Navy directing fire on Allied aircraft and shipping, and the Army directing fire against ground targets, a recipe guaranteed to cause confusion. Allied air attacks had also seriously degraded the Kriegsmarine's U-boat forces in the theater. A series of raids on Toulon in the spring and summer of 1944, culminating in successive attacks on August 5 and 6, had destroyed all but one of the 7th U-boat Flotilla's fifteen submarines, which lacked the massive concrete protection provided in the U-boat pens on the Atlantic coast.

The Third Air Force was responsible for the air defense of southern France and was, if anything, even more enfeebled than the Kriegsmarine. Its interventions during the Anzio and Normandy landings had resulted in heavy losses. Its 2nd *Fliegerdivision* (Air Division)* deployed two offensive elements: the torpedo-bombers of *Kampfgeschwader 26* consisted of three squadrons flying from airfields at La Jasse, Montélimar, and Nîmes with approximately sixty Ju88 aircraft, of which some forty were operational; and the fourteen missile-equipped Do-217 anti-ship bombers of III/KG 100 based near Toulouse. The fighter strength in the theater was provided by the ten operational Bf 109Gs of II/JG (*Jagdgeschwader*), 200 flying from Avignon. In spite of its deficiencies, the Luftwaffe in southern France, flying reconnaissance missions over ports in Italy, Corsica, and Algeria, had provided timely information about the Allied forces concentrating for Anvil.

Hitler's Atlantic Wall had a smaller sibling on the Mediterranean coast, the South Wall (*Südwall*). The region has a long history of fortification, dating back to the pre-Roman era, but the most significant 17th-century additions were the work, around Toulon and Marseille, of the military architect Sébastien Le Prestre de Vauban, commonly known as Vauban. In the 1930s the French Navy had strengthened the defenses around the region's major ports, but immediately after June 1940 the task was left to its Italian occupiers, who were responsible for the Riviera, including the Var department as far as Toulon.

The Italians were timid successors to the great Vauban, sprinkling the coast with many small concrete pillboxes, without steel reinforcement, which would not withstand naval bombardment. In the autumn of 1943, after the Italian armistice, the German Army took over these coastal batteries and incorporated them into the overall South Wall program undertaken by the Todt Organization, the paramilitary

---

* The basic Luftwaffe unit was the Gruppe, identified by Roman numbers, with up to five Gruppen forming a *Geschwader*, the largest flying unit in the Luftwaffe. At full strength each Gruppe contained three *Staffeln*, identified by Arabic numbers, and each Staffel had about twelve aircraft, of which eight or nine were usually operational. Geschwadern and Gruppen carried a prefix indicating their role: *Jagd* (fighter), *Kampf* (bomber), *Stuka* (dive-bomber), *Schlacht* (ground attack), and *Lehr* (Special Test). Although a Gruppe would usually occupy one airfield and operate as a complete unit, its component Staffeln were self-contained entities with their own traditions, ground crew, badges, and sometimes color schemes.

building agency that was also responsible for the Atlantic Wall. At the end of 1943, Hitler ordered an emergency fortification program to install 400 guns in bunkers on the Mediterranean coast. This initiative was only partially successful as the protection in the bunkers from air attack limited the traverse of their guns to 120 degrees for targets at sea and prevented them from firing at targets inland.

These strongpoints were massed around Toulon and Marseille while the rest of the Var coastline was largely neglected. Toulon had 24 strongpoints manned by 1,600 troops and bristling with 141 machine guns, 11 mortars, 23 antiaircraft guns, and 22 field guns. Other coastal defense improvisations involved log-reinforced gun pits and tank turrets, detached from obsolete German and captured French vehicles and mounted on concrete bases (*Panzerturm*). There were 222 of these installations, of which 174 mounted German turrets and the rest French.*

On the Mediterranean coast, many of the bunkers housing the artillery were camouflaged with great ingenuity. One, in Antibes, flush with a handsome villa, was painted to look like an extension with elegant shutters and lace-curtained windows. Another in Antibes sported a fake tree, flowerpots, and a false window. In the harbor at Golfe-Juan, a line of bunkers was transformed into a row of respectable houses. On the Nice waterfront, the addition of a large sign transformed a bunker into a bathhouse. At Napoule, the trick was turned around with a false bunker entrance painted in the wall of a civilian building.

These artistic flourishes failed to impress the keen military eye of General Blaskowitz, who harbored serious doubts about the adequacy of the defenses on the Atlantic and Mediterranean coasts. He observed that the main weakness of the latter was its rigidity: "It tied down locally many weapons and their ammunition. It also tied down at these locations their crews with the necessary supply facilities. It caused the divisions that had become committed for the defense to expand in such a way that they were unable to form local reserves. It necessitated a

* In the early summer of 1944, approximately half of the projected 1,500 Todt Organization fortifications on the Mediterranean coast—everything from ammunition bunkers to field fortifications—had been completed.

widely ramified organization for command and supply. And finally, it aggravated and hindered assembly—and later on timely fusion—of the reserves of the higher command."

Equally sceptical was Major Georg Grossjohann of the 198th Division, stationed near Sète, west of Marseille in the Golfe du Lion and the strongest of the four divisions in 4th Luftwaffe Field Corps, commanded by Lieutenant General Erich Petersen, holding the sector between the Rhône delta and the Spanish border. Grossjohann had joined the Reichswehr in 1928 as a private soldier and had served in Poland, France, and Russia before returning to France in the early summer of 1944. After the war he reflected: "The success of the Allied landings in Normandy proved that Rommel's concept of defending at the beaches was not necessarily the most prudent.* The opponents succeeded in the landing in spite of strong fortifications, large-scale laying of mines, and beach obstacles of all sorts, albeit with considerable losses. With our experience with the Maginot Line in 1940, we should have known better about the value of fortifications, yet, the defensive conditions of the Mediterranean coast could never be realistically compared with those on the Atlantic. There was nothing set up behind the weak coastal defenses at the Mediterranean. It was obvious that this line of defense would be overrun in the first attack. So why should one expose it right there to certain destruction?"[2]

In contrast to the rigors of the Eastern Front, the South of France seemed an idyllic posting. The 157th Reserve Division was the only unit of 19th Army not stationed on the Mediterranean littoral but based to the north near Grenoble in the Drôme. The headquarters of its elite Alpine *Gebirgsjager* (mountain troops) Regiment was in Annecy in surroundings described in lyrical terms by a German historian of the period as a "jewel of nature . . . [Its] fourteen-kilometer lake stretches its arms right into the center of the city, making it into a veritable oasis designed to please the eye. The houses are beautifully maintained and surrounded by groves and vines, which also

* As commander of Army Group B, Rommel was convinced that an Allied invasion of northwest France could only be defeated at the water's edge, a belief that was not shared by other German commanders and resulted in a disastrous compromise.

decorate the surrounding hills . . . The men of the Regiment saw themselves as the fortunate inhabitants of a paradise right in the middle of the Second World War."

This mountain idyll was not so stimulating for other less favored formations in 157th Division. By early 1944, the smell of defeat was in the air and the activities of the French Resistance, operating from the nearby Vercors massif, were becoming more effective. It was noted, in a message to London by a French agent of the Special Operations Executive (SOE), that the men of 157th Division were at pains to keep their distance from the local Sipo/SD* security police for fear of being involved in a Resistance ambush. And another, more sinister element was being added to anti-partisan operations—the arrival from the Eastern Front of units of Ost troops, dubbed "Mongols" by the French, who were to play a baleful role in the reprisals taken against the Resistance.

The presence of the Ost troops was an indication of the heterogeneous nature of the occupation forces in southern France. Most of the men in 148th Reserve Division, part of Neuling's 62nd Corps occupying a stretch of the French Riviera immediately to the east of the 242nd Division running up to the Italian border, came from Silesia, part of the Third Reich in 1944 but handed back to Poland after the war. Some thought of themselves as wholly German while others, considering themselves Polish, could not speak a word of German. The answer was to divide them into four categories depending on how "German" they were. Similar confusion arose in the case of the Czechs, Slovenians, and Croatians who found themselves in the 148th Division. To this mélange of nationalities was added an Ost battalion that was attached to the division.

Josef Kirsner was a Bavarian serving in the division's 164th Reserve Grenadier Battalion stationed between Cros de Cagnes and Beaulieu near Nice. He recalled: "In my company, except for a couple of older

* The Sipo (*Sicherheitspolizei*) and SD (*Sicherheitsdienst*) were field elements of the Gestapo. Another important part of the German security apparatus, outside the control of Army Group G, was *Verbindungsstab* (Field Administrative Command) 800, commanded by Lieutenant General Ludwig Bieringer, which liaised with *Heeresgebiet Südfrankreich*, the overall security command functioning behind the thin crust of coastal defenses, where Blaskowitz's writ did not run.

men, we were all young boys, seventeen and eighteen years old. A lot of men were from Upper Silesia, but in fact they were Poles who had been drafted into the German army. They could speak German, but they stuck together and spoke Polish, and I couldn't understand anything they were saying. Some had been NCOs in the Polish army. They had probably been prisoners of war, and because they had a grandfather or grandmother who was German, they were conscripted into the German army, or they had volunteered for the army instead of staying in prison camps. I was from Bavaria and don't know why I ended up in that unit . . . there was no fighting, and at first it was if there was no war going on. There was a soldier's theater in Nice, and at night we could go out into the taverns to drink coffee or a glass of wine . . . We received our pay in French money, and we paid for everything of course; we didn't steal anything. We didn't notice any great hatred from the French people. Of course there was a war on and we weren't welcome; the French weren't happy to have the Germans occupying them."[3]

There were, however, ominous clouds massing on the horizon. Karl Cyron, a Silesian volunteer in the 148th Division's 164th Reserve Grenadier Battalion, who considered himself wholly German, was stationed in Nice and had less happy memories of the early summer of 1944: "The Americans and the British bombed the railway connection and bridges in all of France. No more supplies were coming from Germany: no equipment, no food, no ammunition, nothing. The food was bad and there was always less and less of it. When I arrived in France, we received one loaf of bread for two soldiers. After a few weeks we had to share one between four men, then six men, and in the last few weeks we received one loaf for ten men. Everyone got one slice. Imagine what that was like for seventeen- and eighteen–year-olds who were still growing and needed strength."

Cyron's morbid view of the overall situation was confirmed by Henri Zeller (code name "Faisceau") head of the Resistance in southeast France. At the end of July 1944, while waiting for an RAF Lysander to fly him to Algiers, he noted, "No train has run since June 15 on the two Alpine lines, Grenoble to Aix-en-Provence and Briançon to Livron. No isolated German car, no courier could travel on the highway, no enemy roadblocks, no control existed outside the garrison towns. No traces of military works or minefields. The Germans are practically prisoners in their own garrisons, from which they emerge in force for supplies or on a reprisal expedition*—and these convoys, these columns are attacked, one out of every two times, by an uncatchable enemy. After two months of this situation, the German soldier is bewildered, demoralized, fooled—we know him, we steal his mail . . . They awaited the arrival of Allied soldiers, like a deliverance . . ."[4]

However, in the upper reaches of the German Army's hierarchy in the South of France, the champagne kept on flowing. The composer Lorenz Rhode was the senior bandmaster in 148th Division. Early in 1944 he attended the premiere, at the Monte Carlo Opera, of his ballet *Snow White* at which he drank champagne with Lieutenant General Otto Fretter-Pico, his divisional commander, and the hereditary ruler of the principality. After several toasts he joined the General, the Prince, and his sister, Princess Antoinette, in a private suite: "The General accepted [the invitation] with pleasure. He brought me with him, but then something awful happened. A German soldier who was taking pictures in the Opera followed us in without us realizing. Since this soldier was wearing a helmet, the Princess received a terrible fright. Poor her! She saw a general accompanied by an armed and helmeted soldier walk in, and probably thought that the evil Germans had something dreadful in mind. Even the photographer seemed to understand the embarrassing misunderstanding and disappeared."[5]

Less agreeable was the sight that greeted the inhabitants of Nice, on July 7, 1944, of two members of the Resistance hung from lampposts in the center of the city. Seraphin Torrin and Ange Grassi were executed as a reprisal for the assassination of a German officer by Maquisards on June 7. The Germans had forced many civilians to watch the execution, and the bodies were left hanging for several days as an example, prompting even the collaborationist prefect of the Alpes Maritime to observe that "Emotion is considerable and the psychological effect is negative." To this day, Torrin and Grassi remain the best-known victims of German brutality in the Alpes Maritime.

---

* One such reprisal was the German punitive raid on the Resistance force on the Vercors plateau at the end of July 1944, from which Zeller escaped.

Nevertheless, complacency reigned in the higher levels of command in southern France. The military governor in the Var Department, Major General Ludwig Bieringer, when interrogated after capture by the Americans in August 1944, noted that, "Until the very day of the invasion a certain cooperation could be observed on the part of the population in the Var Department. Employees could be obtained for internal work as artisans, kitchen personnel, drivers, etc., as well as men for outside work. Thousands of Frenchmen were placed at the disposal of the Infantry Battalions in order to carry out all kinds of earthwork in fortnightly shifts." The ready availability of pastry chefs and hod carriers was about to end.

SIX
READY TO ROLL

"I agree thoroughly with you that Anvil has got to be killed . . ."

—General Sir Henry Maitland Wilson
to Field Marshal Sir Alan Brooke, March 1944

The stop-start progress of Anvil owed much to the diverging expectations of the British and Americans over the thrust of Allied strategy in the Mediterranean from late 1943 to well into 1944. While the British had eventually agreed to subordinate their preoccupation with Italy to the wider goal of Overlord, the Americans were still determined to compel their ally to stand by previously negotiated strategic agreements as essential elements of coalition warfare. However, a cloud of uncertainty hung over Anvil during the first five months of 1944 as the Allies adjusted to shifting strategic perspectives.

The American viewpoint, that the deferring of a decision on Anvil was "almost a disaster," was briskly expressed by the Roosevelt's secretary of war, Henry L. Stimson, who blamed British "sluggishness" for the delay: "I have come to the conclusion that, if this war is to be won, it's got to be won by the full strength of the virile, energetic, initiative-loving Americans, and that the British really are showing decadence—a magnificent people but they have lost their initiative." This damning verdict is the mirror image of the inner doubts expressed by Churchill to Lady Violet Bonham Carter in February 1942.

At this stage in the war, it was impossible to deny American superiority in manpower and industrial muscle, and so it fell to the Americans to supply many of the men and much of the machinery to make the invasion of southern France a reality rather than a piece being pushed to and fro around the strategic board. There were other pressing considerations, which had been pointed out by American planners at the end of March 1944. The abandonment of Anvil would inevitably result in serious political difficulties with the French and deprive Overlord of at least ten divisions, which would remain committed to the laborious and costly crawl up the leg of Italy. This would also leave them pointed toward southeastern Europe and, at war's end, it would be difficult to prevent them from being used in the occupation of Austria, Hungary, and southern Germany. This last point assumes critical importance in the light of Roosevelt's stated reluctance, in February 1944, to see American forces performing an occupation role in southern Europe.

A rough draft of the Allied invasion plan had been drawn up by Eisenhower in December 1943. He had envisaged a two-division assault with a third division coming ashore shortly afterward. It was not until July 1944 that the Combined Chiefs of Staff decided that the assault should be made by three American divisions, followed up by a French corps. In December 1943, at Eisenhower's request, the Seventh Army's headquarters in Sicily was made available for the planning, preparation, and execution of Anvil. In January 1944, under the designation Force 163, a section of the Seventh Army's planners was moved from Sicily and established in Algiers to work on the outline of the invasion plan alongside colleagues from the U.S. 8th Fleet, Mediterranean Allied Tactical Air Force (MATAF), and from March 1944, representatives of the Free French. At the end of January 1944, a logistical planning section, Rear Force 163, was established in Oran, the location of the headquarters of the Services of Supply (SOS) for the U.S. Army's North African Theater of Operations (NATOUSA) commanded by General Devers, who was to play a key role in sustaining Anvil.

March 1944 saw the appointment of a new commander of the Seventh Army, General Patch, who also assumed command of Force 163. Patch set about expanding the North African planning establishment before moving it to Naples in July 1944, where it dropped the Force 163 nom de guerre. It was housed in a former Italian barracks near the city's waterfront that had previously been used as a rest center for American troops. Dubbed the "Block House," the building was a huge quadrangle with an interior courtyard, surrounded by a high wall in which there were only two entrance gates. Inside, two floors accommodated army, navy, and air force staffs, in addition to living accommodations for some officers and all the enlisted personnel. It was an ideal location in which to finalize the plans for Anvil.

The long and winding gestation of Anvil was almost over. That it had survived numerous twists and turns owed much to the quiet persistence of General Devers and his subordinate Major General Thomas B. Larkin, responsible for NATOUSA's Services of Supply, the logistical backbone of the operation. While the Americans and the British bickered over strategy in the Mediterranean, Devers ensured that, by August 1944, all the essential logistical elements of the operation were in place. This was no easy task, as the invasion of southern France had begun life with no clear idea of its size, nature, precise location, and, crucially, the date on which it was be launched.

The first task of NATOUSA's Services of Supply was to draw up a basic plan for sustaining a force of some 450,000 men for a month. The next step was to dispatch requisitions to New York, the port of embarkation, followed by a liaison officer armed with more detailed lists and loading plans. Arrangements were put in hand for convoys, partially loaded for Anvil, to sail to the Mediterranean in the period February to April. At this point it was anticipated that Anvil was to be launched in May 1944. The technical term for the loading process was known as "flatting," in which cargo intended for Anvil was stored up to a fixed level in a ship's hold and then boarded over. Above this level, and on the weather decks, were stored general supplies for the Mediterranean theater. Much thought was given to preventing the diversion of the flatted supplies, when they arrived in the Mediterranean theater, to the ongoing campaign in Italy. Nevertheless, in April 1944, after the arrival of sixty-four of the flatted ships, fundamental Anglo-American disagreement in the Mediterranean over Anvil entered a critical phase.

The British, now dependent on American materiel largesse, had persuaded themselves that it was more or less infinite. But to Eisenhower, surveying the strategic scene in Western Europe in early March 1944, the overall picture was more complicated. The British and Americans were bogged down in the Anzio beachhead and unable to join hands with the Allied Main Force south of the Gustav Line. On March 3, Eisenhower cabled Marshall expressing doubts over his outline for a two-division landing in the south of France and his anxiety over the availability of sufficient assault craft for that operation, and also for Overlord. Marshall concurred; he was now considering the cancellation of Anvil, or its postponement until such time as the shortage of assault craft had been remedied. Eisenhower believed that the best available solution to the problem was to postpone Anvil but retain it as a threat. On March 22, in a letter to Marshall, he regretfully recommended the postponement of the operation, adding that at present "we are striving for the impossible."

Two days later the Combined Chiefs of Staff met to consider the issue. Admiral Ernest J. King, commander in chief of the US fleet and chief of naval operations, a unique double appointment, noted the effect the postponement would have on the French, who had invested such hopes in Anvil, and also on the Soviets, who had favored the idea at Tehran. The British point of view was expressed by Field Marshal Sir John Dill, head of the British Joint Services Mission in Washington, who countered with the argument that if the Germans fought for Rome it would have the same effect as an Allied landing in the South of France. Anvil was, it seemed, trapped by the gravitational pull exerted on it by the twin prospects of the capture of Rome and the Normandy landings.

On April 3, General Wilson was directed by the Combined Chiefs of Staff to prepare for an all-out offensive to burst out of the Anzio beachhead and link hands with the Main Force in the drive on Rome. The directive also required him to develop a threat against the South of France with the caveat that "The undertakings of these preparations for Anvil will in no way preclude a changing of plan by the CCS should an undeniably better course of action be presented by changing circumstances," a form of words that threw doubt on Anvil and gave heart to the British.

Wilson was in the difficult position of having to navigate between the conflicting priorities of London and Washington while simultaneously retaining the confidence of his Anglo-American staff. His attempts to handle the problem in an evenhanded way sparked the ire of Churchill, fretting about the Balkans, and also Brooke, with whom Wilson's relations were usually cordial. In March 1944, Brooke, now a field marshal, wrote Wilson a letter, urging the SACMED, ". . . for Heaven's sake get Anvil killed as early as you can." This blunt intervention came shortly after two of the JCS's senior planners, General John E. Hull and Rear Admiral Charles M. Cooke, had flown out to meet Wilson. After their departure, Wilson's deputy, Devers, informed his superior that the American Chiefs of Staff were determined to bring on Anvil no matter what objections were raised by the British. Wilson's reply to Brooke described his dilemma: "I agree thoroughly with you that Anvil has got be killed. The question is how to do it—to poison it by framing up to the Americans and pointing out its unsoundness on strategical and tactical grounds will not work at the moment I'm afraid, as they will invoke the . . . Tehran Agreements and I am sure that they have visions of getting their troops out of Italy and into France to join up with Eisenhower. The other method is the slower one of strangulation."

Wilson's equivocations over Anvil did not earn him much sympathy among the British high command. The chief of the British air staff, Sir Charles Portal, informed Air Marshal Sir John Slessor, commander of the RAF units in the Mediterranean, that ". . . from here it looks as if his [Wilson's] difficulties over Anvil are largely of his own making and results from his not taking a definite line in which he himself believes even if it displeases the Americans or ourselves." Nevertheless, over the spring and early summer of 1944 Wilson changed from being an opponent of Anvil and an advocate of the primacy of the Italian campaign into a reluctant supporter of the operation, won over by the powerful arguments advanced by Eisenhower and Marshall.

In principle the British were quite happy to tolerate preparations for Anvil, provided the operation did not become a reality. The Americans, on the other hand, were prepared to postpone Anvil but not to abandon it. For Eisenhower, the invasion of the French Riviera was an integral element in Allied grand strategy, the southern element in the "broad front," stretching from Switzerland to the English Channel and one that was not logistically dependent on supplies from the Allied lodgement in Normandy. The two allies were talking completely different military languages but the Americans were now calling the shots.

While Wilson's enthusiasm for Anvil was qualified by his role as SACMED, presiding over an integrated Anglo-British headquarters, no such restraints were felt by his deputy, the American Devers, who was described by Lieutenant General Oliver Leese, Montgomery's successor as commander of the British 8th Army, as a "double-faced" supporter of Anvil. It was Devers who had set the Anvil ball rolling at the beginning of 1944 and had kept pushing it down the track, even when in April it had been put on ice by the Combined Chiefs of Staff. Generals Devers and Larkin, anticipating that Anvil would be revived, decided to freeze all the supplies, afloat or on shore, that SOS had designated for Anvil and to resist any pressure from the War Department to divert them to the Italian campaign. By June, when the prospects for Anvil had brightened, some 75 percent of the Anvil requisition, afloat or on shore, was available for a two-division invasion, enough to sustain operations for a month after the landings. That month requisitions went in for a three-division landing. On June 13, Devers directed SOS to switch the delivery priorities from the Fifth Army in Italy to the preparations for Anvil. They took effect after the reinstatement of Anvil by the CCS on July 2. Two weeks later the first Anvil-bound convoys since April arrived in the Mediterranean. Thereafter an additional 135 merchant ships, sailing in fast and slow convoys, were assigned to Dragoon. Many of these merchant ships were to take part in the invasion of southern France, pressed into service by the shortage of assault ships.

The shortage of amphibious assault shipping in the theater was of some concern to Anvil's planners. In June, Vice Admiral Hewitt lacked 160 Landing Ships, Infantry and Attack Troop Transports (APAs); 24 Large Landing Craft, Infantry (LCI[Ls]; three Auxiliary Troop Transports (XAPs); and 65 Landing Ships, Tank (LSTs). The deficit in the number of LSTs was particularly worrying. The U.S. Navy's response was to dispatch twenty-eight new LSTs to the Mediterranean while Eisenhower made another twenty-four available from his own resources. The LST concept had been pioneered after the Dunkirk evacuations by the British, who had converted three shallow-draft tankers, HMS *Misoa*, HMS *Tasajera*, and HMS *Bachaquero*, into ocean-going vessels fitted with bow doors and ramps that were capable of shore-to-shore delivery of tanks and other vehicles in amphibious operations. The first purpose-built LST design was HMS *Boxer*, developed from an idea suggested by Winston Churchill. The *Boxer* could carry thirteen Churchill infantry tanks, twenty-seven other vehicles and some two hundred men in addition to the crew. But its draft was insufficient to enable easy unloading, obliging *Boxer* and its two sister ships to stow a long ramp behind their bow doors. The three ships were later converted to Fighter Direction Ships for the Normandy invasion.

In November 1941 a Royal Navy delegation arrived in the United States to collaborate with their counterparts at the U.S. Navy's Bureau of Ships. A design swiftly emerged in the form of the LST (2) with a large ballast that combined deep draft for ocean passage and, when pumped out, shallow draft for beaching. An anchor and a mechanical winch enabled the LST to pull itself off the beach after grounding. A high priority was given to the construction of LSTs, and by the end of 1942 construction was well underway. By 1943 the construction time for an LST had been reduced to four months, and by the end of the war it had been slashed to two months.

LSTs made their combat debut in the Solomon Islands, in the Pacific theater in June 1943 and thereafter became a war-winning item of kit in all theaters, their versatility in many roles confirming their basic soundness of design and legendary ruggedness, belying their nickname of "Large Stationary Target." Of the 1,051 built, only twenty-six were lost to enemy action and another thirteen were claimed by bad weather or accident. In a seaway they pitched and rolled violently, inducing seasickness, but they inspired much loyalty among their crews. Claude Miller, a crew member of LSTs 313, 229, and 621 wrote an ode to the vessels in which he served:

"An ugly duckling to some
She 'nay well have been,
Slow of speed
And her armour plate thin . . .

Large slow targets,
They were called with a grin
as with flank speed ahead
They barrelled on in . . .

But I have no regrets.
I'm as proud as can be
To have been one of the crew
Of an LST."

An Allied commander who displayed a keen interest in the LST* was General de Gaulle, who toured LST 358, commanded by George H. Sweet, in the Tunisian port of Bizerta: "One day while docked in Bizerta, General Charles de Gaulle and his staff came aboard—not to inspect but out of curiosity about the ships they had heard so much about, the LST. Of about ten officers, he, of course, stood out among the rest of his entourage with his six-foot-six-inch frame. He was a tall man but not too heavy—extremely military and important in his demeanor and appearance. His curiosity in the LST and its capabilities was very interesting. He did not miss a thing and wanted to tour the entire ship, which he did. He was aboard for about an hour and was very gracious to all of the officers and crew with whom he came into contact. We will always remember him as domineering character."[1]

The D-Day plan envisaged an airborne landing behind the Riviera coast followed by the seaborne delivery of some 84,000 men and 12,000 vehicles on the target beaches. The men and the vehicles of the seaborne assault would carry with them a three-day supply of food. All the assault units would land with five units of fire for all weapons They would be followed, by D+4, by 33,500 more men, including leading elements of the French Army, and another 8,000 vehicles. From D+5, more rations, clothing, equipment, and fuel would be fed in at five-day intervals. On D-Day, the First Airborne Task Force (FABTF), which

* The LST could carry 29 tanks or 350 troops and could accommodate up to 10 LCVPs (Landing Craft, Vehicles and Personnel) on its deck. LCTs (Landing Craft, Tank) could carry five tanks.

had been activated on July 19, was to arrive in its drop and landing zones with the minimum supplies necessary to accomplish its initial mission and would be air-supplied for at least the next two days. To provide an extra margin of safety for FABTF and Seventh Army, seven days of supplies were stockpiled around Rome ready to be flown into the Allied lodgement from D+1. The planners calculated that by D+30 nearly 300,000 tons of arms, fuel, and equipment would have been unloaded over the target beaches, some two-thirds of which was bound for forward units and the remainder held in depots.

The lessons of Anzio and Normandy had been absorbed and strong enemy resistance was expected. With this in mind, particular emphasis was placed by the planners on ammunition at the expense of fuel and rations in the first four days of the operation. Fuel was cut by some 20 percent for these crucial days; and rations were slashed by a third, as was the number of vehicles assigned to haul them inland from the beachhead. This decision was a calculated risk. If the initial assault penetrated further and faster inland than had been envisaged, the reduction in fuel and transport would have a disabling effect on the course of the campaign. However, when one takes into account the limited amphibious capability available to the Seventh Army, the choice of ammunition over fuel provided the Seventh Army's planners with greater confidence that once ashore they would seize and secure a bridgehead in the South of France.

The naval aspects of Anvil were the overall responsibility of the Allied naval commander in the Mediterranean, Admiral Sir John Cunningham. In 1940 he had commanded the Royal Navy's 1st Cruiser squadron during the hastily improvised Allied intervention in neutral Norway in April–May 1940 following the German invasion of that country and Denmark. Cunningham's squadron evacuated some 5,500 French and British troops from Namsos on May 3, accomplishing this tricky operation, under constant threat by German air power, in the course of a single night. A month later Cunningham returned in the cruiser HMS *Devonshire* to extract the Norwegian king, Haakon VII, from Tromso.

At the beginning of August 1940 Cunningham, then a vice admiral, was appointed to command the naval forces in Operation "Menace," the British-French attack on the French West African naval base at Dakar, the capture of which was intended to encourage France's African empire to abandon the Vichy government and align itself with General de Gaulle. Cunningham's considerable naval force included two battleships, an aircraft carrier, five cruisers, sixteen destroyers, and two sloops plus a number of Free French vessels; and a landing force of some 7,000 men. However, Dakar had been reinforced, and when the landing force arrived off the base on September 23, 1940, the port's governor rejected all approaches from the Gaullists and the landings were canceled. British and Vichy French warships, the latter having escaped from the Mediterranean, exchanged fire, during which several French submarines and a destroyer were sunk, and damage was sustained by the battleship HMS *Resolution*, which was hit by a torpedo. Cunningham decided to abandon the operation just as the governor of Dakar was preparing to surrender.

In June 1943 Cunningham became a full admiral in charge of Levant Command with responsibility for the eastern Mediterranean and deputy to Sir Andrew Cunningham (no relation) commander in chief of the Royal Navy's Mediterranean fleet. In September 1943, Admiral Sir Dudley Pound, the First Sea Lord, was forced into retirement by ill health and succeeded by Admiral Andrew Cunningham while his deputy became the new Mediterranean commander in chief, in which post he supported the Anzio landings.

Also present during the Anzio landings was the U.S. Navy's Vice Admiral Henry Kent Hewitt, then commander of the Western Naval Task Force. An expert in amphibious operations, Hewitt had been placed in command of the landings that put Patton's 35,000 troops ashore on the beaches around Casablanca in Operation Torch. In spite of forecasts of adverse weather from London and Washington, Hewitt backed his own judgment and took the word of his fleet meteorologists that there would be a break in the weather. They proved correct, and the landings were successful.

In 1944 Hewitt was given command of the U.S. 8th Fleet, operating in North African waters, after which, commanding the Western Naval Task Force, he put US troops ashore in Sicily and the Italian mainland. At Salerno, when the entire operation was placed in jeopardy by a strong German counterattack on the beachhead, Hewitt went ashore, reconnoitered the situation and requested immediate air and naval support for the assault troops. For his courage, initiative, and leadership under fire, Hewitt was awarded a second Navy Cross to accompany the one he had won during the Torch landings. Now his sights were set on the landings in the South of France. From the time the Western Naval Task force embarked the Seventh Army to the moment when its commander, General Patch, established his headquarters ashore, the ground and naval echelons would be under the command of Hewitt, who was responsible only to General Wilson.

Air support for Anvil was the responsibility of Brigadier General Ira C. Eaker's Mediterranean Allied Air Forces (MAAF). A celebrated prewar endurance aviator, Eaker arrived in England in February 1942 as the commander of the U.S. 8th Air Force's Bomber Command. On August 17, 1942, he flew on the first all-American bombing operation in Europe when twelve B-17 Flying Fortresses of 97th Bombardment Group, under the command of Colonel Frank A. Armstrong Jr., raided the marshalling yards in Rouen in France. At the end of 1942, Eaker succeeded Major General Carl "Tooey" Spaatz as the commander of 8th Air Force. Eaker was a passionate supporter of precision daylight bombing, although he initially underestimated the difficulties of operating over Europe.* During the Casablanca conference, he tangled with Churchill, who had already expressed his doubts about the value of daylight bombing to Roosevelt, and had suggested to General H. "Hap" Arnold, chief of the U.S. Army Air Forces, that the Americans switch to bombing by night.

The next day Eaker had a meeting with Churchill at which the prime minister pointed to the significant losses suffered by 8th Air Force at the hands of the Luftwaffe and the fact that after five months in Britain the Americans had yet to drop a single bomb on Germany. Eaker explained that much of 8th Air Force's strength had been devoted to Torch and that greater precision by day would lead to the accelerated destruction of German industry and population centers, and the degrading of the Luftwaffe and the enemy's war effort. Eaker urged, "If the RAF bombs by night and we bomb by day, bombing around the clock, the German defenses will get no rest." Churchill was

* The overcast skies of northern Europe presented very different operational conditions to the azure desert aerial training environment in the United States.

so impressed that he used the phrase "bombing round the clock" in a speech in the House of Commons on his return from Casablanca. One of the fruits of Casablanca was a directive whose aim was "the progressive destruction and dislocation of the German military industrial and economic system, and the undermining of the morale of the German people to a point where their capacity for armed resistance is fatally weakened." The job of transforming this directive into operational reality was a plan devised by Eaker, code-named "Pointblank," and endorsed by the high commands of the USAAF and RAF in June 1943.*

At the end of 1943, Eaker was reassigned as the commander in chief, Mediterranean Allied Air Forces (MAAF), its previous commander, Air Chief Marshal Sir Arthur Tedder, having been chosen by Eisenhower to plan the air operations for Overlord. Like Mark Clark, Eaker was opposed to the withdrawal of Allied divisions from Italy to participate in Anvil, contending that this would prevent Alexander from breaking through the German Pisa-Rimini defensive line and delay the capture of the Po Valley for use as a base for Allied air operations against Germany. Marshall rejected Eaker's arguments with the wry remark that, in his opinion, Eaker "had been with the British too long."

While Eaker exercised general control and coordination over the air support for Anvil, he operated within a complicated command structure. Under his command were U.S. 12th and 15th Air Forces, led respectively by Major General John K. Cannon and Major General Nathan F. Twining,** plus the British Desert and Balkan Air Forces. MAAF's heavy bombers and their escorts assigned to Anvil were the responsibility of the Mediterranean Allied Strategic Air Force while the Mediterranean Allied Coastal Air Force covered the invasion fleet's staging areas and assault convoys to a point forty miles from the beachheads. The rest of air support was provided by the Mediterranean Allied Tactical Air Force (MATAF) also commanded by Major General Cannon, which was to fly close air support for the

* The effective game-changer for 8th Air Force was the arrival in December 1943 of the P-51B Mustang escort fighter fitted with a 75-gallon drop tank, giving it a range of 1,000 miles. The bubble-canopied P-51D, which arrived in May 1944, had a range of 1,500 miles with drop tanks.

** Twining's principal operational direction came from the U.S. Strategic Air Force based in England and commanded by Lieutenant General Carl Spaatz.

remaining forty miles to the beachheads and over the assault area. In turn Cannon appointed as his tactical air force commander Brigadier General Gordon P. Saville, commander of the 12th Tactical Air Command, 12th Air Force.

From the outset, Allied planners wanted an airborne element for Anvil. It was estimated that a full division would be required for the operation, but in the early spring of 1944 the forces in the Mediterranean available to the Allies amounted to a British parachute brigade, an understrength French parachute regiment, an American parachute battalion, and two batteries of US parachute field artillery. Language and lack of training ruled out the French, leaving Force 163 to contemplate an unbalanced Anglo-American regimental combat team.

In May and June a stream of reinforcements arrived from the United States: a parachute regimental combat team, a second parachute battalion, and a glider-borne infantry battalion. AFHQ and the Seventh Army also assembled a battalion of parachute field artillery; converted a 75mm pack howitzer battalion* to a glider unit; trained two 4.2-inch mortar companies for glider operations; and transformed the anti-tank company of the 442nd Japanese-American infantry regiment into a glider unit. Wearing his North African Theater of Operations, U.S. Army (NATOUSA) hat, General Devers commenced training for support units—engineers, signals, medical detachments—to bring the airborne element up to divisional strength, and on July 19 it became the First Airborne Task Force, commanded by one of the outstanding military leaders of World War II, Major General Robert T. Frederick.

As a young man of fourteen, Frederick had sailed to Australia, lying about his age, and three years later he entered West Point as the youngest man in his class. Apart from his youth, there was initially little to distinguish Frederick from his classmates. He graduated 124th out of a class of 250 and West Point's yearbook, *The Howitzer*, noted only that he had a modest personality. He began his career in the

* Developed in the 1920s, the 75mm howitzer was a gun that could be moved over difficult terrain and designed so that it could be broken down into a number of pieces. In an airborne division there were three 75mm howitzer battalions: two glider field artillery battalions (each battalion with six-gun batteries) and one parachute field artillery battalion (with twelve guns in three batteries).

U.S. Army in the artillery, gaining experience in harbor defense and antiaircraft weapons. In 1930, he underwent flying training but failed to gain any qualifications. In 1933, he was assigned to the Civilian Conservation Corps (CCC), part of Roosevelt's New Deal. In February 1941, as a battery commander at Fort Shafter on the Hawaiian island of Oahu, home of the U.S. Pacific Fleet, he sketched out what had to be done to mount an adequate defense against air attack: ". . . barrage balloons should be obtained to supplement meager antiaircraft artillery . . . Primary targets for attack are Pearl [Harbor], Hickam Field [the U.S. Army Air Corps base on Oahu] . . . no ship to be in Pearl . . . raiding forces steaming towards Oahu during night, releasing planes about daylight . . . ." It was an uncanny anticipation of what happened on December 7, 1941, the day of "infamy," but the planning committee at Fort Shafter was not impressed.

At the end of the summer of 1941, Frederick was assigned, at his request, to the Operations Division of the U.S. War Department, where he was to assess new methods of warfare, a field in which his incisive mind finally made its mark. Marshall and Eisenhower chose Frederick, then a lieutenant colonel, to raise and command a US-Canadian regiment-sized force, the First Special Service Force (FSSF) to be trained at Fort Harrison, Montana. It was originally intended for deployment on commando missions in Norway, training in winter and mountain warfare. However, American commanders, unlike the Canadians, were unwilling to part with their best men. Undeterred, Frederick resorted to recruiting, in addition to some genuine adventurers, a decidedly mixed bag of brawlers, miners, trappers, lumberjacks, and men released from the guardhouse on the condition that they stayed out of trouble.

This unusual formation served in the Aleutians before making its combat debut in Italy in December 1943, attached to U.S. 36th Division in Operation "Raincoat," during the battle for the Bernhardt Line, also known as the Winter Line, the defensive system stretching from the Garigliano River to Castel di Sangro in the Apennines. In three hours of bitter fighting, in which their training in mountain warfare paid off, and from which Frederick's men emerged with nearly 80 percent casualties, the FSSF seized Monte la Difensa, which dominated U.S. Fifth Army's path to Monte Cassino and had held up the Allies for a week.* In February 1944 Frederick was promoted to the rank of brigadier general.

At Anzio the FSSF earned the soubriquet "The Devil's Brigade" after a diary was found on the corpse of a German officer containing the entry: "The Black Devils are all around us every time we come into the line, and we never hear them come," a reference to the silent and deadly night raids conducted by Frederick's men that left behind them a trail of sentries with slit throats. Pinned to the corpses were stickers reminding the enemy: "USA-Canada. The Worst Is Yet to Come."

Frederick was not a soldier in the Patton mold. He seldom spoke to his men except to issue orders, was mild-mannered and mustachioed and looked like a handsome Hollywood second lead, the hero's best friend who never gets the girl. He was wounded on a number of occasions. As the Fifth Army neared Rome, Frederick was crossing a bridge over the Tiber in a half-track when his driver was killed by a German sniper, who also hit him. A US soldier who was on the spot recalled the scene: "Frederick was a bloody mess crawling along a bridge, bleeding from the neck and arm, his pants soaked with blood. I wanted to bandage him up but he kept saying he was OK—here I was an AWOL soldier with a general that I thought was going to die."

Fears of Frederick's death proved premature. He declined to go to a hospital and spent the next two days deploying his men to seize bridges into Rome. It was two days before he submitted to medical attention, resulting in twenty-eight stitches in one of his legs. A week later he was promoted to major general, at thirty-seven the youngest officer of that rank in the U.S. Army. Frederick and his men enjoyed a few days' rest on the shores of Lake Albano, near the Pope's summer residence at Castel Gandolfo. It was noted that at this time a large amount of furniture went missing from the Pope's home, apparently removed by American soldiers.

The manner of Frederick's appointment by Devers reveals much about the respective styles of the two men. The latter was not one of the great fighting generals of World War II but was a deft motivator and talent spotter. Frederick had little or no experience of airborne

---

* This episode is the climax of the 1968 movie *The Devil's Brigade* starring William Holden as Frederick.

operations, but Devers was well aware of his record and was happy to select him as the youngest World War II general to command a division-size formation and, in defiance of convention, to leave the appointment of key subordinates in his hands. Major General John S. Guthrie, the Seventh Army's operations officer, observed Frederick at close hand: "[He] decided to bring in [Major General] Ken Wickham who had been his chief of staff in the First Special Service Force. Wickham was Frederick's exact opposite: the methodical, conservative kind of guy who keeps the show on the road. And, what's more, he knew Frederick intimately . . . As I say, Frederick was not without temperament either. He sort of gave us a hard time on occasion . . . nothing very serious, of course, but he was unquestionably a difficult man to control. But everyone was for him. Because of what he had done in Italy, they felt he was the ideal man for the job."

SEVEN
PLANNING THE LANDINGS

> "The French guerrillas would always avoid confrontation. Instead, disguised as civilians, and without any distinguishing marks, they would lurk in the shadows, waiting for a chance to strike in some clandestine way . . ."
>
> —Major Georg Grossjohann, 198th Division

The location of the Anvil landings was determined by two overriding factors: the need to secure ports on the French Riviera, specifically Toulon and Marseille, capable of sustaining a drive north up the Rhône Valley to link with the Allied forces pushing south from their lodgement in Normandy; and a fervent desire not to repeat the disaster at Anzio, where Wehrmacht control of the high ground beyond the beachhead kept the Allies under continual observation and enemy fire. This time the Anvil planners were determined to select a location where a landing force could quickly seize the high ground beyond the beachhead and establish a firm defensive line.

The planners' first move was to study the coastline to the west and east of Toulon and Marseille as well as the coastline in between them. To the west, the area around Sète-Agde, south of Montpellier, was examined, as a landing there would permit a drive through the Carcassonne Gap and Toulouse toward Bordeaux. However, the planners concluded that poor beach gradients and the many lagoons, lakes, and canalized roads in the hinterland of the assault area would pose too many problems for the Allies. In addition this area was beyond the range of effective air cover from the nearest available Allied air bases in Corsica,* and intelligence had indicated that the approaches to the beaches were heavily laced with obstacles and other defenses. Clearly the Germans had selected this stretch of coast as the most probable point of attack.

The Golfe de Fos, a few miles northwest of Marseille, offered some promising landing beaches, but here the hinterland was flat and swampy and cut by the Rhône estuary. The bay at La Ciotat, a heavily fortified harbor equidistant from Marseille and Toulon, emerged as another candidate but would have exposed any assault force to heavy fire. The same drawback ruled out Hyères, east of Toulon, which could only be approached through shallow waters, restricting naval gunfire support, and was within the range of the port's numerous heavy guns and also those that Allied intelligence believed were stationed on the offshore Hyères islands, the nearest of which was only seven miles away. Preliminary operations against these islands, Port-Cros and Le Levant, would alert the enemy to Allied intentions.

To the east of Hyères lay the Var coastline, not especially well defended but with beaches of widely varying size from 500 to 4,500 yards long and from 10 to 50 yards deep. Behind these beaches were narrow belts of sand dunes, many of which sported small scrub trees. Inland from the dunes were wooded slopes, cultivated fields, interspersed with areas of marsh and soft sand, small streams, farm tracks, and villages. A small macadam road ran along the coast here. Three miles inland was the principal east-west road from Toulon to Cannes, interrupted by a ten-mile section from Sainte-Maxime to Fréjus, where it joined the coastal road.

Rising behind the Toulon–Cannes road was the high ground of the *Massif des Maures* (Range of the Moors) that loomed above the coast from Hyères to Saint-Raphaël, a distance of some thirty-five miles, reaching a maximum height of 1,500 feet and stretching inland for

---

* Corsica, held by the Italians and a German division, was abandoned by the Axis in September 1943, when the Allies invaded mainland Italy, and control was assumed by Free French troops and local Resistance groups.

twenty miles. Heavily wooded and rich in chestnut trees, maritime pines, cork oak, and dense maquis shrubbery, the massif offered the prospect of high ground, the rapid seizure of which was crucial to the Allied planners. To the north of the massif, was the main east-west corridor in the valley of the Argens River with good roads connecting the French Riviera with Marseille. Northeast of the corridor lay the Alpes de Provence that overlooked a smaller massif, the Esterel, which rises above Cannes.

The planners' focus was now drawn to the coastline from Cavalaire east to Saint-Raphaël. Here seemed the most promising point of attack. The beaches on this stretch of coastline were deemed adequate, but no more, with satisfactory gradients and a deep water approach. The beach defenses were not as strong as those to the west, and the Argens River Valley offered the chance of a rapid move to the west to isolate the defenders of the cities of Marseille and Toulon. Nevertheless, the choice of the Cavalaire-Saint-Raphaël coast carried with it several significant drawbacks. Its thirty miles of irregular coastline translated into over fifty miles of shoreline. The potential landing sites were little more more than adequate and were cut off from each other by cliffs and rocky outcrops. Above them hung the Massif des Maures, posing a potentially fatal threat if it was held in strength by the enemy, a repeat of the Anzio debacle. Some of the prospective beaches lacked good exits, and these could be easily blocked by the German defenders, as could the narrow coastal road to Toulon and the highway from Saint-Raphaël to Toulon, which was only marginally wider. The minor roads that fed the main highway were, in large part, no more than a single lane wide and could accommodate only light military traffic.

The planners settled on the Cavalaire-Saint-Raphaël option, but the need to secure high ground as quickly as possible, and to rapidly develop supporting airfields, obliged the Seventh Army's planners to map out a large beachhead with a radius of some twenty miles, at the center of which was Cap Saint-Tropez. Twenty miles to the west, the perimeter of the beachhead, dubbed the "Blue Line," rose from the Rade d'Hyères, snaking through the western tip of the Massif des Maures before looping east just north of Le Luc, near the middle of the Toulon-Saint-Raphaël corridor, and running on past Taradeau and Le Muy, the latter some ten miles inland on the Argens River, from which a good cement road ran down to Saint-Raphaël. Then it curved gently eastward through the smaller Massif de l'Esterel down to the sea at the Golfe de la Napoule, two miles northeast of the town of Théoule. Inside the Blue Line lay important sections of the principal highways and railways leading west and southwest to Toulon, Marseille, the Rhône River, as well as northeast to the cities of Cannes and Nice. The planners were confident that the depth of the beachhead would protect the assault beaches from long-range German artillery; provide space for the development of airfields; and allow U.S. 6th Corps and the leading elements of French 2nd Corps the freedom to maneuver. The two massifs, once taken, would secure the invasion force's western and eastern flanks against a determined enemy counterattack while preparations were made to break out west toward Toulon and Marseille.

The landings by 6th Corps were to be preceded by four key missions: the seizure of the offshore islands of Port-Cros and Le Levant by French commandos and the U.S. First Special Service Force (Operation "Sitka") to neutralize the German batteries thought to be there; assaults by the French African Commando Group (Operation "Romeo") on the mainland north of the islands at Cap Nègre to destroy coastal defenses, establish roadblocks on the coastal highway, secure the high ground up to two miles inland, and block any German attempt to move on the landing beaches; air drops by parachute troops of First Airborne Task Force (Operation "Rugby") around Le Muy aimed at preventing German attempts to mount attacks on the landing beaches from the Argens River corridor. The paratroops were also tasked with securing the area for the glider landings that would follow later that day before joining hands with advanced elements of 6th Corps coming up from the coast. And, finally, on the eastern end of the beach-line, the French Naval Assault Group (Rosie Force) was to block the coast highway on the right, or northeastern flank of 6th Corps. H-Hour for the landings by 6th Corps was set for 0800, markedly later than previous amphibious operations in the Mediterranean. This was to give the pre-assault air and naval forces sufficient daylight in which to reduce the enemy's shore defenses, following which the assault forces could establish themselves ashore and seize the high ground behind the landing beaches to forestall a German counterattack. Particular importance was attached to the formation of twenty-four naval shore fire control parties (NSFCPs) to coordinate fire from the Task Force warships. There was to be a fire control party for each of the eighteen assault battalions, consisting of officers with combat experience gained during the Normandy landings.

In the original plan, 45th Division was positioned in the center, attacking beaches to the northeast of Saint-Tropez; 36th Division was on the left, landing on beaches to the southwest of Saint-Tropez; and 3rd Division was on the right, targeting beaches to the northeast of Fréjus. When these plans were submitted to Truscott toward the end of June, he raised several pertinent objections. He insisted that his most experienced division, the 3rd, should be shifted to the left (Alpha) flank, on the beaches designated 259, 260, 260-A, 261, and 261-A, to launch a swift drive on Toulon or parry a determined enemy counterattack from that quarter. The 36th, which was less experienced, should be on the right (Camel) flank, landing on beaches 264, 264-A, 264-B, 265, and 265-A, to the northeast of Fréjus and deployed in a largely defensive role. The 45th retained its position in the center of the assault landing, concentrating on the (Delta) beaches to the northeast of Sainte-Maxime, 262, 262-A, and 263-A, B, and C. Each division was to have an attached tank battalion, a tank destroyer battalion, three antiaircraft and artillery battalions, a barrage balloon battalion plus three battalions of corps artillery. In addition there was provision for engineers, hospitals, and supply and maintenance troops.

Truscott was also worried that the westward extension of the beachhead ran the risk of repeating the mistake of Anzio, preventing the rapid massing of a force for the westward drive to Toulon. He suggested that the Blue Line to the west be pulled in to accommodate this maneuver. Patch and Admiral Hewitt agreed to these modifications, but Truscott failed to persuade Hewitt to mount a comprehensive reconnaissance sweep for underwater obstacles sown by the enemy in the approaches to the assault beaches. Hewitt was convinced that, in contrast to the Normandy landing beaches, the low tidal range on the coastline chosen for Anvil posed little danger. Moreover, he reminded Truscott that reconnaissance operations carried the risk of alerting the enemy to the landing sites selected by the Americans. Truscott continued to fret about underwater obstructions, and his fears were raised by intelligence reports of such obstructions on the approaches to at least three of the assault beaches. He raised the matter again with Hewitt, who replied, "I believe that the menace of underwater obstacles has been somewhat exaggerated," and that "studied reports from Overlord have lent undue emphasis to a subject new in this theater for the most part . . . I know of no preliminary reconnaissance other than actually running boats through the obstacles, which will ensure that boats can beach." Hewitt rejected the suggestion that pontoon causeways could be used to smash through these defenses but agreed that LCTs (Landing Craft, Tank) could undertake the task, coupled with hand demolitions after the first wave had landed.

Truscott was nothing if not persistent. He dispatched another memorandum: "Without exception every Navy officer with whom I have discussed the subject has expressed the opinion that underwater obstacles constitute a more serious problem for us than was the case in the [English] Channel where the tidal range allowed assault craft to beach and allowed demolition parties to work on dry land. The available information on the nature of the obstacles in our area does not indicate that these obstacles are exceedingly formidable, however, I think that we must assume that these obstacles do have the capability of interfering with the approach of the landing craft to the beaches to some degree at least, and certainly the accomplishment of the troops' mission on the shore depends upon their reaching the beach."[1] Truscott also pointed out that two of Hewitt's subordinate Sub Task Force commanders, Admirals Lowry and Rodgers, had proposed to make an early reconnaissance by speedboat several hours before H-Hour if Hewitt gave the go-ahead. The approach worked. Hewitt agreed to leave the solution of the problem to his subordinates, who would also consult with Truscott's divisional commanders.

Truscott was also preoccupied with 6th Corps's lack of an American armored combat command with which to expand and burst out of the bridgehead. The concept of an armored combat command had been introduced into the U.S. Army in March 1942. It was essentially a headquarters, with no organic combat units, which controlled the armored elements assigned to it for a specific tactical operation, for example the support of an infantry division. The French Army, rebuilt and equipped by the Americans, also featured combat commands (CCs), and one of these, the French 1st Armored Division's Combat Command Sudre, commanded by Brigadier General Aimé M. Sudre, was attached to 6th Corps. CC Sudre comprised a reconnaissance squadron, a regiment of heavy tanks, a battalion of motorized infantry, a group of motorized artillery, a squadron of tank destroyers, engineers, signals units, and elements of transport and service corps—a total of over 3,000 men and some 1,000 vehicles. Each French armored division was divided into three combat commands, any one of which could fight independently from its parent formation in close cooperation with infantry formations.

Truscott hoped to land CC Sudre over 36th Division's beaches around Fréjus and concentrate it for a drive to the northwest. This radically altered the approach to Dragoon, replacing the slow and methodical buildup and progress inland envisaged by the planners with a more ambitious, but potentially riskier, rapid exploitation following the landings. However, the French expected to regain control of CC Sudre on D+3 to shield their right flank from attacks by German armored units as they moved on Toulon and Marseille. This forced Truscott to improvise a solution. On August 1, the day the code name for Anvil was changed to Dragoon, he told his planning staff that he had decided to assemble a provisional armored reserve from 6th Corps assets. It was to be led by Brigadier General Fred B. Butler, 6th Corps's deputy commander, and was designated Task Force Butler (TFB). Because Task Force Butler was almost an afterthought, it could not be added to the invasion force as a separate entity and was scheduled to be assembled in the landing area on D+2.

Butler was a graduate of West Point who had trained as an engineer. He had seen combat commanding 168th Regiment, 34th Infantry Division, in North Africa and Italy. In 1944 he was promoted to the rank of brigadier general and was reassigned to 34th Division as its assistant commander. As Truscott's deputy in 6th Corps, he had been at Anzio, where he became familiar with all his senior's views and, according to Truscott, was "one of the most fearless men I ever met." Butler selected many of his staff from 6th Corps's staff sections. They were veterans of Anzio and the subsequent breakout.

Task Force Butler was to be built around 6th Corps's mechanized cavalry formation, the 117th Cavalry Reconnaissance Squadron,* whose 900 troops rode in jeeps mounting .50 machine guns and 60mm mortars, and forty M8 Greyhound armored cars. Developed by the Ford Motor Company, the 6x6 rear-engined, seven-and-a-half-ton Greyhound entered service with the U.S. Army in 1943. It was quiet and fast, with a top speed of 55 mph, but was vulnerable to mine damage, making it unpopular with its four-man crews, who reinforced its floor with sandbags. Its main armament was a 37mm gun and it also carried a .30 machine gun and a turret-mounted .50 machine gun. The Greyhound did not have the firepower to destroy German heavy or medium tanks, but was effective against less heavily armored vehicles such as half-tracks or armored cars, soft-skinned vehicles, and personnel.

Owing to its dedicated role of reconnaissance, the Greyhound enjoyed a superior communications system. Most Greyhounds carried two radios, one short-range and one long-range, which would in theory enable Butler to communicate with higher headquarters and subordinates, either directly or by relaying transmissions over long distances. Nevertheless, the mountainous interior of southern France would pose a number of problems for rapid and regular radio communication. Butler's Greyhounds may have lacked armored punch but conferred on TFB the ability to locate and report on enemy strength, bypass enemy concentrations, and expand the operational depth and frontage on which it could function in a fast-moving battle.

The 117th Reconnaissance Squadron also fielded a single assault gun troop equipped with six M8 75mm Howitzer Motor Carriages. These assault guns were tracked vehicles that could be used in a number of roles. They were particularly effective in attacking enemy positions in built-up areas and could also be used to provide indirect fire support. The reconnaissance squadron also had an organic company of seventeen M3 and M5A1 light tanks. However, it was in the provision of medium tanks that TFB's profile did not match that of the standard combat command. It had only two companies of medium tanks (from

---

* All the elements of TFB had combat experience, but the Reconnaissance Squadron was the least experienced, although very well trained. It had seen about a month of fighting in Italy.

the 753rd Tank Battalion) each with seventeen M4 Shermans armed with a 75mm gun, plus one M4 mounting a 105mm howitzer that gave close support to medium tank formations. To offset this deficiency in firepower, TFB was assigned a company of twelve open-topped M10 tank destroyers (Company C, 636th Tank Destroyer [TD] Battalion) armed with a 3-inch high-velocity gun in a turret capable of an all-round traverse. The M10 was not a true tank but was often used in this role when no M4 Shermans were available. More indirect fire support was provided by the self-propelled field artillery battalion (59th Armored Field Artillery) attached to Task Force Butler. The battalion was equipped with eighteen M7 open-topped Howitzer Motor Carriages, carrying a 105mm howitzer and a pulpit-mounted Browning .50 antiaircraft machine gun to the right of the main armament.

Task Force Butler was also assigned a single motorized infantry battalion (2nd Battalion, 143rd Regiment) riding in two-and-a-half ton (deuce-and-a-half) trucks rather than the more maneuverable M3 half-tracks used by units organic to armored divisions. Half-tracks could follow tanks wherever they went, but Butler's trucks were relegated to the roads. The motorized infantry deployed fewer machine guns than their armored counterparts but were equipped with more mortars, the most responsive indirect fire available to commanders in the field. Moreover, in heavily forested or mountainous terrain, as was the case in the South of France, tanks were often forced to advance by road, losing their cross-country mobility. When one compares the inventories of an American combat command and that assembled at extremely short notice by Brigadier General Butler, one can only conclude that his organizational skills had created a formation with capabilities that exceeded those of a regular armored combat command, not least in the conduct of reconnaissance and security missions. In all, Task Force Butler fielded some 3,000 men and 1,000 fighting vehicles.

At the beginning of July, Truscott reflected that "Our plans were based upon a thorough knowledge of terrain and beaches in southern France, particularly of the assault area, and on an unusually complete intelligence concerning enemy strength and dispositions. Not even the Normandy invasion had better advance information."[2] This information principally flowed from three distinct sources: aerial reconnaissance, the French Resistance, and Ultra, the last the code name for the decrypts of intercepted German radio traffic, made at Bletchley Park and forwarded to senior Allied commanders and their staffs in the field. Ultra-derived information gave Allied intelligence an overall picture of German capabilities and dispositions in the run-up to Dragoon, but the speed of German redeployments after Overlord, combined with the time-lag inevitably involved in the process of decryption and its correlation with other intelligence—prisoner of war interrogations, air mosaic analysis, captured documents, Resistance reports—sometimes clouded the Allied assessment of precise enemy intentions. Moreover, the German practice of making many key decisions at military conferences, and the transmission of detailed orders by officers entrusted with documents, made Ultra a less than perfect, albeit indispensable, tool in the Allies' intelligence toolbox. It was rare that an Ultra decrypt had an immediate effect on an unfolding battle, as happened at Mortain in early August 1944. Nevertheless, a series of intercepts after the August 15 landings were to prove critical to the course of the campaign.

Old-fashioned human intelligence (HUMINT), derived from agents on the ground, provided an alternative to Ultra's insights. Here the OSS came into its own. One of their outstanding agents, based in Algiers, was Henry Hyde, born in Paris and the scion of a wealthy American family, who had been educated at the British public school Charterhouse and Cambridge University. Hyde was the epitome of the sarcastic OSS sobriquet "Oh, So Social," and had been recruited in 1942 by spymaster Allen Dulles, who later became the director of the Central Intelligence Agency (CIA). From Algiers, Hyde ran the "Penny Farthing" network, which from July 1943 controlled agents, ranging from anarchists to aristocrats, in northern and southern France. In February 1944, Hyde spotted that the German 2nd Panzer Division had arrived in southwest France to refit, but had not been picked up by Ultra. In early June 1944, informed by Hyde, members of the Resistance had disabled much of the division's replenished armor and delayed its arrival in Normandy by two weeks. By the late spring of 1944, Hyde had established an extensive network of agents in the South of France, supplying a mass of information by radio and maps, diagrams, drawings, and photographs smuggled through Spain. His agents also accumulated significant amounts of information about roads, bridges, and German installations and troop movements, all of which were supplied to the Anvil planners. A final piece of the intelligence jigsaw came from a wealth of prewar tourist photographs of the assault beaches, which provided planners with detailed insights into the target area as significant landmarks loomed behind the tanned, smiling faces of vacationers.

Up to and during the landings, the Seventh Army's G-2 (Intelligence), Colonel William W. Quinn, ensured that he received a constant stream of information from OSS reports on enemy dispositions and strength. On August 13, two days before the landings, a French OSS agent, bicycling from Cannes to Hyères, was able to make a detailed survey of the landing areas, which was cabled to Quinn aboard the Seventh Army's command ship, *Catoctin*. After the landings, the OSS assigned teams to each of the three US divisions involved in Dragoon to provide information on the enemy's order of battle.

In the weeks preceding the Allied landings, the FFI in the Var was encouraged to do all it could to hamper German movement into the Anvil assault area by destroying bridges, cutting railway lines, blocking roads, and creating major diversions inland after August 15 to distract enemy forces maneuvering to counterattack. On the face of it, the prospects looked promising. The FTP was active throughout the region; the ORA was particularly strong in the northwest of the department; the Gaullist AS operated principally in Toulon and Draguignan, the department's administrative center; and by mid-August many of these groups had joined forces to form the CFL (*Corps Français de La Libération*).

The most successful unification was achieved in the Massif des Maures, where the *Brigade des Maures* was created by a young architect, Marc Rainaud, who had forged an alliance between members of the FTP, the ORA, and the AS, merging them with local Maquisard and Resistance groups farther afield in the Saint-Tropez peninsula. However, Rainaud was not informed that the 3rd Division was going to land on beaches to the west of the peninsula. In addition, Allied attempts to supply the Brigade des Maures with air-dropped containers and packages were sporadic. After June 6, only eight deliveries were successful, and one of these occurred after August 15. In the days immediately leading up to the Dragoon landings, frantic efforts were made to step up the landing of agents and teams who had been training in Algiers into zones just beyond the Allied Blue Line. One of the agents was Lieutenant Geoffrey M. T. Jones, a twenty-four-year-old, French-speaking OSS training officer who had been instructing recruits at Blida airfield, outside Algiers, since June. He was accompanied by a French naval officer Capitaine de Corvette Léon Allain, the leader of a counter-scorch team bound for Toulon with orders to open the port for Allied shipping.

At this stage in the war the Germans seldom ventured in force into the Provençal countryside, but they could still make life difficult for the Resistance active in major conurbations. In the spring of 1944 an entire network had been penetrated in Nice, in the Alpes Maritimes, the department adjoining the Var. German countermeasures were particularly effective in Marseille, where a number of Resistance leaders had been identified by colleagues "turned" by SIPO/SD operative Ernst Dunker, a shady trilingual character with a prewar background in international catering. The Résistants were arrested in two raids, at Oraison in the Basses-Alpes, and Marseille itself. On July 18, twenty-six Résistants were taken to a lonely spot near the hamlet of Signes, some fifteen miles north of Toulon. There, in an unfrequented copse, they were shot and buried in a shallow grave. Just over a month later, their corpses were joined by ten more executed Résistants.

In the remote countryside of southern France, the Resistance was less vulnerable. In the hilly, forested regions of the southeast, the Maquis had so rattled the Germans that, with the exception of anti-guerrilla operations, like that in the Vercors, and heavily escorted convoys, they rarely ventured beyond the relative safety of their urban garrisons, leaving tracts of countryside open to bands of Résistants. The corrosive mixture of fear and contempt felt by many German soldiers toward the Resistance was captured by Georg Grossjohann in his memoirs: "In my experience, these guerrillas only appeared where and when they could do so. Typically they would liquidate small German rearguards or scattered groups, and then mostly from ambush. Even then, the German OKW allowed them the status of combatants if they complied with two conditions—to come forward as an integral military unit and to wear clearly visible armbands to identify themselves. Nevertheless, the French guerrillas would always avoid open confrontation. Instead, disguised as civilians, and without any distinguishing mark, they would lurk in the shadows, waiting for a chance to strike in some clandestine way . . . German soldiers disappeared again and again without a trace. The most common victims of French 'resistance' included lone messengers or communications people who were sent out in small parties to repair cables."[3] Later in his memoirs Grossjohann records his grim satisfaction at the summary execution of an armed Résistant reconnoitering his position without displaying a white armband marked with the Cross of Lorraine insignia of the FFI. Grossjohann signally failed to comprehend that when the Resistance went toe-to-toe with well-armed and disciplined enemy troops, it always came off second-best. Nevertheless, the drip-drip effect of the hit-and-run tactics he found so contemptible steadily undermined German morale.

As Army Group G's strength diminished with the transfer northward of many of its most capable units, the FFI became increasingly emboldened, threatening the Germans' two most important lines of communication, the Carcassonne Gap and the Rhône Valley. The operation to secure the upper Rhône Valley, the harrowing of the Vercors, proved only a partial success as it prompted an explosion of brush fires in other parts of southern France. Sabotage of roads, railways, and bridges reached epidemic proportions. In the first two weeks of August, the FFI cut the railway lines in the Carcassonne Gap and the Rhône Valley some forty times and damaged or destroyed thirty-two road and rail bridges. The cutting of underground and overhead telephone and telegraph lines shredded Army Group G's communications with its forces on the Atlantic coast and OB West. Because the mountains in southern France significantly interfered with radios—a phenomenon also endured by the Americans after the landings of August 15—Army Group G resorted to going through Berlin rather than OB West in Paris. However, the increased radio traffic was now rendered more vulnerable to interception and subsequent decryption at Bletchley Park. A week before the landings, Blaskowitz complained that the Resistance was no longer a negligible terrorist threat but constituted an organized and full-blown army threatening his rear.

The degrading of German road and rail communications was a task also undertaken principally by the Allied air forces in the weeks preceding the Dragoon landings. By August 15, MAAF had destroyed almost all the important rail and highway bridges over the Rhône, Durance, and Var Rivers, severely disrupting communications with Lyon. This came at a heavy cost of French civilian lives. One example will suffice. On August 13 the Americans had bombed the railway bridge at Crest, missing the bridge—which in any case had been rendered useless by the Resistance two months earlier—but killing 530 civilians, wounding another 713, and destroying 1,221 buildings.

In July, the weight of the Allied air offensive had been thrown against Italy and the Balkans, but thereafter the priorities switched to the South of France. The bridges on the Var were particularly badly hit. Josef Kirsner, with 164th Battalion, 148th Reserve Division, was a member of the detail guarding the western side of the Var bridge in Saint-Laurent. "There were some Italian soldiers or workers who were constantly repairing the bridge after it had been damaged in air raids so that cars and trucks could keep on using it. They had a trumpet, and whenever an air raid was coming they blew the trumpet before our own *Fliegeralarm* [air raid siren] sounded. Beside our house in the orchard we had dug real foxholes, almost two meters deep. When there was an air raid we ran like crazy and jumped into these holes. It was bit safer there than on the bridge. Once there was a train stopped in the train station at Saint-Laurent and they bombed it. It was only a couple of hundred meters away from where our foxholes were."[4]

The bane of Kirsner's life was an NCO from the battalion headquarters who was constantly checking the bridge guard to see if they were sleeping. The NCO insisted that Kirsner and his comrades take shelter during a raid in a flimsy Italian bunker built on the bridge. The detail members, preferring the relative safety of the shelter in the orchard, refused to use the bridge shelter. The NCO, setting an example, made a point of using the shelter, which, soon enough, took a direct hit and was blown into the river below. Kirsner recalled, "We practically found nothing of him. He died in his bunker and that was the end of him. Other than that we had no losses."

Between April 28 and August 10, MAAF had dropped over 19,500 tons of bombs on southern France. The second phase of the air effort, Operation "Nutmeg," began on August 10 and targeted enemy coastal batteries and defense formations with the overall aim of isolating the invasion area. To retain tactical surprise, an almost impossible task, the aerial bombardment stretched over the Mediterranean coastline in an arc from the Spanish border to Viareggio in Italy.

On the ground in the Dragoon target area, one particularly important operation was launched by the OSS man Geoffrey Jones and his French colleague Capitaine Allain, both of whom had made a series of successful rendezvous with Maquis leaders and some two hundred Maquisards at Draguignan, Montauroux, and Les Arcs. On the afternoon of August 14, less than twenty-four hours before the launching of Dragoon, Jones, Allain, and the Maquis leaders met at the village of Mons, thirty miles from Draguignan, where at 2000 they received a BBC message, "*Nancy a le torticule*" (Nancy has a stiff neck) indicating that Dragoon was imminent.

Jones and Allain decided to knock out the German radar installation at Fayence, a "*village perché*," overlooking the plain south of the Esterel Massif. The radar had been erected at an abandoned reservoir above Fayence with its antennae perched atop a huge boulder from which it could survey the Allied landing beaches at Saint-Raphaël, some fifteen miles away. Jones, who had heard about the radar in Algeria, was well aware of its importance, and with his Resistance team crawled up the old reservoir's water mains, placed explosives, and blew it up. Jones's and Allain's next task was to proceed to the landing zone of First Airborne Task Force and to prepare it for the arrival of Frederick's airborne American and British troops.

EIGHT

CHESS GAME OF THE GODS

> "Organizing this vast armada, planning and directing its routes, coordinating and protecting its movements, so that each of a thousand pieces fell into place at the exact time, fully prepared for its manifold duties was something of a gigantic jigsaw puzzle—or a chess game of the gods with the broad Mediterranean as a board."
>
> —General Lucian Truscott

In the days leading up to Dragoon, two important visitors arrived in Naples to inspect the Allied preparations. The first, on July 23, was King George VI, who stayed as the guest of Admiral Cunningham at the latter's residence in Posillipo where, some 150 years before, Emma Hamilton had conducted a notorious affair with Admiral Horatio Nelson. The next day, in brilliant sunshine, the King, accompanied by General Wilson, Admiral Cunningham, and Rear Admiral J.A.V. Morse, inspected officers of the Royal Navy and WRNS (Women's Royal Naval Service) drawn up in parade-ground formation at Fort dell'Ovo.

Then, embarking on Cunningham's barge, and accompanied by Royal and U.S. Navy escorts, the king passed along the line of warships and merchant vessels at anchor in the Bay of Naples. Later, George VI went aboard the Leander-class light cruiser HMS *Orion*, a warship with twelve battle honors, to meet Vice Admiral Kent Hewitt, commander of the Western Naval Task Force, and then proceeded to the American headquarters flagship for Dragoon, the USS *Catoctin*, an Appalachian-class command ship for amphibious operations.

On August 12, Winston Churchill arrived in Naples in his Avro York* aircraft *Ascalon*, still furious about the protracted Anglo-American tug of war over Anvil and still obsessing over the Balkans. A few days later he would meet Marshal Tito,** leader of Yugoslavia's Communist guerillas who were by far the largest Resistance recipients of Allied aid. But now Dragoon held the prime minister's attention. On August 13, resplendent in a white linen suit and looking relaxed and jovial, he assumed control of Admiral Morse's barge as it sailed around the Allied shipping bound for the South of France. Good humor had replaced his dark mood and he stood up in the stern, waving and giving the V-sign to sailors on deck who waved back shouting, "It's Winnie. It's the old man himself!"

Back in London, Field Marshal Brooke, who throughout the war handled Churchill with a mixture of admiration and exasperation, reflected in a diary entry of August 15: "Life has a quiet and peaceful atmosphere about it now that Winston is gone. Everything gets done twice as quickly, everybody is not on edge, one is not bombarded by a series of quite futile minutes and the whole machinery settles down to smooth efficient running. I feel that we have now reached the stage that for the good of the nation and for the good of his own reputation it would be a godsend if he could disappear out of public life."[1]

However, life was anything but peaceful in Naples and its adjacent ports, which were the scene of a great gathering of Allied warships, assault ships, landing craft, and escort vessels. The assembly of such a display of military and naval hardware was in grim contrast to the utterly debilitated state of one of Europe's great cities. Allied air raids

---

* The York was a transport aircraft produced by taking the wings and engines off the Lancaster bomber and attaching a new fuselage and tail unit. After the war, Yorks played a significant part in the Berlin Airlift of 1948.

** Tito liberated Belgrade in October 1944 and formed a coalition government.

had torn Naples apart, and to Norman Lewis, a British Field Security officer who had been there since October 1943, the port was "literally tumbling about our ears." Manhole covers had disappeared, leaving the streets pockmarked with yawning mantraps. Lewis noted an abandoned tank that was melting away day by day, like a block of ice in the sun, as its armor plating was prised off by the locals. Entire ships had been spirited out of the harbor and broken up. The tanks in the city's aquarium had long since been drained and the fish that swam in them eaten. The aquarium's prize exhibit, a manatee, arrived on the dinner plate of General Mark Clark. Lewis met a countess who had filled her ballroom with earth and grew vegetables where once aristocrats and courtesans had danced the polka. Like Victorian London, Naples was a city of teeming and insanitary rookeries in which the Camorra, the Neapolitan Mafia, reasserted its grip and one of its bosses, Vito Genovese, became for a time a trusted source of intelligence for the American military. Naples was a blowsy old whore effortlessly capable of catering for all tastes, from GIs seeking sexual pleasure—Audie Murphy was rumored to have had three prostitutes in one evening*—to more sophisticated servicemen seeking spiritual nourishment. The British actor Alec Guinness, then serving with the Royal Navy as the commander of an amphibious vessel, later recalled seeing performances of *Faust* and *Tosca* at the opera house while awaiting shipment home.

In the Bay of Naples on August 9, however, all was discipline and determination as warships, escorts, and merchantmen awaited orders to set sail for the divisional Dragoon landings: Alpha (3rd Division), Delta (45th Division), and Camel (36th Division), and the operation against the offshore islands (code-named Sitka). The last was the responsibility of Task Force (TF) 86, commanded by Rear Admiral L. A. Davidson. Gunfire Support to TF 86, was to be provided by the American heavy cruiser USS *Augusta*, the British cruiser HMS *Dido*, the destroyers USS *Somers* and USS *Gleaves*, the British destroyer HMS *Lookout*, and the French battleship *Lorraine*. Launched in 1913, *Lorraine* had been extensively rebuilt in 1934–35, her midships turret

* In the Naples area troops on pass received a kit that included not only prophylactics but also six sulphur tablets to be taken after sexual activity. Many troops did not observe these precautions and contracted sexually transmitted diseases.

being replaced by an aircraft catapult. When France surrendered in 1940, *Lorraine* had been in Alexandria with a number of other French ships. The commander of the French squadron, Admiral Godfroy, reached an agreement with Admiral Sir Andrew Cunningham by which the French ships were disarmed but remained under French control, and in May 1943 the squadron joined the Allies. In all, there were some 300 landing craft and 75 assault transports, assault cargo ships, and merchant vessels in the area of Naples, a presence that no amount of attention to security and deception could conceal from German aerial reconnaissance and on-the-spot informers, although the enemy had no resources to mount an effective preemptive strike.

In the heel of Italy, at Brindisi and Taranto, some forty merchant transports were loading Moroccan and Algerian troops of the French 2nd Corps. Also at Taranto was the Gunfire Support Group to Delta Force, under Rear Admiral C. F. Bryant, the principal components of which were the battleships USS *Texas* and USS *Nevada*. The *Texas*, launched in 1912,* was a veteran of D-Day, closing to within three thousand yards of Omaha Beach and firing her main guns with little or no elevation. The *Nevada* had been described in 1916 as "the greatest battleship afloat" and was the first of her kind in the U.S. Navy to boast triple turrets and geared turbines. She was badly damaged and run aground at Pearl Harbor in December 1941, and after a major refit served on Atlantic convoy duty, during the Normandy landings and the bombardment of Cherbourg. The two battleships were supported by the cruiser USS *Philadelphia*, the French cruisers *Montcalm* and *Georges Leygues*, and eight American destroyers. The French destroyers *Le Fantasque*, *Le Malin*, and *Le Terrible* were to join them later.

At Malta were the escort aircraft carriers of Task Force 88, commanded by Rear Admiral Thomas Hope Troubridge, RN. Task Group 88.1 comprised five carriers, HMS *Khedive*, HMS *Attacker*, HMS *Pursuer*, HMS *Emperor*, and HMS *Searcher*, all of which had been built in the United States and transferred to the Royal Navy under the terms of Lend-Lease.** They carried crews of 646 men and, depending on mis-

* The *Texas* is the only surviving dreadnought-era battleship.

** From March 1941, the United States had been supplying the British with weapons and war materials under the terms of the Lend-Lease Act. After the Japanese attack on Pearl Harbor, the aid was extended to the USSR.

sion, could each put in the air some twenty-four aircraft, a combination of Hawker Sea Hurricanes, Supermarine Seafires—Spitfires modified for use from aircraft carriers—Fairey Swordfish torpedo carriers, Grumman F4F Wildcats and F6F Hellcats, Vought 4FU Corsairs, and Grumman TBF/TBM Avenger torpedo bombers. In American fashion, food was served cafeteria-style in the carriers in a central dining area, and all of them were equipped with modern laundries and barber shops. Hammocks were replaced by three-tier hinged bunk beds, eighteen to a cabin. In April 1944, the *Pursuer* and the *Searcher* had taken part in Operation "Tungsten," in which the German battleship *Tirpitz*, moored in Kafjord in northern Norway, was badly damaged by the Home Fleet Strike Force.

Task Group 88.2, under Rear Admiral Calvin T. Durgin, had just completed a deception exercise, sailing to Alexandria before returning to Malta. Durgin deployed four carriers*: the USS *Tulagi* and USS *Kasaan Bay*, both Casablanca-class escorts launched in 1943; and HMS *Stalker* and HMS *Hunter*, Attacker-class escorts transferred to Britain under Lend-Lease. Also in Malta was the Alpha Gunfire Support Group, under Rear Admiral John Mansfield. It consisted of the British cruisers HMS *Orion*, HMS *Aurora*, HMS *Black Prince*, and HMS *Ajax*, the last a veteran of the Battle of the River Plate in December 1939 in which the German pocket battleship *Graf Spee* was bottled up in Montevideo harbor by Commodore Henry Harwood's cruiser squadron and scuttled by its commander, Captain Hans Langsdorff. The Group also fielded the cruiser USS *Quincy*, which had supported the D-Day landings, the French cruiser *Gloire*, the British destroyers HMS *Terpsichore* and HMS *Termagent*, and the American destroyers USS *Livermore*, USS *Eberle*, USS *Kearny*, and USS *Ericsson*. On its way to join the Group was the British battleship HMS *Ramillies*, one of the five Revenge-class battleships built for the Royal Navy in World War I. Interwar modification to the *Ramillies* had been hampered by her relatively low

* The nine Allied aircraft carriers earmarked for Dragoon could fly off some 216 Spitfire, Wildcat, and Hellcat fighters under the control of the 12th Tactical Air Command. Flying from Corsica, within range of Provence, the 12th Tactical Air Command deployed sixteen bomber squadrons, thirty-seven American, British, and French fighter squadrons, and three photo-reconnaissance squadrons, a total of 2,100 aircraft flying from fourteen airfields.

displacement and narrow hull, preventing the installation of machinery to increase her speed, which by 1939 was an absolute maximum in an emergency of twenty knots, comparing badly with German capital ships, which could reach twenty-eight knots at top speed. Nevertheless, the *Ramillies* proved a doughty warrior in World War II, serving in the Mediterranean and the North Atlantic on convoy duty and providing fire support for the Normandy landings, during the course of which she fired 1,002 15-inch shells.

Assembling at Palermo was the Gunfire Support Group for the Camel Attack Force (TF 87), led by American Rear Admiral Morton Deyo. It consisted of the American New Orleans–class heavy cruiser USS *Tuscaloosa*, which had served on the Arctic convoys as part of the Royal Navy's Home Fleet and later in Operation Torch, during which she had tangled with the Vichy French battleship *Jean Bart*. She had served on the Atlantic convoys and in May 1943 had escorted the liner RMS *Queen Mary* carrying Churchill to New York. Later she had operated in the North Sea as part of the force covering air strikes in Norway, and off the coast of Normandy during Overlord. The Group also included the light cruiser USS *Brooklyn*,* a veteran of the Torch landings, where she survived submarine attack, and the landings at Anzio; and the light cruiser USS *Marblehead*, which had been badly damaged in the Dutch East Indies in 1942 in an encounter with the Imperial Japanese Navy, and after extensive repairs served on Atlantic convoy duty. Also in the Support Group were two American light cruisers and two French light cruisers plus eleven destroyers The heaviest hitter in the Support Group was the Wyoming-class dreadnought USS *Arkansas*, launched in 1911, which had taken President Woodrow Wilson to Europe in November 1918. Extensively modified in the mid-1920s, the *Arkansas* was present at the Atlantic Charter conference in August 1941 at which Churchill and Roosevelt set out their position on self-determination, free trade, joint economic development, freedom from fear and want, freedom of the seas, and the abandonment of the use of force. After Pearl Harbor, the *Arkansas*'s antiaircraft armament was overhauled and, in addition to convoy duties, she fought

* The comedian Lenny Bruce served on the *Brooklyn* from 1942 to 1944 as a forward gun turret shell passer.

alongside the USS *Texas* off Omaha Beach and subsequently took part in the bombardment of Cherbourg. On July 21, 1944, she arrived in Italy. Making up the rest of the Camel Attack Force's gunfire support were the British cruiser HMS *Argonaut*, the French cruisers *Duguay, Trouin,* and *Émile Bertin*, and eleven US destroyers.

In overall command of Task Force 87 was Rear Admiral Spencer S. Lewis, Hewitt's chief of staff, who was a last-minute replacement for its original commander Rear Admiral Don Moon, who had led the Utah assault group in the Normandy invasion. Moon was an exhausted and demoralized man who on August 4 had implored Hewitt to postpone the assault on the South of France to allow more time for training. Hewitt denied the request while failing to spot the depth of Moon's depression. The next day Moon committed suicide. On August 6, Lewis stepped into the breach and took over the late Admiral Moon's command. Fortunately, TF 87 was an amphibious force composed of battle-hardened veterans who, in the opinion of Rear Admiral Lowry, commander of Task Force 84 (Alpha Force), "could have made the landing without an operation order."

Oran, in North Africa, was the embarkation point for French armored and infantry divisions together with their assigned escorts. The signs in Italy, Sicily, Malta, Corsica, and North Africa were there for everyone to read: the accumulation of Allied shipping from Naples to Oran, moored under billowing canopies of barrage balloons; the transfer of Allied close-support aircraft to Corsica and Sardinia; the withdrawal of seasoned American formations from the Italian front; and the embarkation of French troops in Oran, another development noted and reported by Blaskowitz. The American journalist David Schoenbrun, who was to cover Dragoon, observed that a Neapolitan youth who was hustling for handouts from GIs asked him, "You going to France?" Invasion fever reached a peak in early August and rumors were rife that an attack was planned for August 15, the birthday of the Emperor Napoléon. On August 12, Admiral Theodor Krancke, the Kriegsmarine's C-in-C West, noted that "the assembly of ships in Ajaccio and in the Bay of Propriano confirms the assumption of a landing in southern France in the near future." When, on August 13, German reconnaissance aircraft spotted a mass of shipping moving north from Corsica, another development reported by Blaskowitz, Army Group G was placed on full alert.

Because of the different speeds and characteristics of the many vessels involved in Dragoon, it was not possible for the three major assault units—Alpha, Delta, and Camel—to sail to the assault area as a single integrated force. Rather, they were dispatched by types in convoys, with the slowest departing first. Each of the convoys was divided into three sections proceeding at ten-mile intervals, the first in each case being being made up of Camel Assault Force vessels; the second of Delta vessels; and the third of Alpha vessels. All three would sail north, up the west coast of Corsica, before turning left, section by section at the last possible moment, into their respective approach lanes. The aim of this maneuver was part of the Allied deception plan to convince the enemy that the Allies' intended target was Genoa. This meant that, for the invasion fleet's slowest types, the crucial turn would have to be executed just before nightfall on the eve of the attack.

At 0930, on August 9, Hewitt activated the Dragoon attack plan, Western Naval Task Force Plan 4-44, leading up to an H-Hour of 0800 on D-Day, August 15. On August 9, at 1000, the first of the assault forces, Task Force 84, Alpha, moved out of Naples bound for Ajaccio in Corsica, through the Strait of Bonifacio, where minesweepers were already hard at work. The convoy consisted of 145 LCTs (Landing Craft, Tank), with 72 other craft and escorts under the command of Rear Admiral Frank J. Lowry in the USCGC *Duane*, a coast guard cutter converted into a combined operations communications headquarters. The speed of the three-part convoy was 5.5 knots. Lowry's convoy was to stage through Ajaccio for replenishment, fuel, and supplies, and to give troops and crews a brief rest before they went into action. Task Force 84 was the first of ten convoys to set sail, their routes converging off the west coast of Corsica and, in Truscott's words, flowing "like a mighty river toward the transport areas where the troops would disembark and head ashore."

Throughout the days before they set sail from the harbor in Pozzuoli, the men of 36th Division had been entertained by an attractive blond American girl who came aboard ship to serenade the men, prompting sentimental tears with her renditions of patriotic songs. She was almost certainly Ann Goplerud, who was with the Red Cross and was remembered by one veteran as "just about the sweetest thing you ever saw . . . She was equally good at both sweet and torch stuff. She sang to nearly every unit in the 36th Division . . . she meant so much to the boys in one regiment [143rd] that they had a scroll engraved to express their appreciation. It was presented by the colonel at a special ceremony." Goplerud exerted the same spell on the GIs as the singer Vera Lynn had on British servicemen, appearing as a surrogate sister before they went into action.

By the time the sun had set on August 10, two more convoys were at sea, sailing from Taranto and Brindisi, and from Oran, both carrying French troops. The convoy from Brindisi-Taranto comprised forty merchantmen and twelve escorts, proceeding at 7.5 knots along another convoy route to the southeastern Sicilian coast near Augusta, then westward through mineswept channels before turning north along the west coasts of Sardinia and Corsica toward the Dragoon approach channels. The convoy from Oran comprised fifteen merchant transports plus nine other ships carrying personnel and six escorts. It was to sail east at 7.5 knots, hugging the Algerian coast until making a northeasterly turn at Philippeville toward Sardinia and a junction with the Brindisi-Taranto convoy.

By the end of August 11, more pieces on the chessboard were in play. At midday the transports of the Sitka force, five LSIs and five APDs (aged US destroyers converted to high-speed transports) escorted by a single destroyer set sail, working up to fourteen knots. These crowded vessels were to stage at Propriano in Corsica, south of Ajaccio. After nightfall, another convoy consisting of one large transport, one LSI, two fast British LSTs, and two destroyers carrying Combat Command Sudre set sail from Oran at twelve knots. The Delta Gunfire Support Group, minus three French destroyers with which it was to rendezvous off Bizerta, left Taranto following the same route taken by the convoy that had sailed the day before.

On August 12, Alpha, the first of the assault forces that had set sail three days earlier, was staging as planned at Ajaccio while the two remaining three-section convoys, Delta and Camel, were sailing the same route from Naples. The first, an LCI convoy, consisted of 115 LCIs and 30 other vessels. It was followed by an LST convoy, comprising sixty-nine LSTs and sixty-three other vessels under the command of Rear Admiral B. J. Rodgers in the USS *Biscayne*, a seaplane tender converted into a communications ship. At 2000 Rear Admiral Davidson got underway from the Bay of Naples with the Sitka Gunfire Support Group, following in Rodgers's wake before changing course off Propriano to avoid the main assault force lanes and proceeding to the Sitka assault area. Meanwhile, Troubridge's carrier force sailed from Malta toward the assigned assault area through mineswept waters and the Tunisian War Channel, the ten-mile-wide protected channel between Cap Serrat and Cap Bon, before changing course to the northwest.

On August 13, the remaining ships and landing craft of the Western Naval Task Force got underway. The weather was superb; clear skies bestowed excellent visibility and the sea was like a millpond. Sergeant Frank Andrews was with Alpha force, serving in a battalion headquarters in 3rd Division, which had set sail on August 12. He recalled the outward journey: "We spent a few days on the ships, which were loaded heavy with equipment on the top deck. For the trip from Naples to southern France, it was more like time on a luxury cruise with beautiful weather with everyone laying around, playing cards, or listening to radios . . ."

Enemy air reconnaissance was spotted, and radio intercepts suggested that the German 19th Army was anticipating an Allied amphibious assault in the Genoa area. At 0530 a convoy carrying the rest of French 2nd Corps left Taranto following the same route as that taken to the assault area by the Brindisi-Taranto convoy of August 10. Four hours later Rear Admiral Deyo's Gunfire Support Group left Palermo, passing south of Sardinia and then turning north on its way to the assault area.

At 1400 the three sections of Western Naval Task Force's combat loader convoy,* comprising twenty-five assault transports and assault cargo ships and escorts plus sixteen other ships and escorts, under the tactical command of Rear Admiral Spencer S. Lewis in the attack transport USS *Bayfield*,** were sailing at twelve knots from Naples following the course set by Admiral Lowry on August 9. As the third section of the combat loader convoy moved out of the bay in columns

* The combat loading concept was driven by the rapid development of amphibious operations in World War II. It gave troops immediate access to weapons, ammunition, and supplies in opposed landings. Vessels designed specifically for the purpose were given the designations APA (transport, attack) and AKA (cargo ship, attack).

** The Baseball Hall of Famer Yogi Berra was a gunner's mate on the *Bayfield*.

before assuming cruising formation, it was passed by the Admiral's barge carrying a jaunty Winston Churchill.

Later that day, the *Ramillies* was on the move, sailing under escort from Algiers to join the Alpha Gunfire Support Group. Simultaneously, another large convoy, comprising forty-eight merchant transports and ten other vessels with escorts followed in the wake of the transport loaders at a speed of nine knots. As darkness fell, the slow LCT convoy that had left Naples at 0930 on August 9 moved out of Ajaccio on the final leg of its journey to the assault area. Watching the transport loaders leaving Naples was a gaggle of senior Allied commanders and political figures aboard the USS *Catoctin*, which bristled with state-of-the-art communications systems and was the dedicated amphibious flagship for Dragoon. Rear Admiral Lewis was accompanied by Generals Patch and Truscott and Gordon P. Saville, of the 12th Tactical Air Command, the French Admiral André-Georges Lemonnier, and U.S. Secretary of the Navy James V. Forrestal, the last an immensely wealthy prewar investment banker who as undersecretary of the Navy until May 1944 had overseen a massive expansion of American sea power.

The previous two weeks had seen a frenetic burst of activity. On August 1 the code name for the invasion of the South of France had been changed from Anvil to Dragoon. The same day saw the 3rd Division's rehearsal for the operation and the completion of the final army, navy, and corps orders for Dragoon, and those for the sub–task forces, which were packaged for distribution onboard ship but not before the invasion fleet had put to sea. At this stage only commanders and their staffs knew their precise destination. On July 28 Patch and his staff had briefed Generals Wilson and Devers on the final army plans for Dragoon; and on August 3 Admiral Hewitt and his sub–task force commanders and their staffs presented a rundown of the Navy's operational plan. On August 7, the 36th and 45th Divisions conducted their assault rehearsals, the so-called "Dry Run" before the real thing, the "Wet Run." According to Truscott, the staff at the Invasion Training Center, "constructed obstacles similar to those which intelligence indicated we would expect, and used every aid to reproduce battle conditions and to make the rehearsals entirely realistic: live ammunition, naval gunfire with reduced charges, rockets, bangalore torpedoes, mines with simulated charges, smoke, and the like."[2]

Not everyone was impressed. Private First Class Ralph Fink, of D Company, 157th Regiment, 45th Division, recalled the chaos that descended on his unit's rehearsal: "All went well until we were in the landing craft. For some reason, the second ship was late in arriving, so we kept on circling for about an hour at a slow speed. Even though the sea was calm, that small craft seemed to rock in so many different directions and many of us got violently sea sick. Finally, when all was coordinated, we made our gung-ho charge across the beach, directly into a field of ripe watermelons. Discipline broke down at this point . . . we probably had the greatest orgy of water melon eating in the history of mankind."[3]

On August 8, the day after the 36th and 45th Divisions' rehearsals, Generals Truscott, O'Daniel, and Dahlquist presided over a final briefing on the 6th Corps's plans. The three divisions of 6th Corps had been reviewed, Truscott noting with pride that the 3rd Division was reviewed on the same ground and in the same formation in which he had reviewed them before the Anzio operation. He later recalled: "It was a magnificent and inspiring sight. I addressed the officers of each division to impress upon them their individual responsibilities for the success of our forthcoming venture, and to offer them words of advice from my own experience."

By August 12, 6th Corps was fully loaded, and at 2100 Truscott was piped aboard the *Catoctin*. Both he and Patch eagerly awaited the action that lay ahead. Patch reassured Truscott: "I am coming along on the *Catoctin*, but I want you to know I do not want to embarrass you in any way. I am not going to interfere with the way you fight your battle. I want you to know it." Charts and maps in the *Catoctin*'s war room revealed the scale of the Allied armada bound for the South of France. Admiral Hewitt later wrote: "All the elements of the Western Naval Task Force were now at sea converging on the assault area. Ten divisions of troops were afloat, with their equipment and supporting services, probably nearly a quarter of a million men. Involved in transporting them, protecting them, and landing them safely in the face of enemy resistance, and supporting them when ashore were nearly a thousand (974) ships and craft of many types, of which 851 were naval-manned, and the remainder merchant-manned. Of the naval ships and craft, 534 were American, 266 were British, 35 were French, and seven were Greek."

Truscott's quarters on the *Catoctin* were stiflingly hot, as the command ship's ventilation system had broken down. The comings and goings of the senior Allied commanders aboard the command ship were noted by Truscott's aide, as was the tension building up to the Dragoon landings. On Monday, August 14, the day before the troops went ashore, Truscott's aide noted: "Another bad night in oven-like cabin. Day quiet and almost uneventful, with ship passing through the Sardinia-Corsica strait at noon and skirting western coast of Corsica all afternoon. Gen. Saville in during morning to straighten out questions of bombing enemy CPs. Destroyer alongside. Gen. Somervell [head of the US Services of Supply] and Secty Patterson [U.S. Secretary of War] request permission to come aboard tomorrow. Msgs from Gen. H. M. Wilson and Adm. Cunningham wishing all good luck. In late evening begin to pass through the LCIs . . . Jitters cooling off a little, and General writes letter to wife before starting to bed." That night Truscott reflected: "Organizing this vast armada, planning and directing its routes, coordinating and protecting its movements so that each of a thousand pieces fell into place at the exact time, fully prepared for its manifold duties, was something of a gigantic jigsaw puzzle—or a chess game of the gods with the broad Mediterranean as a board. Our admiration for the professional ability of our Naval colleagues was boundless, and our respect for their achievement in this complicated operation was profound."[4]

A more earthy reflection on the hours leading up to the invasion of the South of France was subsequently offered by Sergeant Frank Andrews, who was with the headquarters of 1st Battalion, 7th Infantry Regiment, 3rd Division. Andrews was an Anzio veteran who remembered marching to his embarkation point through back alleys in Naples's red-light district as the main thoroughfares were filled with tanks and heavy equipment. Around the column swarmed prostitutes enticing the GIs into the shadows as the soldiers stared straight ahead. On the subsequent sea crossing the troops listened to Axis Sally[*] telling them "how easy it is to surrender any time we wanted to. She named all the units in the convoy and told us where we were at . . . and that sure makes your hair stand on end."

---

* A German propaganda broadcaster, possibly Mildred Gillars.

NINE
LE MUY FOLLIES

> "It was quite still, and I remember looking out of the door—we appeared to be flying over the sea. I wasn't too happy about jumping, but we'd been drilled to go on the green light; so I thought, 'Here we go.' The 'sea' was early morning mist—really white mist—and as I came down I saw trees poking through it. I wasn't sure if they were islands or trees."
>
> —Major Dick Hargreaves, 4th Parachute Battalion, 2nd Independent Parachute Brigade

From the outset, Allied airborne operations in World War II had a record that mixed triumph and tragedy in equal measure. In the invasion of Sicily in early July 1943, airborne troops were tasked with the taking of key points on the Ponte Grande, over the canal at the entrance to the port of Syracuse, and the principal coastal bridge on the approach to Catania, the Ponte Primosole, to block the enemy's escape route across the Straits of Messina. On July 9, airborne forces, drawn from the U.S. 82nd and British 1st Airborne Divisions, suffered heavy casualties when inexperienced pilots dropped them into the sea and antiaircraft gunners shot down their aircraft. On July 13, a key mission by British paratroops to seize the Primosole Bridge, south of Mount Etna, proved particularly costly when they were counterattacked by the German 1st Parachute Division. The 1st Parachute Brigade's drop had also been dispersed over a wide area after being fired on by ships of the Royal Navy, a muddle that forced the American aircrews to take excessive evasive action. Just three hundred men were dropped with sufficient accuracy to enable them to seize the Primosole Bridge and hold it against fierce counterattacks until the arrival of the British 8th Army. Nobody needed reminding that the operation in the South of France, entrusted to First Airborne Task Force commanded by Major General Robert Tryon Frederick, was fraught with risk.

First Airborne Task Force (FABTF), code-named "Rugby," had been activated on July 19. It consisted of 9,732 men from the paratroop, glider, and regular units that were available in Italy at the time. Its order of battle was as follows: landing by parachute were the 517th Parachute Infantry Regiment (517th PIR); the British 2nd Independent Parachute Brigade, consisting of the experienced 4th, 5th, and 6th Battalions of the Parachute Regiment; and a number of supporting units, such as 127th Parachute Field Ambulance; 509th Parachute Infantry Battalion (509th PIB); 551st Parachute Infantry Battalion (551st PIB); 460th Parachute Field Artillery Battalion; 463rd Parachute Field Artillery Battalion (463rd PFAB); and 596th Parachute Combat Engineer Company (596th PCEC). The glider-borne units were an American infantry battalion (550th GIB); a British light artillery battalion (64th) and an anti-tank battery (300th); an American anti-tank company (442nd) and 602nd Field Artillery Battalion; and a number of auxiliary units, among them signals and medical companies; airborne engineers; two companies from chemical warfare battalions, one of which was attached to the British 2nd Independent Parachute Brigade; an ordnance maintenance company; a military police platoon; and the headquarters company of First Airborne Task Force.

From the start, relations between the British and American formations in FABTF were less than cordial. In a postwar interview Frederick admitted, "I began to worry about the British back in Italy during the planning stage. They seemed to be devoting more time to getting together all the creature comforts to take with them than they were to tactical readiness."[1] Colonel Bryant Evans, Frederick's intelligence officer, was unimpressed by the British commanding officer, Brigadier Charles Pritchard, an immaculately turned-out officer of the old school. Bryant recalled, "I had told Frederick what was going to happen because before we jumped in. I'd been over to see Pritchard to arrange artillery support, and he told me that there was no necessity to discuss it because he didn't intend to fight after he landed. I was perfectly furious about that."[2]

A possible reason for British guardedness about the operation was later offered by Major General John S. Guthrie, who was the Seventh Army's G-3 (Operations) during Dragoon: "I have the feeling that Jumbo [Wilson], the theater commander, was reluctant to get the British involved in the operation. When he did lend us the brigade, he had them on a string of some kind to be sure that they would be returned: in other words, he wanted to be sure that the British participated, but he wanted to get his paratroopers back again as soon as possible. In any case, we gave him what we considered the simplest part of the operation and we expected that once we had landed and consolidated that he could exploit the operation as did others in the area. But I suspect that Pritchard had [private] instructions to conserve his forces."

Frederick was now faced with the seemingly impossible job of turning this composite group, some of whom had no airborne training, into an effective fighting force within less than a month. The task was daunting, but to the man who had made the Devil's Brigade, this presented few problems. The 700-strong 509th PIB, commanded by Lieutenant Colonel William Yarborough and formed in 1941, was a battle-tested formation that had jumped into action four times and seen much hard fighting in Sicily and on the Italian mainland. The 517th Parachute Regimental Combat Team (517th PRCT) commanded by Colonel Rupert Graves, comprised the 517th PIR, 460th PFAB, and 596th PCEC—some 2,800 men. These units had trained together and were all-volunteer outfits with an aggressive esprit de corps. However, they had seen only about ten days' combat in Italy, in June 1944. The 742 men of 551st PIB, commanded by Colonel Wood Joerg, had seen no combat, and probably for this reason were tasked with jumping into the target area in the afternoon of August 15, to reinforce the units that had jumped early that morning.

Frederick had never gone into action by parachute, but this did not deter General Devers, who told him in Algiers: "I have no idea that you have jumped out of any airplane . . . but I know you sure as hell are going into Southern France by air, whether it's by glider or by jumping . . . and that's what your men are going to do too!" Of the glider units assigned to Rugby, only one—the 550th GIB—was glider-trained when FABTF was formed. Men from other units were "volunteered" in the old Army sense of the word. One of these was of particular interest—442nd Anti-Tank Company whose men were Japanese-Americans who had distinguished themselves in hard fighting in Italy. Along with the 602nd Field Artillery Battalion, and a clutch of aviation engineering, chemical, and medical units, they attended a hastily established glider school near Rome where they learned to load and lash their equipment in Waco CG-4A gliders,* dubbed "flying coffins" by their aircrews.

The training center for the parachutists, the glider-borne troops, and the 51st Troop Carrier Wing, which was to fly or tow them into battle with its Douglas C-47 Dakota transports, was established near Rome between the Ciampino and Lido di Roma airfields. Frederick set up his headquarters at Lido di Roma on July 17, and three days later detailed planning for the operation began. The Troop Carrier staff undertook the aspects of the airborne landings that involved high-level coordination, timing, routes, corridors, rendezvous, and traffic patterns, while the details of the Drop Zones (DZs), Landing Zones (LZs), and composition of lifts were jointly handled by the Airborne and Troop Carrier staffs.

An early proposal for a pre-dusk airborne assault on D-Day was ruled out, as was a plan for the air drops and landings to be made after the amphibious assault on the French coast had been launched. A third proposal, that the operation be staged through Corsica, was

* The Waco, which had a wingspan of 83.6 feet, was the only US glider to see combat service in World War II. In the last two years of the war some 12,000 were built. The entire nose could be hinged upward for loading wheeled vehicles or weapons, although not all the Wacos used in Dragoon had this modification. The Waco could carry fifteen fully-equipped troops or 3,750 lbs. of cargo The British air-landing elements of FABTF went into battle in towed Horsa gliders, introduced in 1942 and the first British glider to use a tricycle undercarriage, the two side wheels of which were jettisoned after takeoff, leaving the nosewheel and skid to support the landing. The Horsa could carry thirty men or approximately 7,700 lbs. of cargo. Some 6,600 were built during the war. The FABTF planned to use 332 Wacos and 71 Horsas in the South of France operation.

also rejected on the grounds that there were insufficient airfields available on the island and the flight over its 9,000-foot mountains by towed gliders posed too great a risk. A final plan had emerged by July 25. The airborne assault would go in before H-Hour, starting with the dropping of Pathfinder crews equipped with Eureka beacons at 0323. The beacons, introduced in 1943, were short-range radio navigation aids used in the dropping of airborne forces and their supplies, and also for supplying the European Resistance movement. The Eurekas (from the Greek "I have found it!") were linked to airborne "Rebecca" transceivers, whose name was derived from "Recognition of Beacons."

The main parachute lift, flown by 396 aircraft, was to begin at 0412 and end at 0509. The first glider landings were to be made at 0814 and end at 1859. Resupply of FABTF was to be undertaken by 112 aircraft flying from Italy on D+1 with the residuals retained around Rome to meet any emergency that might arise. The route flown by the airborne assault force was to follow the Italian coastline from Rome to the island of Elba, the first overwater check point, followed by the northern tip of Corsica. Thereafter it would proceed on an azimuth course over U.S. Navy checkpoints to landfall just to the north of Fréjus and Agay.

Three drop and landing zones had been chosen. Two miles northwest of Le Muy was A, the target for 517th Parachute Regiment Combat Team (PRCT). Some two miles to the north of Le Muy was O, the target for British Independent 2nd Parachute Brigade. And C, two miles to the southeast of the town, was the target for 509th PIB. Maps and models of the target area proved problematic for the planners. A useful terrain model, a photo-model on a scale of 1:25,000, was available in only one copy, and large-scale blow-ups of the drop and landing zones arrived too late to be of general use.* However, some of these photographic studies revealed the previously undetected presence around Le Muy of so-called "Rommel asparagus," glider-smashing networks of twelve-foot poles wired together with explosives and sunk two feet into the ground, which the Allied airborne forces had previously encountered in Normandy.

* The British 2nd Independent Parachute Brigade produced an excellent terrain model of the target area.

By mid-July, nearly all the units earmarked for Anvil had been assembled outside Rome and an intensive training program had been initiated by FABTF. The Pathfinder platoons rigorously tested their Eureka sets, M/F beacons (radio compass homing devices), and light panels, which were topped with a frosted pane, making them visible from above. They then practiced working as a team in every conceivable situation they might encounter. The final phase concentrated on parachute drops with full equipment. Small groups of parachutists were dropped onto simulated drop zones to test the accuracy of the Pathfinder aids. However, due to the extremely tight schedule imposed on Anvil, and the difficulty of repackaging parachutes in large numbers before D-Day, it was not possible for FABTF to stage a full dress rehearsal of the operation. Nevertheless, a limited combined training exercise was conducted with the U.S. Navy and the USAAF to acquaint the former with the timing, schedules, routes, and altitudes established for the operation and to test the provisions made for air-sea rescue and fighter cover.

For the airborne troops waiting to go into action, the precise destination remained a mystery. Guy Carr, who was a Pathfinder with 1st Company, 517th PIR, remembered: "Behind the closed doors of the S-2 [battalion intelligence] and the guarded war tents, details were taking shape on maps and sand tables marked 'Top Secret.' Then, during the second week, all the men of the regiment were sent into the war tents in small groups. We were to memorize what we saw on the sand tables and maps. We still had no knowledge of the locations shown on the sand tables, as S-2 had reproduced only that portion of the terrain covering the area of the drop zone. We were required to etch each mountain, river, valley, power line, road, town, forest, and any other object that would be of use behind enemy lines . . . not on paper, but in our minds which could not be read by the enemy."[3]

In the run-up to the air drops around Le Muy, Frederick once again demonstrated his idiosyncratic command style. He chose as a bodyguard to jump alongside him Duffield W. Matson Jr., a soldier who had spent more time either absent without leave or in various stockades on numerous charges than he had on the front line. Matson was in the stockade near Lido di Roma when an emissary from Frederick's headquarters, a Native American of Apache descent named Leonard

Cheek, arrived to spirit him out. Cheek made Matson an offer he could not refuse: serve with FABTF or stay in the stockade. Matson had no idea why Frederick had singled him out beyond the fact that he was told that his new CO had a reputation for turning old lags into good soldiers. It seems that Frederick had discerned that although Matson was a man of with an unenviable record, his college education, high intelligence, and low criminal cunning made him an ideal candidate for FABTF's intelligence section. Matson later recalled: ". . . this kind of treatment was a godsend at this particular time of my life. Just before they took me out of the stockade I had made up my mind to bust out come hell or high water. I didn't give a damn if I had to shoot anyone or if anyone shot me, but I was going to get out. So Frederick's willingness to take me changed my whole life."[4]

The middle of July saw the more conventional arrival in Italy of thirty-six staff officers, most of them from 13th Airborne Division, dispatched by the War Department to make up a divisional staff for the planning of the airborne invasion of southern France. Extra airlift and pilots were also provided by two wings of 4th Troop Carrier Command, then stationed in the United Kingdom. The British 2nd Independent Parachute Brigade had sufficient Horsa operational gliders in the theater for the operation, but in mid-July the Americans could only lay their hands on approximately 130 operational CG-4As. Happily, an order for 350 Wacos had already been placed with the US manufacturers, and by August 5 the shipment had arrived in theater, had been reassembled, and was ready for operational employment along with 350 extra pilots. However, only 40 percent of the new Wacos were fitted with hinged noses. By D-4, August 11, the extra requisitions for cargo parachutes and freight had also reached the quartermaster depot in Italy.

On the afternoon of August 14, the order came through to FABTF to get ready. Guy Carr recalled the preliminaries to takeoff: "We put on our jump suits and proceeded to Service Company, where we were sprayed completely with camouflage paint from hoses. What a wild looking lot we were, as the boys with the hoses made no effort to spray only our suits, but the rest of our bodies as well. All types of pistols and knives appeared from nowhere, and the so-called name 'Butchers with Big Pockets' seemed appropriate . . . Chutes were passed and fitted, and ammunition and 'K' rations* issued. Machine guns, rifles, pistols, mortars, and anything that could destroy the enemy were given a final inspection. We were also given pamphlets containing French phrases and escape kits, native currency, compasses, silk maps, and matches (this was our first clue as to where we we would be landing). We were given camouflage paint to be applied to our hands and faces . . . and some very interesting designs were worked up."[5]

The Normandy landings had demonstrated the problems of dropping airborne forces at night, given the limitations of existing navigation technology. In spite of this, the Dragoon planners stuck to script and the initial air drops were scheduled to go in while it was still dark. However, on the night of August 14 the weather took a hand. Much of Western Europe was now covered by a large, flat high-pressure area swirling down from the North Sea. A large chunk of this high pressure had settled over the Dragoon target area. While this precluded the possibility of storms and heavy winds disrupting the progress of the invasion air forces and fleet, it brought with it another threat, that of accumulating fog or stratus clouds. Meteorologists had forecast clear weather to Elba followed by steadily decreasing visibility as FABTF neared the DZs and LZs. The forecast turned out to be over-optimistic. Visibility on the DZs was now less than half a mile and the dense summer mist enveloping the target area and its approaches would not disperse until 0800.

The airborne operation began shortly after midnight on August 15. Aircraft were loaded, engines warmed up and by 0300 marshaling for takeoff had begun. At this point the first troop carrier aircraft took off carrying the Pathfinder teams whose job was to mark the target area for the Main Force. Nine aircraft divided into three serials** were tasked with dropping three teams on each of the DZs. The lead serial

---

* The K ration was the US soldier's daily combat food ration in three separate boxes for breakfast, lunch, and dinner. The rations were mass produced by Heinz and other food corporations. Some of the components, notably fatty pork and acidic lemon powder, were not universally popular with troops and were often discarded. The three meals in a daily ration provided some 3,000 calories.

** A serial was a formation based on three aircraft, with one aircraft leading and the others flying a little behind and below the leader. This configuration could be built up into a formation 45 aircraft strong.

was to drop Pathfinders from 509th and 551st Battalions, plus those of 550th Battalion, at 0323 hours, but lost its way in the fog and had to circle back to sea to make a second run at its DZ. The serial's SCR-717 radar* proved of little help and its pilots had to resort to navigation by dead reckoning. After circling for about thirty minutes, it dropped its Pathfinders and turned for home. By now, the two other serials had separated and the second dropped its team at about 0400 hours. The third team jumped about fifteen minutes later on the aircraft's sixth run into the Drop Zone. None of these teams was able to reach the Drop Zone in time to perform their designated role of guiding in the main force.

The second serial dropped Pathfinders from 517th PRCT at around 0330, but they jumped three minutes early, landing in a wooded area three and a half miles east of DZ A and Le Muy, attracting enemy fire. They did not reach DZ A until 1630 but set up Eurekas, M/F beacons, and a light panel that helped some of the later glider landings. The third serial, carrying British Pathfinders from 2nd Independent Brigade had better luck, parachuting into DZ O at 0334, precisely on schedule. By 0430 they had two Eureka beacons working some 300 yards apart along FABTF's approach path. One of the British Pathfinders was Jim Chittenden, who recalled: "Over the Mediterranean, we flew across the Navy ships, which were sending out a Eureka beam. We got our bearing from that. Once we passed over that ship, we flew on a certain bearing, for a certain distance of time, and they dropped us spot on the target . . . We were only jumping from an average of 500 feet and were down in about seven seconds. We landed at about 0320 in the morning, and the Germans didn't even know we were there. Our first person to get killed was Eric Morley. His parachute never opened because his static line had broken. We got different reports about this. Some of them said his static line was ruptured by the acid in the batteries we carried and others said different tales. But his parachute never opened, so you can say that he was the first man killed because he went straight down."[6]

* The SCR-717 airborne radar sender/receiver scanned the landscape below the aircraft with its beams and their reflections appeared on a screen as a crude outline map on which water was shown as black and land and shipping appeared lighter. It was similar to the British H2S system.

❖

The Pathfinders were followed in over the coast after 0400hrs by Mission Albatross, 396 aircraft divided into ten serials and carrying 5,600 paratroops and 150 field guns. In one of the leading C-47s was Frederick, immaculate in his jump suit, white silk scarf, and .45 automatic on his hip. The first serial of C-47s from the 442nd Troop Carrier Group (TCG) with elements of 509th Parachute Infantry Battalion and 463rd Field Artillery Battalion arrived over Drop Zone C at around 0430hrs to find none of the Pathfinder navigation aids in place. Hilltops dimly discernible through the murk had to serve as navigation aids. Terrell E. Stewart of the 509th waited for the green light signal to jump from his C-47. Then he was out of the aircraft, striving to make a quarter turn to the left as he went out of the door, clasping his reserve parachute with both hands. Immediately afterward he was caught roughly by the Dakota's propeller backwash, pushing him violently backward, before he dropped down, as if in a funnel of air, his body inclining first to the left and then to the right. Then he was jerked up sharply. His parachute had opened and he was suspended quietly in the night air, but still seeing stars as his head spun from the shock of the parachute opening: "I could still hear the drone of the planes, but growing fainter. I looked around. On both sides of me chutes were drifting silently, as if in a kind of dream world. . . . As the plane drone finally died, we were engulfed by complete silence. I looked below. At first I could see nothing . . . I accepted this as normal and reflected that the ground would show up eventually Then, as I continued to fall, a dull whitish expanse began slowly spreading below me. It grew larger and larger as my chute descended. . . . The whitish mass gradually expanded to such a degree that I was able to see that it had no density . . . it looked like a kind of vapor. Then suddenly I knew what it was—a cloud! We had jumped above the clouds. Gently the friendly mass received me. I was encompassed by a dull, damp whiteness, surrounded by a pleasant glow as from subdued fluorescent lighting . . . Innumerable tiny crystals seemed to break against my skin."[7]

Stewart's peaceful reverie was rudely interrupted when he hit the ground. He struggled out of his harness, slicing through its belt—known as the "belly band"—with his knife before he heard the sounds of stealthy movement around him. As figures loomed out of the darkness, he was challenged with the password "Democracy," to which he rasped the reply, "Lafayette." He was among friends. Duffield Matson was not so lucky, breaking a leg as he landed. He was later evacuated. Frederick, however, had landed safely and was attempting to read a map with the aid of a blue flashlight. Peering through the mist, he identified the small town where he planned to establish his command post. He made for it but had only gone a few yards when he spotted the dark shape of a man in the mist. Taking no risks, Frederick circled behind the figure before grabbing him around the neck in a death grip he had been taught in the Special Service Force.

When the stranger spluttered "Jesus Christ!" in an English accent, Frederick relaxed his hold and discovered that he had been attempting to strangle a man from 2nd British Independent Parachute Brigade. He ordered the paratrooper to rejoin his unit, but his new comrade declined, saying that he had lost his rifle in the jump and, as Frederick was in possession of a .45, he was not going to take any chances. When the two men arrived at the command post, they learned that all Frederick's equipment, including the radios, had been dropped thirty miles away.

The dispersal of Frederick's paratroops had in large part been caused by the mist hanging over the target area, frustrating the Pathfinder aircrews and then imposing jumps by the Main Force from around 2,000 feet rather than the 600 feet envisaged at the planning stage of the operation. At 0430 the first sizeable American units to jump, 509th PIB and 463rd FAB, managed to deliver two companies of infantry and two artillery batteries on to the DZ, which lay in broken and partially wooded country some two miles southeast of Le Muy. A second serial strayed off course and dropped one infantry company and two batteries into the hills south of the coastal resort of Saint-Tropez, approximately fifteen miles southeast of Le Muy. Only half of 509th's Battalion Combat Team had landed in or close to the DZ.

The problem was compounded when 517th Regimental Combat Team arrived over its DZ, two miles west of Le Muy, at approximately 0435. The greater part of 1st Battalion, the 517th Infantry, was strung out from Trans-en-Provence, four miles northwest of Le Muy, to Lorgues, six miles farther to the west. Many of the regiment's 2nd Battalion came down some two miles northwest of Le Muy, near La Motte, while one third of the battalion landed on rising ground east and northeast of the target town. The 3rd Battalion of the 517th landed on a six-mile line thirteen miles northeast of Le Muy, and a battery of the regiment's Field Artillery Battalion landed northwest of Fréjus. By now, many other individual soldiers and small groups of men were scattered seemingly at random across the Provençal countryside with little or no idea where they were.

Thanks to the success of two of its Pathfinder beacon teams, British 2nd Independent Parachute Brigade, whose assault began at 0450, was faring better. Just under two-thirds of the brigade landed in Drop Zone O. The rest of their comrades were strewn over countryside some ten miles to the northeast and northwest of Le Muy. Major Dick Hargreaves of the 4th Parachute Battalion later described the mist that plagued the air drop as they flew into the DZ: "It was quite still, and I remember looking out of the door—we appeared to be flying over the sea. I wasn't too happy about jumping, but we'd been drilled to go on the green light; so I thought, 'Here we go.' The 'sea' was early morning mist—really white mist—and as I came down I saw trees poking through it; I wasn't sure then if they were islands or trees. I actually landed on top of a fir tree, which wasn't a bad way of coming down, except I nearly knocked myself out tugging my kit bag down. But I was very lucky because I landed in the right place, while Dan Calvert who commanded A Company was dropped miles off target. He reckoned there was no way he was going to walk it, so he ended up by getting a bus in!"[8]

Major Bill Corby of the 5th Parachute Battalion came down on the DZ: "There wasn't much shooting but a few seconds after landing, when I'd stuffed my parachute under a bush, I heard somebody coming through the undergrowth. I quietly cocked my automatic and waited. When he got really close I challenged him and he answered in what was obviously a Welsh accent—he was a Welsh battalion signaller! He could easily have been one dead Welshman. Meanwhile one of my platoon sergeants [Sergeant Tucker] had dropped on the roof of a local German headquarters. Of course the opposition came out and started shooting at him so he shot back with a Sten gun,* killing the German adjutant and wounding two others. Eventually they made a hole in the roof and came up through and warned him that if he didn't surrender they'd chuck grenades into his bit of the roof valley—so he decided to call it a day. They took him down to the guard room where there were another two people who had landed in the same position. He told the Germans that they were surrounded by two divisions of airborne troops so they might as well chuck it in. He was right. At 9:00 A.M. the gliders with the gunners and sappers [engineers] had come in along with another American battalion. It was marvelous drop—the whole lot were in the air at once. When the Germans holding the sergeant saw this they surrendered straight away and Tucker led all eighty Germans out as prisoners."[9]

Walter Perkowski, a BAR (Browning M1918 light machine gun) man of F Company, 517th PIR, was another soldier who enjoyed a lucky escape. He landed near a German strongpoint and was captured by the enemy after being stunned by a hand grenade explosion. He recalled that the German who took him prisoner "seemed like a nice guy" and offered him a cigarette. Perkowski declined the offer, prompting his captor to proffer a candy bar. This was also declined as, understandably, Perkowski was in no mood for a snack. Then he was taken to an officer: "He asked me how many guys jumped. I told him 60,000 and then he hit me, grabbed hold of me, and threw me inside a trench. Mortars and shells were coming in and they pulled me out and put me and two English paratroopers in a garage and lined us against a wall. The door opened and two Germans came in with a machine gun. All of a sudden another one comes in with a bicycle, and he said something to them, so they picked up the damn machine gun and the guy on the bicycle and took off and left us in there. I just came out and waited for the guys to come in. The whole thing lasted for about an hour or two."[10]

The paratroops who had landed around Le Muy heavily outnumbered the Germans garrisoned there. Aside from patrols and

* The Sten gun was a British 9mm submachine gun developed by Shepherd and Turpin at the Royal Small Arms Factory, Enfield, from which combination the name was constructed. Simple and cheap to manufacture, some 3.25 million were produced during the war for British troops, commandos, and Resistance fighters in Occupied Europe.

headquarters units, the only significant German presence in the vicinity of the town was a horse-drawn transport battalion. Moreover, the scattered nature of the paratroops' descent gave the enemy an exaggerated picture of the scale of the drop. The Germans' alarm was increased when, shortly after 0800 the gliders arrived, carrying infantry, artillery and anti-tank units, support troops, and elements of FABTF headquarters. Riding in a flimsy towed glider was a particularly uncomfortable experience. The roar of its C-47 tow's twin radials was deafening, and the paratroops, who unlike the aircrew were not provided with parachutes,* sat on flak jackets as a protection against upward small arms fire. The unsettling concertina-like effect of formation flying frequently induced air sickness, and landing was little more than a barely controlled accident with the added risk of inadequately secured items like small vehicles, ammunition, and artillery pieces working loose and crushing airborne troops and crew.

When the first wave of gliders crossed the coast on Mission Bluebird, fog still blanketed the target area, prompting half of the C-47 pilots, flying in Troop Carrier Group 435 (TCG 435), to turn back to the airfields around Rome without cutting their 300-foot tow ropes. They were towing the larger Horsa gliders and their fuel consumption was greater than that of the C-47s towing the lighter Wacos of TCG 436. The TCG 435 was not to return until late afternoon while TCG 436, after circling for an hour over LZ O, released its gliders. TCG 436's aircrews immediately ran into problems that had not been revealed by photo reconnaissance. On the photographs, the landing fields, ringed by low stone walls, looked flat and benign, but they were smaller than had been anticipated, surrounded by fifty-foot trees and criss-crossed by vineyards and hedgerows. In addition to the Rommel asparagus, the Germans had dotted the landing area with many large mounds of earth and flooded parts of it. The glider pilots had been trained to fly in low, clearing three-foot walls and hedgerows, but now faced rising over the trees fringing the landing areas, overshooting the target, and contending with the trees surrounding the next field. Even if they survived landing, many of the airborne troops were weakened by the

* At least one FABTF officer, Lieutenant Karl Wickstrom of the 602nd FAB, on noticing this, drew his revolver to ensure that the pilots would not bail out of the glider.

rigors of the flight. Frederick's intelligence officer, Colonel William Blythe, recalled: "We landed in a vineyard while firing was going on all around us. But the men were so sick [from the violent motion of the maneuvering glider] that many of them fell out of the glider on their faces, lying there vomiting. It took a while for their officers to get them up and moving."

During the course of the day, two more waves of towed gliders flew into the LZ: Mission Canary, carrying men of 551st PIB; and Mission Dove, delivering 550th GIB. Both formations were augmented by supporting units. As more serials came in to an increasingly crowded landing area, the pilots found themselves competing with each other for landing space. The 602nd FAB, made a landing run at 1820. One of its men, Marvin McRoberts, remembered the sight that greeted the pilots: ". . . we could see there were gliders on the ground that had landed before us. They were scattered every which way. Some were crashed for unknown reasons . . . we stopped just short of the east side of the field. A paratrooper standing next to a GI was taking motion pictures with his camera on a tripod and was watching us come in. The glider that came in just south of us came in the same way and did real good until it hit some of the flooded area, flipping as the nose dug into the ground. This in turn threw the front of the glider open. The pilot and the co-pilot were thrown forward out of the glider like two peas in a pod. They were bruised and scratched up but alive. All the GIs in that glider were killed, as the [badly secured] gun was pushed forward where they were sitting and they were crushed."[11]

The Rommel asparagus was to prove particularly hazardous. In the small hours of August 15, Geoffrey Jones, an OSS colleague, and seven French gendarmes had descended from the Montagne de Malay to Le Muy to uproot as many of the air-landing obstructions as they could before the arrival of the gliders. (The gendarmes were with the OSS men as a ruse. If the party was stopped by a German patrol, Jones and his comrade would be identified by the gendarmes as prisoners.) However, as they neared the LZ, the greatest danger to the little party came from marauding Allied fighter-bombers, attracted by the headlights on the truck in which they were traveling rather than jittery enemy patrols. One bomb exploded only yards away, lightly injuring two of the party. By dawn, as they neared their objective, the first paratroop units had arrived.

When they were followed by the glider-borne troops, the Rommel asparagus took a heavy toll, snapping the wings off many of the gliders as they slithered to a halt, turning the landing zones into a shambles. After the operation, only some fifty of the approximately four hundred gliders that had flown in the operation were salvageable. However, damage to crews and cargo was markedly less severe. In the entire operation, by parachute and glider, sixteen glider pilots were killed and thirty-seven were injured; and 230 parachutists and glider-borne troops died or suffered serious injury—some 2.5 percent of the 9,000 airborne troops who arrived in southern France on August 15, 1944. In addition, 213 artillery pieces, 221 vehicles, and over 1,000 tons of equipment had been delivered to the battlefield, as had approximately 95 percent of the glider-borne troops and some 50 percent of the parachutists.

Throughout August 15, the American and British parachutists who had dropped outside the Le Muy area strove to rejoin their parent units. Many did not make it until D+1, and a few failed to find their way back until D+5. Nevertheless, by dawn on August 15 about 60 percent of the first parachute lifts had assembled in the vicinity of Le Muy. Here Geoffrey Jones and his party made contact with Colonel Graves's 517th PRCT, but not without incident. Jones recalled: "It seemed that I was in the wrong uniform. When I took off my blue civilian suit, I was wearing khakis underneath, and everyone in the invading force was wearing olive drabs. Almost every soldier we saw wanted to take a shot at me. You see, these parachutists were landing all over the place instead of being exactly where they were supposed to be, so understandably many of the Americans were quite jittery. Many of them shot at each other rather than the Germans. The first few Americans I saw were convinced that I was a German spy, but I got away. Finally, I made my identification by yelling through the fog to some sergeant. We got to the point where he was willing to let me come over so long as I held my hands up as high as they would go. Somehow . . . I talked the sergeant into telling me the name of his unit, and to my relief it was a parachute artillery battalion where I was quite familiar with many of the officers because they had been with me in either the 11th or 82nd Airborne. After throwing their names around, he agreed to take me to meet some of their fellows. After I established identification, I brought out my gendarmes." Shortly afterward, Jones met Major General Fredrick, asking him, "What did you want to know?" Jones did this with some assurance because he and the gendarmes knew where everyone was, and the conditions of the local roads and bridges, the location of power lines, and "just about everything else he needed to know that night."[12] Then Jones grabbed some much-needed sleep in a nearby hayloft. It felt good to be surrounded by fellow Americans.

In the afternoon of August 15, Frederick organized attacks on Le Muy and Les Arcs, four miles to the west of Le Muy. Les Arcs had been briefly occupied by the FFI after the withdrawal of its German garrison. It was later occupied and secured by all three battalions of the 517th PIR, who beat off a succession of German counterattacks on the following day. It was a small-scale but grueling battle. Colonel Zais's 3rd Battalion, which had landed some twenty-five miles away, was the last on the scene, on August 15, gathering strength as it marched on its objective, following a power line that took it in the right direction. By the time 517th arrived near Les Arcs, the battalion was almost back to full strength. However, the rigors of the jump and a night march had been exhausting. Moreover, because they had no transport the men were carrying all of their equipment on their backs. After snatching some sleep, the 3rd Battalion went in later that night, supported by howitzers and mortars of 406th FAB. When the sun came up, the town had been cleared of Germans, who had left behind their dead and wounded. Later that morning Zais was paid a visit by Colonel Graves, and the two men ate Provençal tomatoes in the backyard of a farmhouse while they discussed the consolidation the defenses at les Arcs and moving against the Toulon-Saint-Raphaël corridor.

The task of taking Le Muy had been given to the British, but Brigadier Pritchard decided that the scattered parachute drop of the 2nd Independent Parachute Brigade and the delayed arrival of his artillery and anti-tank guns left him too weak to launch an attack on what appeared to be a strongly defended town. The British had taken the bridge over the main road into the town but held back from moving into Le Muy. The exasperated Frederick ordered the 550th GIB to take the town, and by the early afternoon of August 16 Le Muy had been cleared and secured.

The Germans had not been surprised by the arrival in their midst of several thousand airborne troops. On August 13 Major General Ludwig Bieringer, the district commander of *Verbindungsstab 800* (Field Administration Command 800) headquartered in Draguignan, seven miles northwest of Le Muy, and responsible for security behind the thin crust of coastal defenses in the Var Department, warned a staff conference in Avignon that the long-awaited invasion of the southern coast of France was imminent and could be launched within two days. After the war, Bieringer wrote a lengthy account of events during the initial days of Dragoon for the benefit of the Americans in which the tone is one of weary resignation. He reflected that no order had been issued as to the course of action to be taken by district commanders in the event of an Allied invasion. Furthermore, he observed that the district commander responsible for the landward defenses of Marseille had informed him that "effective defense of the sector was impossible with the forces he had at his disposal, which were absolutely inadequate for fighting enemy troops with up-to-date equipment. The only reply he received was a shrug of the shoulders."

The first concrete indication that a major Allied assault was imminent came toward midnight on August 14, when warships of the Western Task Force bombarded shore installations in the Marseille area and MAAF aircraft dropped dummy parachutists in the same sector as an integral part of the Allied deception plan. The bait was not swallowed by the Germans, however, and the deception was discounted within an hour. Two hours later Bieringer received a report that enemy paratroops had jumped in the area of Le Muy-Saint-Raphaël and he was ordered to assemble Alarm Companies to deal with the threat. By 0400 hours, the Alarm Companies, ill-armed formations consisting of rear area troops, had been dispatched. An hour later Bieringer's headquarters had been transformed into a strongpoint manned by administrative staff hastily armed with rifles, machine guns, and grenades. First aid packages were distributed and files burned. Simultaneously, the 19th Army headquarters at Avignon was receiving reports of the Allied landings at Cap Nègre and the Hyères islands. But it was not until 0600 that coastal defense units began to send reports of the enemy commandos coming ashore on the mainland.

At about the same time news arrived in Avignon of the air drops around Le Muy. Simultaneously wire and radio communications in the Var department began to break down, thanks to sabotage by the FFI and FABTF, forcing General Wiese, commander of 19th Army, to rely on information from the OB West network. The weakness of the communications system was the disabling flaw in 19th Army's entire command sector. Its telephone network was based almost entirely on the infrastructure of the French Post Office. The trunk lines of the telecommunications cables ran through the aptly named "terrorist regions" in the Rhône Valley, and were cut with such regularity by saboteurs that by mid-August 1944 teletype and telephone communications had been abandoned. Radio communications were not an adequate substitute, as equipment capable of long-distance transmission was not available and, as the Americans also discovered, radio messages were badly affected by atmospheric and topographic conditions in southern France. It was not until 1030 that General Wiese, commanding the 19th Army, received confirmation through local channels of the Allied airborne assault. By then Bieringer's Alarm Companies had disappeared without trace. With no orders to withdraw, their commander was stranded at Draguignan.

Also at Draguignan was the headquarters of 62nd Corps, one of 19th Army's three corps, commanded by General Ferdinand Neuling and consisting of the 242nd Infantry Division and 148th Reserve Infantry Division. The corps headquarters had been established at Draguignan in late 1942 and had been used principally as a training and occupation command. On August 9, 1944, it had dropped the designation "reserve," but the change in nomenclature was purely cosmetic and the headquarters never acquired the staff sections and corps troops essential to perform effective combat operations. General Neuling's health had broken down on the Eastern Front in the spring of 1942 as had those of his two divisional commanders, Major General Johannes Baessler (242nd Division) and Lieutenant General Otto Fretter-Pico (148th Division).

Nevertheless, Neuling was able to dispatch the 148th Division's reserves toward Le Muy before his communications were cut off. On August 13, Neuling had been ordered to move these reserves into the Argens Valley between Le Muy and Saint-Raphaël. Had he done so, the task of FABTF would have been much harder. However,

Blaskowitz, at the head of Army Group G's chain of command, was afflicted with the same communications breakdown that was bedeviling his subordinates. Throughout the day radio traffic between his headquarters and those of the 19th Army was seriously disrupted, obliging him to obtain information from OB West headquarters near Paris, relayed via the Kriegsmarine net. As dawn broke on August 16, Major General Bieringer was gloomily surveying his improvised defense force at Draguignan, now cut off and kept under continuous rifle fire by the FFI, and concluded that it was not up to the job: "The fighting spirit of the officials, specialists and men . . . and their will to resist a superior enemy was not to be rated very high . . . On the invasion day, they could observe the landing of enemy airborne troops near Le Muy for several consecutive hours without any chance on the part of the Germans to offer any resistance."

The final indignity occurred when the FFI brought a captured artillery piece to bear on Bieringer's strongpoint and forced some of its German crew to open fire. As darkness fell, Bieringer could hear cries of distress coming from the site's hospital, where wounded men were still keeping the Maquis at bay. At 2300, the strongpoint was subjected to a sustained burst of rifle, machine gun, and artillery fire as Bieringer vainly strove to establish telephone contact with the outside world. There was a sudden lull in the fighting before Bieringer heard one of his subordinates shout, "The Americans are in the strongpoint. Cease fire!" Bieringer ran outside to see his men emerging to lay down their rifles. After a moment's hesitation, he joined them on their way into American captivity. His escort was Major General Frederick, who later remembered: "He [Bieringer] told me he wanted to take his orderly and two suitcases full of clothing (at least I guess it was clothing) but I said, 'No, the orderly doesn't go with you,' and threw his suitcases over to the side and left them there. Then I put him in my jeep to take him down to Patch's headquarters. Before we started the engine, I told him to take off his German military cap and pull a tarpaulin over his head and shoulders. He said no. So we drove away but when the French alongside the road started throwing things at him, that's when he took off his cap and wanted the tarpaulin. That's when he put it over his shoulders."[13]

TEN
THE ISLANDS

"What else could I do? You engage, you fight, you win. That is the reputation of our Navy, then and in the future."
—Commander John Bulkeley, U.S. Navy

One of the essential preliminaries to Dragoon was the seizure by Sitka Force of the two small offshore Îles d'Hyères, Le Levant and Port-Cros, situated on the southern side of the landing zones, and the silencing of the 164mm batteries thought to be positioned on Le Levant. The guns posed a considerable threat to the main divisional landings. In the interwar years, the island of Port-Cros had been the haunt of literary luminaries André Malraux, André Gide, and Paul Valéry. (Today some 90 percent of Le Levant is now given over to a French weapons testing establishment and the remainder has a thriving tourist industry, much of it devoted to nudism.) Both islands are rocky and pine-covered, with sandy beaches on the landward side and fifty-foot cliffs on the seaward shore. The decision was taken to attack from the seaward side of the islands as it was anticipated that the Germans had discounted the possibility of an assault from this quarter.

The mission was entrusted to Rear Admiral Lyal A. Davidson's Task Force 86 and its associated Special Forces formations. The task of Sitka Force, consisting of the First Special Service Force (FSSF) commanded by Colonel Edwin A. Walker, and the Naval Task Unit 86.3, was the elimination of the threat to the Alpha assault area posed by the German guns and the opening of the approach to the Rade (Roads) d'Hyères, which was to be used by warships supporting the westward drive on Toulon. The men of the FSSF, all hardened veterans, had spent several days preparing for the mission at Propriano Bay in Corsica, where there was "little to do but swim and fish." The "Black Devils," as they were known, were unfazed by their new assignment, and many of them relaxed by sleeping or jitterbugging to the dance band music played over the loudspeaker systems.

The man in operational charge of the Sitka operation was Rear Admiral T. E. Chandler, flying his flag in *Prince Henry*, a converted Canadian vessel similar to a US destroyer transport, plus the Royal Navy landing ship HMS *Prince Baudouin*, five more destroyer transports, and gunfire support vessels. Just before midnight on August 14, Chandler's squadron anchored five miles off the islands, and shortly afterward the first of Sitka Force's boats were in the water. Low-profile LCAs (Landing Craft, Assault) towed the rubber boats of First Special Service Force to within 1,000 yards of Le Levant and Port-Cros before casting them off. Ahead of the first wave were scouts paddling in one-man kayaks or lying prone on surfboards to check the target beaches and guide the first wave in with hooded lights. It was, to the very hour, the first anniversary of the Allied occupation of Kiska, in the Aleutians, in which FSSF had played a part. True to their first commander, Robert Frederick, the men of FSSF were as contrarian as ever. Before they clambered down into their boats on the debarkation netting hung on the side of the destroyer transport USS *Tattnall*, every man was handed two fragmentation grenades by sailors on the orders of the *Tattnall*'s captain. The Black Devils took a dim view of carrying the extra weight onto the shore and, after obediently accepting them, quickly found convenient ways of discarding the unwanted grenades on their downward journey.

The 2nd and 3rd Regiments, FSSF, some 1,300 men, landed without opposition on the southeastern side of Le Levant. Having scaled the cliffs, the 2nd Regiment struck southwest while the men of the 3rd Regiment battled through head-high maquis overgrowth, forging north to deal with the 164mm battery at Pointe Titan on the northeastern tip of the island only to discover, to their great disappointment, that the guns were cleverly constructed dummies. Shortly afterward, they came under fire from German mortars and machine guns concealed in a complex of caves on the other side of the narrow tip of the island. Colonel Walker ordered his men to move on the enemy position, which was held by men from a static unit of 242nd Infantry Division, while gunfire support came from the British destroyer HMS *Lookout*. In the late evening the German garrison surrendered, having inflicted about seventy-five killed and wounded casualties on Walker's force, all of whom were evacuated to the *Prince Henry*, along with 110 men from the Le Levant garrison and 57 badly burned German sailors from a torpedoed German auxiliary destroyer.

In the small hours of August 15, the U.S. Navy was in a sharp naval action off Le Levant. Patrolling off the island, the destroyer *Somers*[*] picked up on her search radar a contact of two ships at about 16,000 yards. They were challenged but the ships did not identify themselves. When, at 0440, one of them did not respond to a searchlight challenge, the *Somers*, having closed to 4,750 yards, opened fire, fatally damaging one of the ships and pursuing the other until it stopped dead in the water at 0520. At dawn the *Somers*'s captain, Commander W. C. Hughes, identified the first ship as a former Italian corvette *Escabart* (UJ6081) and the second as another former Italian ship *Camoscio* (SG21), which sank an hour later. Hughes sent a boarding party across before she went down, and rescued a total of ninety-nine men from both ships. Homer Bigart, a war correspondent embedded with the Black Devils on Le Levant, witnessed the *Somers*'s engagement with the corvette: "We were just getting into the underbrush when the sky suddenly went red and we turned to see a ship convulsed in a violent explosion four miles up the coast. We thought at first one of ours had struck a mine, but it later developed that the ship was a German corvette that had left Toulon a few hours earlier on a nightly coastal patrol. She was carrying several tons of gasoline and machine gun bullets and the cargo was afire before the corvette could lash back at her

* The *Somers* was the lead ship in her class and named after Richard Somers, a hero of the Barbary Wars.

tormentors. The skipper was killed but more than forty members of her crew, some horribly burned, were picked up and brought to our ship."

To the west, on Port-Cros, the plans of FSSF's 1st Regiment were about to unravel. Here the garrison had retreated to a château in the island's northwest corner and two stone forts dating from the Napoleonic era, the most formidable of which was the Fort de l'Eminence, the garrison's headquarters, which boasted a roof protected by gravel and earth twenty feet thick and was ringed by machine gun nests. All three positions beat off infantry assaults, obliging the shore fire control party to call for gunfire support, which arrived at about 0900 from the 8-inch main batteries of the heavy cruiser *Augusta*. By mid-afternoon, the *Augusta* had fired ninety-two unavailing rounds that failed to persuade the Germans to throw in the towel. According to an eyewitness, "The rounds bounced off the heavy forts like tennis balls." A sustained rocket and bomb attack on August 17 by RAF Typhoon fighter-bombers was no more successful. Eventually, one of the forts was infiltrated and forced to surrender, but the others held out.

Much of this was witnessed by Secretary of the Navy Forrestal, who had come aboard the *Augusta* on August 15 accompanied by Admiral Davidson. After he expressed a desire to take a closer look at the action, Forrestal was taken ashore in a landing craft and coolly watched the fight for Port-Cros from under the shade of a tree. German resistance was finally broken when, on August 17, the Royal Navy battleship *Ramillies*, supported by the *Augusta*, was brought up to batter the fortresses with twelve rounds from her 15-inch guns. Shortly before 1400 on August 17 the Germans, seeing that further resistance was futile, surrendered. In the fight for Port-Cros FSSF had five men killed and ten wounded, while the German losses were ten killed and 105 captured. The British destroyer *Dido* sent the elderly battleship a saucy signal, "Many a good tune can be played on an old fiddle!"

In the small hours of August 15, a number of dedicated deception exercises had been launched on both flanks of the assault area. The first aimed to suggest an airborne landing at Baie de la Ciotat between Toulon and Marseille, as C-47s dropped three hundred life-size dummy parachutists festooned with demolition charges near La Ciotat. The deception achieved some initial traction but was swiftly discounted by Army Group G. The dummy parachute drop was followed by an operation conducted by the Special Operations Force's Western Diversionary Unit. Eleven air-sea rescue craft, two motor launches (MLs), eight patrol torpedo boats (PTs), and the destroyer USS *Endicott** raced into the Baie de la Ciotat, deploying radar reflecting balloons and loudspeakers to create the impression of a larger force, the effect being enhanced by aircraft dropping chaff. On the *Endicott*'s bridge was Commander John Bulkeley, who had won a Medal of Honor captaining the PT boat that had extracted General MacArthur, his staff, and his family from the Philippines in March 1942. On the eastern flank of the assault area, the prewar movie star Douglas Fairbanks, now a lieutenant commander in the U.S. Naval Reserve and, appropriately for the man who played Rupert of Hentzau in *The Prisoner of Zenda*, an expert in the art of military deception, led a small force of PT boats and other craft making a feint toward Genoa and a demonstration off Cannes. These ships were part of the Eastern Diversionary Force, Task Unit 80.4.2, also known as Rosie Force, which was commanded by Fairbanks. The elderly British Insect-class gunboats HMS *Scarab* and HMS *Aphis*, also elements of Rosie Force, shelled German positions near Antibes, aiming to plant the seeds of doubt in German minds as to the precise location of the anticipated landings. These measures undoubtedly caused some confusion in the minds of German commanders in the South of France, but as Army Group G had few mobile reserves it possessed only a limited ability to respond to threats real or imagined.

Bulkeley was involved in a second deception operation off La Ciotat on August 17 when seventeen PT boats, and the *Scarab* and the *Aphis*, followed by the *Endicott*, sank a German merchant steamer in the harbor. The warships then bombarded the town before spotting two German ships, the former Italian Gabbiano-class corvette *Antilope* (UJ6082), whose sister ship the *Escabart* had been sunk off Port-Cros on August 15 by the *Somers*, and a former Egyptian armed yacht *Nimet Allah* (UJ6081). The German boats were engaged by *Scarab* and *Aphis* which forced them to withdraw. The *Endicott*, which could deploy only a single 5-inch gun during the action, then opened fire from within 1,500 yards. In a duel lasting nearly an hour both German vessels were

* Named after another hero of the Barbary Wars.

sunk while the *Endicott*'s side was torn open by a shell that failed to explode. When later asked why he had chosen to take on a fight with two vessels that at the time outgunned him, Bulkeley replied, "What else could I do? You engage, you fight, you win. That is the reputation of our Navy, then and in the future."

The first assaults on mainland France were the task of Romeo Force, consisting of the French Commandos d'Afrique, who were to land at Cap Nègre, a thickly forested promontory jutting into the Mediterranean on the western end of the assault area five miles from the town of Le Lavandou. The vessels carrying them broke off from Task Force 86 at 2155 and launched the commandos shoreward at approximately 2230. However, the operation was complicated by some fussy planning. Sixty commandos were to land on a rocky beach at the bottom of a 350-foot cliff at the southeastern corner of Cap Nègre while a single scout was to go ashore to mark landing sites for the main body of commandos at Rayol Beach, two miles to the east. Two small parties would follow at 0050 to secure rocky points on both sides of the Rayol landing area before the main force went in at 0100.

Then the weather made its presence known. A gentle westerly current nudged the leading landing craft off course while the haze that was later to hamper the parachute landings of First Airborne Task Force made it impossible for coxswains of the landing craft to positively identify landmarks as they drifted westward, landing their troops, and those in the landing craft that followed, about a mile from their objective. The commandos came ashore at Cap Nègre under heavy fire, while the jeeps and heavy equipment intended for Rayol Beach were delivered to another beach, Canadel, which lacked suitable exits; the equipment was reloaded and taken off, again under fire. Nevertheless, the commandos who had landed at Cap Nègre overran artillery positions, cleared pillboxes, and bunkers, and set up a roadblock at the base of the promontory before beating off a German counterattack launched toward midmorning on the 15th. The men who had landed at Rayol cleared the beach, with gunfire support from the cruisers *Dido* and *Augusta*, and established a second blocking position on the coast road, which was shortly to be reinforced by men of the U.S. 3rd Division advancing from their landings in the Baie de Cavalaire. The

Commandos d'Afrique lost eleven men in the operation, with some fifty wounded while killing three hundred Germans and taking one thousand prisoner. A third group of commandos advanced a little over three miles inland toward the small town of La Môle, nestling in thick forests in the heart of the Maures Massif. By midday La Môle had been cleared of scattered German opposition and an artillery battery had been established on high ground at the edge of the town.

On the eastern flank of the of the assault area, on the western edge of the Golfe de la Napoule, lay the coastal town of Théoule-sur-Mer, boasting the vivid red stone of the Esterel Massif and the target of sixty-seven marines of the French Naval Assault Group, who landed as part of the Rosie operation at 0140 from rubber assault craft at Deux Frères Pointe, a mile south of the little port. The marines had advanced only a few hundred yards inland when they walked into a freshly laid and extensive minefield, taking casualties and alerting the Germans, who took them prisoner at daylight.* Although it had not set up a blocking point along the coastal road, the Rosie operation, combined with the successful Romeo landings to the west, drew German attention away from the main assault beaches, where the principal blow was about to fall.

* They were soon to be liberated by troops of U.S. 36th Division.

ELEVEN
THE ASSAULT

> "We are told to expect casualties. Ten troop ships joined our TF [Task Force] this morning. The signal corps Lt. who is aboard will be in contact with a group of spotters ashore. They will signal targets for us. Just finished a good book *Journey into Fear.* Found it hard to concentrate on the book at times. Maybe I'm scared—never felt this way before. Empty feeling in stomach—comes and goes. All the boys seem in good spirits. Things should go well tomorrow."
>
> —August 14, 1944, entry in the diary of William J. O'Leary, a gunner's mate on the destroyer USS *Hambleton*

Dawn broke at 0638 on August 15 as the main assault force closed on the landing area between Cap Bénat and the Golfe de la Napoule. The sea was calm, the air was warm and the Maures and Esterel Massifs on the distant coast were dimly visible through the morning haze. On the left was the transport area of 3rd Infantry Division, which was to land on the two Alpha beaches, Beach Red in the Baie de Cavalaire and Beach Yellow to the north of Cap Camarat. Behind was the Gunfire Support area of Task Force 84. In the center, Delta sectors, was the Transport Area of 45th Division, targeting Beaches Red, Green, Yellow, and Blue to the north of Sainte-Maxime with gunfire support provided by Task Force 85. On the right, in the Camel sector, was the Transport Area of 36th Division, aiming at Beach Red near Fréjus, Beach Green near Cap Drammont, and Beach Blue to the northeast, with Gunfire Support coming from Task Force 87. Within a matter of hours, the Allied invasion fleet would deliver some 80,000 men and thousands of vehicles to the shores of the French Riviera.

The Dragoon planners were aware that the waters in the assault area might be heavily mined and had reinforced the invasion fleet with a significant number of minesweepers, both large and small, to clear transport areas and sweep paths for the hundreds of LCIs, LCTs, LCVPs (Landing Craft, Vehicle, Personnel), and LCMs (Landing Craft, Mechanized), bringing men, weapons, and materiel ashore. In the Alpha sector, a shallow-waters sweep squadron, consisting of six submarine chasers, was tasked with operating ahead of larger Admiral-class (AM) sweepers. This unit was also augmented by LCVPs equipped with Oropesa sweep gear, a device developed by the British in World War I. The Oropesa consisted of a pair of small torpedo-shaped vanes towed on the surface by the sweeping vessel and connected to each other by cables equipped with cutters. The cables and cutters sank below the surface to cut the cables of moored mines, bringing them to the surface where they could be destroyed by gunfire. These LCVPs were assigned to the Alpha, Delta, and Camel assault forces. Also operating in Alpha sector on August 15 were four US minesweepers (the USS *Prevail*, the USS *Pioneer*, the USS *Seer*, and the USS *Dextrous*) and eighteen vessels of the British 13th Minesweeping Flotilla, comprising sixteen minesweepers and two danlayers, the last converted trawlers, which followed the minesweepers as they cleared an area and laid marker buoys (dans) indicating the swept channels.

The Delta beaches were covered by eight minesweepers and two danlayers. The waters off the Camel beaches were the responsibility of a minesweeping squadron comprising the Auk-class USS *Strive*, USS *Steady*, USS *Speed*, and USS *Sustain*, six American auxiliary wooden-hulled YMS minesweepers, durable and versatile vessels, six British Lend-Lease BYMS sweepers, two danlayers, six motor launches (MLs), and the repair ship HMS *Product*. One of the *Strive*'s crew, Alfred Case Jr. wrote in his diary on August 14, "1630, left Ajaccio. This is just about it again. This makes the fourth invasion we've been in. We have a new radar jammer and rocket gun on the ship this time. We all hope this will be the last one." In addition to the minesweepers, the assault forces fielded a relatively new weapon, radio-controlled Apex or drone boats, LCVPs packed with explosives and guided by Naval Combat Demolition Units (NCDUs). They were designed to blow gaps in the underwater obstacles fringing the approaches to the assault beaches. There were two types of Apex: the "male" version, which carried a ton of explosive to create an initial breach in the obstacle, enabling the following "female" version to blow a bigger gap with her four-ton load. In the Dragoon landings the Apex boats were to enjoy only a qualified success. Another new weapon deployed during the assault was the so-called "Woofus" 7.2-inch rocket launcher mounted in 120-round batteries aboard LCRs (Landing Craft, Rocket). Finally, there were the DD (Duplex Drive) M4A1 Sherman swimming tanks, which had been used with some success in the Normandy landings by five British, two Canadian, and three American armored battalions.

The 3rd Division's southernmost beach was Alpha Red, in the Baie de Cavalaire, backed by low, bare sand dunes, behind which lay a narrow belt of pines about thirty yards deep. The coastal road, N-559, ran behind the pines parallel to a narrow-gauge railway before the latter swung inland near the center of Alpha Red. The eastern half of the beach fronted farmland. At the back of the western half there were stony, pine-clad slopes. Farther to the west, was the resort town of Cavalaire-sur-Mer and six miles down the N-559 lay Cap Nègre, target of the Commandos D'Afrique on the night of August 14. To the northeast, the stubby Saint-Tropez peninsula thrust into the Mediterranean. At the tip of the peninsula, six miles northeast of Alpha Red, was the 3rd Division's second beach, Alpha Yellow. This beach was some two miles long and could easily have accommodated the 3rd Division in its entirety but for the fact that its exit points to the interior were unsatisfactory. Behind the beach, running northeast to Saint-Tropez, was a narrow one-lane road unsuitable for heavy military traffic. There was no direct westward route to connect with the N-559.

The assault on the Alpha Red and Yellow beaches was preceded by an intense naval and air bombardment. Commander O. F. Gregor, leading Task Group 84.1, the Alpha Red assault group, noted that "Many shells of all calibers were fired at the beach, beginning at 0615 hours. This lasted for over an hour. About 0700 hours many waves of medium bombers came over and dropped numerous 100-lb. anti-personnel bombs on the beach." In *Command Missions*, the usually taciturn Truscott painted the picture seen from the bridge of the *Catoctin* in almost lyrical terms: "Flight after flight of bombers appeared against the morning sky like birds flying shoreward. Bright flashes and towering clouds of smoke and dust marked distant locations, as the rumble of the bombardment drifted out to sea. Minutes passed, and guns from battleships, destroyers, and cruisers, and a host of lesser craft, poured a hail of steel onto the landing beaches."[1]

In the Delta Fire Support Area, the elderly battleship *Texas* opened up with her 14-inch guns. Her main armament used an old powder that belched out billows of dark red smoke amid a cacophony that brought all conversation on the bridge of *Catoctin* to a halt until everyone's ears stopped ringing. Crewman Bob Ferris, serving on the LST-91, was awe-struck by the power of the *Texas*'s main armament: "The 91 was directly between the beach and the battleship *Texas*. When the *Texas* let go with her big guns, you could feel the concussion on the bridge. Your dungaree pants would move as if they were in a very strong breeze." By the time the naval bombardment had ended, the *Texas* had fired 172 rounds of 14-inch ammunition.

Admiral Hewitt later concluded that "Aerial bombing before and on D-Day and naval bombardment were so effective that by H-Hour all major [enemy] guns had been damaged and most of the coastal defense crews had deserted their posts, been put out of action, or were willing to expose themselves in order to man their guns properly. The success of pre-D-Day pinpoint bombing was so considerable that the anticipated threat from coastal defenses never materialized and was easily disposed of on D-Day by the closely coordinated naval and aerial attack." Before 0800 on August 15, MAAF had flown over nine hundred missions, hammering the landing areas to a depth of four hundred yards with the loss of only six aircraft. By the end of the day, MAAF's bombers and fighter-bombers had flown 4,200 sorties, of which a quarter had been ground-attack missions.

Off Alpha Red, minesweepers were followed in at about 0715 hours by the Apex boats launched from LSTs to detonate the mines hanging on the seaward side of the big concrete tetrahedrons guarding the assault beach. At around 0750 hours, twenty-one LCRs, racing ahead of the first assault wave, began a ten-minute bombardment of Alpha Red to detonate mines on the beach. Audie Murphy, a sergeant with 3rd Division's 15th Infantry Regiment, recalled that the rockets were "more intimate than the naval cannon. Fired in batches, their missiles sail hissing through the air like schools of weird fish. They hit the earth, detonating mines, blasting barbed-wire entanglements, and unnerving the waiting enemy." Doubtless the enemy found the rockets less intimate than did Sergeant Murphy.

The LCRs closed to within six hundred yards of the shore before making a 180-degree turn while laying smoke to screen the approaching landing craft of the first assault wave from hostile fire. Their crews had anticipated that they would come under murderous enfilade fire from the shore as they executed this battle turnaway maneuver, but they met only spasmodic enemy response as they plowed back from the beach. The leading assault wave on Alpha Red had set off for the shore at about 0630, preceded by four amphibious M4A1 Shermans of the 756th Tank Battalion. One tank sank when it hit a mine, and the other three parked in shallow water and began firing on targets of opportunity. The tanks were followed in by thirty-eight LCVPs carrying the men of 3rd Division's 2nd and 3rd Battalions, 7th Infantry Regiment, working as regimental combat teams (RCTs).* Held in reserve was 7th Infantry's 1st Battalion.

As they approached the shore, two of the LCVPs struck mines, resulting in some sixty casualties. At this point the mines were proving a greater hazard than the gunfire of the defenders of Alpha Red—men of 242nd Infantry Division, the majority of whom were reluctant warriors, Russians, Poles, and Turkomen under German officers and NCOs. They did not emerge from their bunkers until about 0825, to be confronted by the DD tanks. Twenty-five minutes later the beach was reported to be neutralized and shortly afterward the divisional reserve, the 30th Regimental Combat Team (30th RCT) had come ashore.

* An RCT was a provisional formation assembled for a specific mission and in this case equipped with DUKWs (amphibious trucks), armored and artillery units, naval shore fire control parties, an engineer section, plus reconnaissance, signal, medical, quartermaster, military police, and other support units to make it a self-supporting formation in the field.

At 0950, after eight waves of landing craft had hit the beaches, the beachmaster* on Alpha Red declared the beach closed on the advice of engineers concerned about the danger posed by mines. However, none of the DUKW amphibious trucks carrying the sector's artillery had arrived at Alpha Red, and a forty-minute argument broke out on the radio between the army commander and the beachmaster that was resolved at 1030 with the arrival of the artillery. Nevertheless, the whole beach was not declared open until 1350. Had enemy opposition been more determined, the delay might have had serious consequences.

The orders of 7th Infantry were to fan out, spearheaded by special "battle patrols" of 155 men assigned to specific objectives. On the left, the 7th Regiment was to push inland, securing the dominant high ground before swinging southwest along the coastal road, the N-559, toward Cap Nègre. In the center it was to advance north along the N-559 to the point where it joined Route N-98 and strike to toward La Môle in the interior. The men on the right were to probe into the Saint-Tropez peninsula. Due to come ashore at 0930 was the 30th RCT, tasked with advancing across the base of the peninsula to secure the road junction at Cogolin, three miles from the head of the Golfe de Saint-Tropez. Thereafter it was to push westward along a minor road toward Collobrières, fifteen miles to the south of the Massif des Maures.

Landing at the second Alpha beach, Alpha Yellow, which was overlooked by Ramatuelle, a picturesque village perché, was the 15th Infantry Regiment, tasked with clearing the peninsula, seizing Saint-Tropez, and then assembling in reserve at Cogolin, six miles inland. Private First Class (PFC) Robert Gehlhoff landed at Beach Yellow with the headquarters of 3rd Battalion, 15th Regiment: "Those Higgins boats [LCVPs] were lowered in the water, and then by rope ladders the troops got over the side of the ship and climbed down. That can be a little tricky with the rising and falling ship and the waves. One might be ready to step off the rope ladder into the landing craft only to find the craft had dropped 15 feet and was coming up to meet you

---

* The officer in charge of the disembarkation phase of an amphibious landing. The beachmaster at the Anzio landings was Denis Healey, later to become Britain's chancellor of the exchequer.

with a backbreaking slam." The men were heavily loaded with gear, including rifle, helmet, field pack, gas mask, ammunition belt, canteen, entrenching tool, bayonet, C-rations, extra ammunition bandoliers, and grenades. Heavier items, parts of mortars, mortar rounds, bazooka anti-tank guns, light machine guns and boxes of ammunition, had been prepacked in the landing craft. Rifles, carbines, BARs, and pistols had been wrapped in cellophane bags to protect them from salt water in the event of the assault craft not making it to the shore. Once closed, the bag was watertight, and if the soldier blew into it before it was sealed, it retained enough buoyancy to keep it afloat.

Before being swung over the side or clambering down the ropes into the bobbing landing craft, the men were checked by junior officers to see that they were "rigged" properly. This involved ensuring the long straps of their helmets were held in the men's teeth; their packs, rifle belts, and rifles were positioned to enable them to be jettisoned if they fell into the sea; opening the mouth would also detach the helmet. If you could not detach yourself from your equipment, plunging into the sea could be a death sentence. The lifebelts designed to save them, worn around the waist and inflated by CO2 cartridges punctured by a trigger, were of little use in an assault landing as the troops were loaded above the device's safety limit.

Audie Murphy landed on Alpha Yellow with the 1st Battalion of the 15th: "Under the rocket barrage, scores of landing boats churn toward the shore. I stand in one; and the old fear that always precedes action grapples with my guts. Seeking to distract my mind, I glance at the men huddled in the boat. They look as miserable as wet cats. Though the water had been smooth enough, several are seasick; and others have the lost, abstract expression of men who are relieving their bowels."

The Alpha Red timetable was slipping when 30th Battalion set off for the beach twenty minutes behind schedule, closely followed by most of its artillery and, at 1045, General O'Daniel. By the time the general arrived, Alpha Red had been cleared and 7th Infantry, screened by tanks and tank destroyers, was pushing west to Cap Nègre to join hands with the French commandos before both were held up by a German strongpoint at Pointe du Layet, seven miles southwest of their landing beach. In the center, the 1st Battalion of the 7th moved out from Alpha Red at about midday, marching over the rocky coastal slopes of the Maures Massif to reach Route N-98, about a mile east of La Môle, shortly after mid-afternoon. On its right, the 2nd Battalion moved into Cogolin and then set off southwest, having made contact with the French commandos, who had cleared La Môle. Meanwhile, 1st Battalion, 30th Infantry Regiment, sliced across the base of the Saint-Tropez peninsula to link with elements of 15th Regiment and advanced units of 45th Division, which had come ashore in the Delta sector. The 3rd Battalion, 30th Regiment, then pushed on westward to Collobrières, which it took at 2000, a full twenty-four hours ahead of schedule, while the rest of the battalion pressed on northwest, through the Maures Massif, in the late afternoon. By the time darkness fell, the battalion's leading elements were just five miles short of Le Luc, on the perimeter of the Blue Line and a vital point in the Toulon-Saint-Raphaël Corridor.

At Alpha Yellow, things did not go entirely to plan. The barrage of rockets launched between 0750 and 0800 misfired and detonated the mines on only half of the Cavalaire beach. The LCVPs overtook the DD tanks on the approach to the beach, swamping one of them in their wake. Another tank was disabled on the beach by a mine. The 1st and 3rd Battalions, 15th Infantry Regiment, came ashore under desultory fire from a few German 88mm guns about ten minutes behind schedule at 0810. Thirty minutes later the submarine chaser SC-1029 was narrowly missed by a rogue Apex boat that struck a nearby buoy and exploded, badly damaging her. The chaser's 40mm ammunition boxes were set ablaze and casualties were strewn over her deck, four of them seriously wounded, while a surviving sailor managed to raise her ensign on a halyard.

Nevertheless, these mishaps did not dislocate the landing schedule at Alpha Yellow, and the 15th Infantry's assault went like clockwork. Again, mines rather than determined opposition caused most casualties. PFC Gehlhoff recalled, "We tried to get off the sandy beach as fast as we could. The beach was mined with many small foot mines that just blow off your foot and Bouncing Bettys that, when stepped on, would bounce head high and burst. We tried to follow the footprints of the men ahead. Many lay wounded, some dead. We went by one soldier laying on his side with his foot a bloody mess."[2] Audie Murphy also remembered the moment when his battalion came ashore: "We jump from the landing craft and wade ashore through the swirling waters. From the hills the German guns begin to crack. An occasional shell lands in our midst. The medics roll up their sleeves and get busy. An explosion sounds on my left, and when the smoke lifts I see the torn body of a man who stepped on a mine. A medic bends over him, rises, and signals four litter bearers that their services will not be needed."

The clearing of mines and underwater obstacles went ahead unhindered and aided by the actions of the FFI, who had marked the minefields on the beach in the small hours of August 15. By 0910, seven assault waves had landed on Beach Yellow, and 1st Battalion, 15th Infantry, was advancing to seize the high ground on the Saint-Tropez peninsula.* On the right, men of 3rd Battalion were rounding up surrendering Ost troops dazed by the weight of the bombardment. At 0955 the beach was declared secure and LSTs moved closer in to deliver vehicles. From their decks light observation aircraft (dubbed "flying fosdicks") were launched, one of which, L-4 flying off LST-906, was shot down. Happily its pilot was recovered. Nevertheless, LST-906's crew were less than happy with her ten-aircraft cargo for Dragoon, which condemned her to some twelve hours off the contested coast of southern France, outside the beachhead's umbrella of antiaircraft fire and with little overhead fighter protection cover. The men aboard the LST were anxious that a German fighter ace might be eager to paint the symbol of the ship on to his tail rudder, but the Luftwaffe did not put in appearance until dusk.

While LST-906's crew fretted about about marauding Luftwaffe fighters, Saint-Tropez was being seized, in a remarkable departure from the original Dragoon plan, by a combination of FFI fighters and B and C companies of 509th PIB who had been mistakenly dropped near the seaside town earlier in the day. Lieutenant Mike Reuter of B Company recalled the jump: "We dropped into Saint-Tropez by mistake. When we flew into that area, of course, it was dark, and I was the jump master of the plane. So I looked out of the door and I couldn't see anything except the clouds. I was looking for some kind

* It was during this passage of arms that Sergeant Audie Murphy was awarded the Distinguished Service Cross.

of terrain feature. Then the green light went on and I still couldn't see anything, and I waited and waited, and finally somebody said: 'Lieutenant, the green light is on, we gotta go . . .' So I said, 'OK let's go.' But that delay evidently put us on land, because the company commander, Captain Miller, and his whole plane went into the ocean and they all drowned."[3]

Displaying their usual initiative, and also keenly aware that help from the D-Day assault force would soon arrive, the paratroops sent small patrols to the outskirts of Saint-Tropez, where they were informed by French civilians that the Germans were pulling out and were withdrawing into the Citadel, a medieval fortress on the eastern outskirts of the town. This placed the paratroops in a dilemma, as they were now pinned between the sea and the possibility of a German armored counterattack launched from the interior. An uphill assault on the Citadel was an equally uninviting prospect. Meanwhile, firefights were still flaring in the town and around the Citadel. The decision was taken to move out of the town and into the hills, but no sooner had this been made than a white flag appeared in one of the Citadel's windows and its sixty-seven German defenders emerged to discuss terms of surrender. By the time two battalions of 15th Infantry Regiment arrived on the scene, Saint-Tropez had been secured and the defenders of the Citadel had been handed over to the FFI.

In the center of the landings was Delta Force, consisting of 45th Division, commanded by Major General William W. Eagles, and Rear Admiral B. J. Rodgers's Task Force 85. Its target beaches, Red, Green, Yellow, and Blue, lay on the Baie de Bourgon, eight miles north of Alpha Yellow and on the opposite side of the Golfe de Saint-Tropez. The landing areas were defended by a battalion of 242nd Division, supported by a single field artillery battalion and a naval coastal battery. Weather conditions were perfect, with no wind or surf, and the preliminary bombardments had destroyed most of the beach obstacles. The southernmost of the Delta beaches, Red, was just over a mile north of Sainte-Maxime while the others, Green, Yellow, and Blue, lay a few miles to the northeast, separated by rocky outcrops. Behind the beaches ran Route N-98, hugging the contours of the coast and pointing the way back southwest to Sainte-Maxime and northeast to the port of Fréjus. Behind the beaches, farmland rose gently away for about half a mile before it met the steeper, wooded slopes of the Massif des Maures.

Lieutenant Leonard A. Faustino served with an engineer battalion, the 111th, attached to the 45th Division. After the war, he left a crisp account of his unit's journey from ship to shore in an LCA (Landing Craft, Assault), which had a British crew: "As we settled into the LCA, the British coxswain standing in the bow said, 'Welcome aboard, mates.' An LCA does not have seats, you either sat on your gear or squatted on your haunches. There were other sailors, one in the bow, the other in the stern, inserting hooks on cables from the crane into eyes welded on the gunwhales. When this was done, and all thirty-seven of us were settled down, the coxswain waved his arm [and] the boat started to rise and swing over the side. I was in the bow, squatting on my haunches, and Sergeant Shuster was on my right. As we swung over the side, I noticed there were rope ladders hanging. I thought, gosh, for once we lucked out. When the coxswain returns for a second trip, they [the assault troops] would have to scramble down the ladder. I don't believe any of us regretted that we did not get to show our expertise on the ladder. When we reached the water, the coxswain and the sailor unhooked us from the crane and he started the engine. Turning toward us, he said, 'Here we go lads, hang on tight.' We didn't have to hang on very tight, because the surface of the sea was almost like a sheet of glass. I was still on my haunches, experiencing mixed anxieties. There was an inclination to rise up to see what was happening and where we were heading; but the ships were still firing over our heads and when an eight-inch shell passed over, I ducked quickly. I never noticed any return fire coming from the shore. There were anxious moments as I recalled reports I had read about some men making the landings in North Africa at Oran, leaving the boats in ten feet of water. You don't do much swimming with a full field pack and weapons in water that deep. In fact these reports were corroborated by people in the 343rd [Engineer General Services Regiment] who told me that the first job they were given, after landing in North Africa, was the worst and most gruesome. That job was fishing drowned soldiers from the surf. I immediately put these thoughts from my mind."[4]

There were no offshore obstacles guarding the Delta Beaches, and the air and naval bombardments had played havoc with the German artillery emplacements, leaving a solitary 75mm gun to fire a few forlorn rounds before it was silenced by an American destroyer. Three 81mm mortars on Cap des Sardinaux loosed off some sixty rounds before they were suppressed. Dazed and disorientated by the naval and air bombardments, the gun crews defending the beaches were quick to surrender. Beach Blue, the northernmost of the sector's four beaches, was protected by an elaborate trench system that was linked to underground shelters and ammunition stores. The men holding this sector had been almost driven out of their wits by the fury of the bombardments and emerged to surrender "in their grey-green uniforms covered with masonry powder and looking as though sacks of flour had been dumped onto them, bleeding from mouths and eyes . . . staggering out of dugouts and bunkers with hands raised."

The Delta Beaches Red and Green were hit by the 157th Infantry Regiment, preceded by four DD tanks, all of which were disabled by mines they struck when coming ashore. Sergeant Ralph Fink, a veteran of tough fighting in Italy, led a machine gun section in the regiment's 1st Battalion and found the going easier than he had in Italy. After circling the mother ship for about thirty minutes, a flare went up and Fink's landing craft turned toward the shore: "This was the moment of truth, and the feelings of exhilaration and fear are indiscernible. Up to this time we had drawn no fire from the shore. As we neared shore, some artillery shells started to hit the water around us, but it soon became obvious that it came from just one small battery and danger was not too great unless we took a direct hit. The craft took us to about seventy yards off the shore and dropped the front gate, and we plunged into the water about waist deep and made our way to the shore. The sea was calm, the weather was warm, and the beach was almost level, although it sloped up slightly toward the seawall, which was eight feet high, fifty yards to our front. At this time we were hearing small arms fire at a distance to our right and left, but we were drawing no fire at all."[5]

Once ashore, the men of 157th ran to the seawall and reorganized into squads and sections. Then they spotted a break in the wall, through which Sergeant Fink led his men, breathing a sigh of relief that the gaps, possibly left to allow seawater blown over in a storm to run back to its source, relieved his section of hauling their heavy weapon over the top. Simultaneously, the men discarded their climbing ropes and gas masks before pushing on to a small wooded area several hundred yards away to await orders. Fink reflected: "On the surface, this whole operation seems like a piece of cake and, in a way, it was. However, considering the rush of preparation on board the ship the night before, the sleeplessness, and the intense mental rush of storming the beach left us exhausted. I vividly remember resting there in the trees and my body was trembling. We had carried out our mission once more and were still alive."[6]

The engineer Lieutenant Faustino had also reached land without incident. Some 150 yards beyond where they had splashed ashore, Faustino assembled his men near an intersection in the road running parallel to the beach. His orders were to bivouac near Fréjus, to the northeast, make contact with company headquarters, and await further orders. Before Faustino and his men set off, "we noticed, coming down the road from our right about forty Kraut POWs, with their hands joined in back of their heads, being herded toward the beach by three GIs with rifles. These were the only live Germans we saw that day."

Faustino's company bivouacked on a wooded hill overlooking Fréjus. Faustino unrolled his pack, slung a hammock between two trees and went to sleep. He was dozing off in the hammock when Sergeant Shuster suddenly appeared and said, "Lieutenant you gotta come to see this." Faustino followed him into Fréjus, where the two Americans were confronted by a scene they would both never forget. Faustino recalled: "There was screaming and finger-pointing. The French are known to be emotional people and these were surpassing any idea I had of their temperament. When a group would scream and point their fingers at a comely young female, being held by two males, two others with clippers shaved her head and let her locks fall to the pavement. Immediately the shaved one's appearance was altered as she cried despondently with tears rolling down. As we watched, a man came up and said, 'Welcome, Americans.' . . . I asked, 'What did she do?' He replied, 'They are accused of collaborating with the les Boches [the Germans].' This was interpreted as sleeping with the Germans." Faustino reflected, "In Italy we could tell the gals who were willing to share their favors because of their two-toned tresses. The roots were dark while the rest was blond because it had been dyed to please the Germans. Now, in France, we would be able to spot them because of their short, bobbed hairdos. I contrasted this scene with the one that had greeted us on our entrance into Rome, when the men offered us wine and the girls kisses. After watching this spectacular show for a while we made our way back up the hill and found the cooks had set up a lunch of C and K* rations."

In France the deep, festering wounds left by defeat, occupation, and collaboration were to linger well into the postwar era. The official purge of collaborators, known as *l'épuration* (purification), lasted from September 1944 to the end of 1949. Faustino and his sergeant had witnessed the spontaneous eruption of hate and shame that gripped the populations of European countries immediately after their liberation from Nazi oppression. However, Faustino's day was by no means over. After taking a brief nap, he was woken up by the company runner, Corporal Weiss, and taken to see his captain. The captain ordered Faustino to go back to the beach where he had landed, and with one of the unit's bulldozers bury the corpses of Germans killed in the pre-assault bombardment. It was a hot day and the bodies were beginning to stink.

It was now about mid-afternoon, and Faustino had no trouble finding a bulldozer and a flat-bed transporter. Back at the beach, he stumbled on a hive of activity: "LSTs were discharging all sorts of vehicles and equipment. DUKWs were shuttling from ship to shore loaded with ammo, rations, guns, and artillery pieces. There were also some Sherman tanks being discharged from LSTs and other armor already ashore. This had to be one of the most amazing feats in the history of warfare. The infantry had assaulted this beach at 0800 this morning; and now, just hours later, all this."

The last resting place of some of the defenders of this small stretch of the Riviera was a villa with extensive grounds on a bluff overlooking the sea. Here, Faustino found some men serving with the 747th GRS

---

* The K-ration was introduced in 1942 at the request of the USAAF and was originally developed for paratroops as it was lighter than the C-ration. As with the C-ration, the K's components varied over the course of the war to offer greater variety while meeting the need for compact size and balanced nutrition. In 1944 over 105 million K-rations were produced.

(Graves Registration Services) of the Quartermaster Corps, all of whom were African American. In charge of them was an imposing staff sergeant. The staff sergeant told Faustino he was from Selma, Alabama, to which Faustino replied that he too was a Southerner, from Mobile in the same state. “As we walked we counted dead Germans scattered helter skelter around the grounds. We came to the building and noted two lying in front of an opening that led to the storm cellar. The doors that were on a slant to the building and hinged were laid back, showing steps that led down to the cellar. These two unfortunates must have been running for the shelter of the cellar and reached it together at the same instant that a shell landed behind them. The backs of their heads had been blown off. The ground was stained with blood and gray matter beneath their heads. Apparently they had been pitched forward by the blast.” Inside the villa Faustino and the staff sergeant, whose name was Bryant, found twenty-six bodies, “some lying in the most grotesque positions. We returned to the grounds and selected a spot under two large sycamore trees. Sergeant Bryant said, ‘This is a nice peaceful spot. It’s a long ways from the Fadder-land, but they can rest awhile here.’” Faustino replied, “Okay, the dozer blades can give you a trench ten feet long and five feet deep, do you want it?”

The bulldozer went to work while the men in the GRS detachment gathered the corpses and stacked them around the excavation. Faustino was then informed that five more bodies had been found: “These guys had probably been on perimeter guard duty. Four of them had been mangled by shells bursting in the trees; but the fifth, found some distance further away, only showed evidence of having taken a rifle slug in the chest. This one had been dead much longer than the others. He was starting to decompose. The sockets where his eyeballs had been were pits of squirming maggots where flies, looking for moisture, had laid their eggs. A very gruesome sight. We suspected that he had been shot two or three days earlier by members of the French Maquis . . . the stench coming from him was enough to make up for all the others.”

The sun was going down and a cool breeze was stirring the trees as the corpses were laid out alongside the trench and a melancholy roll call began. Two GRS soldiers searched for identification on each of the dead men. When they found a tag on a chain around the neck, similar to the American dog tag, they read a name, Josef Fromm, Hans

Braun, Manfred Goethe, and so on, with the relevant rank if they could determine it. If no tag was found, they searched the man's pockets for identifying papers. As each name was read, Sergeant Bryant recorded them on a pad, while the two GRS soldiers lifted the body and carefully placed it in the trench. When about twenty of the corpses had been deposited, it became clear that there was insufficient room left to accommodate all the men in a neat row. Sergeant Bryant declared that there was no need to dig another trench and indicated how the rest of the Germans should be interred, by folding them into the fetal position. He observed, "That's the way they came into this world. Why not leave it the same way." Bryant's men obeyed his instructions, some of them singing spirituals, others trading jokes. When they manhandled the corpses into the fetal position, there was a loud smell of escaping gas. Faustino observed, "Sarge, this is one helluva job you have," to which Bryant replied, "Somebody's gotta do it."[7] Back in his bivouac, swinging gently in his hammock, Faustino could not get the faces of the dead Germans out of his mind.

In the northernmost assault sector, Camel, General Dahlquist's 36th Division was assigned four landing beaches: Red, to the west of Saint-Raphaël in the Golfe de Fréjus; Green, three miles to the east of Saint-Raphaël, overlooked by Cap Drammont, with its its ruined 16th-century watchtower pointing skyward like a ragged exclamation mark; Yellow, at the base of the Rade d'Agay on the eastern side of Cap Drammont; and Blue, a much smaller beach with a frontage of only eighty yards, three miles to the northeast of Cap Drammont at the head of Anthéor Cove.

The port town of Fréjus, with its backdrop of the Massif d'Esterel, has a military history stretching back thousands of years. It was founded by Julius Caesar in the 1st century B.C.E.; Napoléon landed there in 1799 on his way back from his Egyptian campaign; and in World War I it provided winter quarters for French colonial troops. It was not surprising, therefore, that in early 1944 the Germans, concerned above all with coastal defense and the protection of key ports in its *Atlantik* and *Süd* Walls, had paid particular attention to the strengthening of this sector. Fréjus and Saint-Raphaël, the resort on the eastern shore of the Golfe de Fréjus, provided direct access to the Argens River valley, and Le Muy and Draguignan in the interior. The

Italians, the first to occupy this area in 1940, had grasped the sector's significance and installed six batteries, boasting twenty-four Ansaldo field howitzers, on the heights above Fréjus. Following the 1943 armistice, these guns were manned by Italian volunteer crews as "Abteilung Coniglio," after their commander, before being redesignated in 1944 as part of the overall German defense plan for the Côte d'Azur. Just weeks before the launching of Dragoon, the Kriegsmarine had embarked on the installation of a powerful battery of Schneider M17 220mm guns on the Pointe des Issambres, south of Saint-Aygulf, but these had been wrecked on August 11 by an American bombing raid before they became operational. In Saint-Aygulf itself, a casemated strongpoint had been set up equipped with French 75mm guns. Farther to the east, on Cap Drammont, three 150mm guns salvaged from destroyers had been installed. The Luftwaffe had also positioned several batteries of 88mm antiaircraft guns around Anthéor Cove, eight miles beyond Saint-Raphaël.

The Golfe de Fréjus had been established as the heavily fortified *Stutzpunkt Gruppe* (Strongpoint Group) Saint-Raphaël, containing four separate bastions consisting of resistance nets (*Widerstandsnester*). These were clusters of bunkers, each manned by a platoon from the 242nd Division armed with an unusually heavy complement of machine guns, mortars, and light artillery, with support from reserves held back in Fréjus. Additional firepower was provided by a tank destroyer (*Panzerjäger*) battalion fielding towed 88mm guns. Northeast of Saint-Raphaël, from Anthéor Cove to Théoule-sur-Mer, the six miles of coastline was defended by an Ost battalion of the 148th Infantry Division.

The 36th Division's primary assault beach was Camel Green, at the back of which was a steep embankment carrying the N-98 and the mainline railway, which from Saint-Raphaël headed east along the coast toward Cannes and Nice. Behind the embankment, the landscape was scarred by deep quarries gouged out of the shrub-covered foot-slopes of the Esterel Massif. The 141st Infantry Regiment was tasked with taking Camel Green and Blue Beaches on the crucial right shoulder of 36th Division's assault area. The two beaches were outside the heavily fortified Golfe de Fréjus but were nevertheless well within the range of much of the German artillery.

Minesweepers swept the areas off Beaches Red, Blue, and Green before the naval bombardment of the sector began at 0600 hours. In the

Task Force 87 Fire Support Area were the battleships *Nevada*, *Arkansas*, and *Texas*. At 0750 the rocket barrage was unleashed. According to Lieutenant Larry Carr, U.S. Navy, the mission of the LCT(R)s was "to completely saturate an area 700 yards wide by 300 yards deep with 5-inch projectiles. Defenders not completely knocked out should be neutralized sufficiently to aid the first wave in getting ashore and taking cover." However, the unfortunate side effect of the combined aerial and naval bombardments was to reduce visibility to about fifty yards, posing problems for the first wave of LCVPs heading ashore at 0800 hours.

The plan was for the LCVPs to be led into the attack by eight M4AI DD amphibious tanks of the 753rd Battalion, but the tanks had been launched some 4,000 yards offshore and were overhauled by the first wave of landing craft before they arrived on Camel Green. Only desultory small arms fire greeted the men of 141st Infantry as they came ashore, but the Ostruppen defending the beach were in no mood for a fight, and by 0900 began to surrender, as they did at Camel Blue to the east. The principal threat to the 141st came from the enemy artillery to the west but without forward observers the German fire had little impact.

Camel Blue, the target of 1st Battalion, 141st Infantry, was ringed by bunkers and pillboxes projecting into the sea on either side of the eighty-yard strand, a potential killing ground. Sergeant Jack Wilson and his machine gun squad were part of the seventh wave. Wilson was also armed with a bangalore torpedo, a five-foot metal pipe packed with eight pounds of TNT, which could be extended by adding extra tubes and was capable of blasting a twenty-foot hole in a section of barbed wire or a minefield. As Wilson's Higgins boat neared the beach, machine gun bullets thudded into the landing craft's gunwhales. The ramp went down, along with the Navy man who lowered it. Wilson, with his bangalore torpedo, was the first man into the waist-deep water: "Holding my rifle over my head with my left hand, and the bangalore over my head with my right, I felt a slight sting in the hand holding the bangalore, and noticed blood running down my arm. If the bullet had hit the torpedo instead of my hand, it would have been over for me and several of the fellows behind me." Wilson had had a lucky escape, but the majority of Camel Blue's Ost defenders, a battalion from 148th Division, quickly emerged from their defenses with their hands over their heads, having abandoned their weapons.

Towering over the exit from the beach was the Anthéor railway viaduct, surgically severed by Allied air raids. Edward Stoermer was with the 1st Battalion and remembered the shells from a US battleship whistling over his head as his LCVP neared the beach, "sounding like a freight train going right over the top of us." Lieutenant Carl Strom, executive officer with 1st Battalion's B Company, went ashore with the second wave, got off the beach unscathed, moved his men through the remaining arches of the viaduct, and pushed up the valley beyond, climbing a hill to place his company behind some German mortar emplacements he had spotted. Moving on to the attack, Strom encountered an enemy dugout held by about fifteen men, all of whom surrendered. The troops, who were Ostruppen, told Strom that their officers had departed that morning when they saw the invasion coming. He recalled that the Ostruppen had abandoned their mortars: "They all had their helmets on and were happy to see us; they were all smiles." B Company's mission was to clear the valley behind the viaduct and then advance on Cannes on the left flank of the battalion's C Company. "We didn't have any resistance. However, at one point we did come to a cave, and we flushed probably twenty or twenty-five Germans, including two officers, out of the cave. They were ready to surrender too. They had their helmets on but again no weapons . . . I think that last group was real Germans. They were all infantry but they didn't want to fight. I think they recognized that the Normandy forces were pushing on past Paris. They were happy to give up."[8] At this stage, 141st Infantry's principal mission of was the twofold task of securing of the calm, sheltered water of the Agay roadstead and the occupation of the high ground of the Esterel Massif that lay behind it. The regiment was swiftly followed ashore, at 0945, by the 143rd Infantry, which had been tasked with swinging westward toward Saint-Raphaël. However, by late afternoon the 143rd was brought to a halt when it ran into the bunkers of one of the Stutzpunkt strongpoints on the eastern outskirts of the town.

The landings at Camel Red were scheduled for the early afternoon, and it was here that the 36th Division met the only sustained opposition of the day. Recognising the significance of this sector, the

Germans had established a formidable network of coastal defenses. They had laid a minefield across the Golfe de Fréjus and had sunk single and double rows of mined tetrahedrons close to the shore. Behind the tetrahedrons, on the heavily mined beach, were two rows of double-apron barbed wire, and a seven-foot-high, three-foot-thick concrete anti-tank wall fronted by an anti-tank ditch twelve feet deep. The nearby airfield and the roads and paths leading inland were also seeded with mines. There were machine gun nests in the anti-tank wall and pillboxes and strongpoints behind it. Enfilading fire was delivered by 88mm guns positioned at the Saint-Raphaël harbor front, and inside the town the Germans had turned numerous buildings into defense points peppered with booby traps and mines. On the rising ground to the north and northwest of the town were batteries of 105mm guns and 100mm howitzers supported by numerous light antiaircraft batteries and the towed 88mm guns of the 1038th Anti-Tank Battalion, which had escaped damage by all the previous naval and air bombardments. The infantry in the area of Saint-Raphaël consisted of at least two companies of the 2nd Battalion, 765th Grenadiers of 242nd Division.

At 1100, the minesweepers clearing the deep-water approaches to Beach Red came under heavy fire from German artillery that drove them off. An hour later over ninety Consolidated B-24 Liberators flew in to drop nearly 200 tons of high explosive on the Camel Red sector. This encouraged the minesweepers to resume their work, but under renewed enemy fire they were forced once again to withdraw. LSTs towing Apex boats were the next to go in. Under heavy fire, they released their drones about 1,000 yards from the shore, but the female drones began to behave erratically and only three exploded, damaging underwater obstacles but failing to make any adequate breaches. Four destroyers and the 12-inch main armament of the battleship *Arkansas* followed up with a forty-five-minute bombardment, which lifted as the first assault wave of LCVPs, led by rocket craft, headed for the shore. At 1400 it was some 3,000 yards from Camel Red and coming under sustained fire from the enemy guns.

Reconnaissance Sergeant Thomas S. Sherman of A Company, 636th Tank Destroyer Battalion, was on an LST preparing to land on Camel Red. The LST was carrying Sherman's "jeep, a half track, and four tank destroyers and the crews." Sherman recalled: "As the assault boats started toward the shore, a terrific artillery barrage greeted us and there seemed to be a solid wall of water thrown up by the artillery and the underwater demolitions being set off in front of our landing craft."

Watching from the *Catoctin* was General Truscott, who had arrived in his headquarters ship at about noon and now had a grandstand seat at the unfolding drama at Beach Red. Truscott had already witnessed the aerial and naval bombardments, and was convinced that they had broken the enemy's spirit. He was untroubled by the malfunctioning drones and was relishing this display of American military might: "These were exciting moments to those of us who watched from the deck of the *Catoctin*. But suddenly the whole flotilla of landing craft halted just a few thousand yards from the beach. What was wrong?"

The sequence of events that led to Truscott's dismay, and subsequent display of temper, was an object lesson in the making of command decisions. At about 1400 the naval officer in command of the Beach Red assault group, Captain Leo B. Schulten, had temporarily halted the landing by the 142nd Regimental Combat Team until 1430, informing Rear Admiral Lewis, commanding Task Force 87, of his decision and requesting instructions. Lewis now faced a dilemma. He was reluctant to cancel the landing, but it was clear to him that pressing ahead with the assault on Camel Red could result in heavy losses comparable to those that U.S. 5th Corps suffered on Omaha Beach during the D-Day landings in Normandy. The air and naval bombardments had failed to suppress the enemy artillery, and the Apex craft had failed to accomplish their mission. The defenders had scrambled out of their shelters and were manning their guns. All hope of achieving tactical surprise had been blown to the winds.

Lewis had immediately decided to contact the commander of the 36th Division, General Dahlquist. Before D-Day, both men had prepared a fall-back option for this sector, which involved the landing of 142nd RCT on Camel Green. However, Dahlquist had gone ashore at 1000 and Lewis was unable to confer with him by radio as ship-to-shore communications had not been established. At 1415, reluctant to wait any longer, Lewis ordered Schulten to land the 142nd over Camel Green, which had now been secured by the 141st Infantry. The Beach Red Assault Group had turned back to sea and was now heading for

Camel Green to the east of Saint-Raphaël, prompting further protests from Truscott.

At 1515, the leading elements of 142nd came ashore on Camel Green. A potential disaster had been avoided, but Truscott, General Patch, and Admiral Hewitt were furious. Hewitt promised Truscott that an investigation would be launched before handing him a message referring to the alternative landing plan. The admiral then lowered an LCVP for Truscott, who set off to Beach Red to find Dahlquist. Truscott's displeasure at the turn of events was exacerbated when he discovered that Dahlquist had not been consulted about the switch of assault beaches and that the decision had apparently been made by the navy because of the failure to breach the underwater obstacles. Fuel was added to the flames when Truscott subsequently discovered that Dahlquist had sent a message to Admiral Lewis congratulating him for his prompt action in changing the landing plan when the underwater obstacles could not be overcome. Truscott later recalled, with some understatement: "I made known to Dahlquist my complete displeasure with this procedure. It was in fact almost the only flaw in an otherwise perfect landing. Failure to carry out this delayed landing as arranged was to hold up the clearing of Beach 264A [Camel Red] by more than a day. It was to necessitate a change in the landing of CC Sudre and ground echelons of the Tactical Air Force. It was to delay the seizure and occupation of the air fields near Fréjus and in the Argens Valley, which in turn were to prevent our having close air support east of the Rhône when we began our drive a few days later. It was in my opinion a grave error which merited reprimand at least, and most certainly no congratulations. Except for the otherwise astounding success of the assault, it might have had even graver consequences."[9]

In spite of Truscott's stern words, the right decision had been made. At the time it was taken he had been ignorant of the strength of the defenses on Beach Red. The 36th Division did not secure the Saint-Raphaël-Fréjus sector until the middle of the afternoon of August 16, and the lingering threat posed by offshore and beach obstacles made it impossible for army engineers and navy demolition experts to conclude their operations until the early evening of August 17, potentially delaying the planned arrival at Beach Red of CC Sudre's armored component. In fact, CC Sudre was able to land over 45th Division's beaches on the night of August 15, enabling it to assemble earlier than had been anticipated in Truscott's original plan. Moreover, 45th Division had already established contact with FABTF, and CC Sudre could have been dispatched over the Sainte-Maxime-Le Muy road, as the 45th Division's 191st Tank Battalion had already reached Le Muy over the same road. Nevertheless, the possibilities remain lost in the fog of postwar argument, as Patch had already decided that control of CC Sudre would revert to de Lattre shortly after the Dragoon landings. It was on this basis that Truscott had decided to assemble an ad hoc formation, Task Force Butler, for a north or northwest drive from the beachhead. As originally planned, CC Sudre would attack west toward the primary objectives of Toulon and Marseille. Nor do Truscott's assertions about the delay in airfield construction hold much water, as the speed of the Allied advance after the landings gifted 6th Corps with sites in the Argens Valley well ahead of the anticipated schedule. In contrast, congestion in the beachhead frustrated the best efforts of engineers to rapidly construct an emergency strip and four dry-weather fields. Both projects fell behind schedule, and the rapid advance inland led to the cancellation of the fourth dry-weather field. The thrust inland from the beachhead after August 16 ensured that forward air bases at Sisteron, Le Luc, and Cuers, the last in the Toulon-Saint-Raphaël corridor, were all operational by the end of August.

Camel Force had negotiated the landings on August 15 without suffering any major setbacks. However, there was a sting in the tail to come, delivered from an unlikely source, the hitherto inactive Luftwaffe. The Tank Landing Ship LST-282 was a Normandy veteran, having operated off Utah Beach on June 6. Just over two months later, off Beach Green, its crew passed what one of its officers, Hans E. Bergner, the LST's assistant gunnery officer, later remembered as an easy day: "We waited offshore after watching the H-Hour bombing of the beach and saw our LCVPs return safely after landing assault forces on Beach Green. We saw no enemy planes. With our binoculars we could see resort homes and the hills behind them. In a sense we sunbathed on the Riviera that day as the ship circled and waited in the transport area for our turn to go in. Our turn came late because there was no immediate requirement for the primary cargo we were carrying, 155mm Long Tom artillery pieces of the 36th

Infantry Division. The main deck and tank deck of the LST-282 was jam-packed with those guns and their trailers full of ammunition."[10]

LST-282 was some 1,200 yards off Beach Green at 2030 when a radio red alert was received and gun control and battery were informed. An enemy aircraft had been spotted and LST-282 cut its speed by two-thirds. LST-282's commanding officer, Lieutenant Lawrence E. Gilbert, was on the ship's conning tower and was alerted by his executive officer to "a bright red, flaring, rocket-like object . . . seen about 100 feet directly under a twin-engine, twin-rudder plane. The object was apparently motionless. The object began to move ahead of the plane and downward on the same course as the plane until its elevation was approximately 25 degrees. At this point it turned approximately 90 degrees to starboard and apparently headed for LST-282. Bright red flame and white smoke were seen coming from the tail of the object, which resembled a miniature plane."[11]

Gilbert's ship was under attack from an Hs 293 rocket-boosted glide bomb released by a Dornier Do 217 of Kampfgeschwader 100 "Wiking" (KG 100) flown by *Oberfeldwebel* (sergeant major) Kube. The Hs 293 had been introduced in August 1943 and had been used with some success against Allied shipping at Salerno and Anzio. The bomb was steered by radio commands from the aircraft that released it, and the Allies had quickly developed countermeasures to jam the control system. The German response was to devise tactics that overrode the jamming. Instead of guiding the missile on a path perpendicular to launch, the Do 217 flew on to the target with the radio guidance system burning through the jamming signals, tactics that placed a heavy burden of the missile operator sitting next to the pilot.

LST-282's forward guns opened fire but scored no hits before the Hs 293 plunged through the ship's main deck and exploded below, setting the tank deck ablaze and igniting ammunition boxes. Lieutenant Gilbert was blown out of the conning tower into the water. The elevator platform collapsed, fortuitously forming a ramp from the tank deck to the main deck and providing a means of escape for many of the men trapped below, most of whom emerged with their uniforms on fire. With all pressure lost on her fire pumps, LST-282 was now a doomed ship, heavily listing to port as the bomb blast had blown a hole in her hull big enough to accommodate a truck. Her bow doors, halfway open when the bomb sliced through her main deck, were frozen, and the LST was abandoned some fifteen minutes later. Hans E. Bergner recalled: "There was never any formal order to abandon ship but people saw the obvious and jumped overboard. I tried to warn some soldiers to stay on board, because we had been taught in midshipman school not to leave the ship until directed because conditions might be even worse in the water. But soldiers get nervous on board ship, where there were no foxholes, so they said to me 'F--- you,' and off they went."[12]

The burning hulk of LST-282 eventually ran aground on some rocks. LST-1011 passed around her as she burned and found a batch of wounded men on the shore waiting to be transferred to a hospital ship. LST-1011's commanding officer, Bob Wilson, anxious about the threat posed by enemy artillery and keen to pull out, was told by his executive officer that the wounded could not be loaded because they were "niggers." Wilson later reflected that the officer had raised no objection when their ship had taken on Nazi prisoners. Perhaps, he thought, his subordinate hated black comrades in arms more than he did the Nazis.

LST-282 was the only ship lost in Operation Dragoon, sustaining forty casualties in the attack by the Do 217. The ship burned and lit up the sky for hours. Lieutenant Gilbert was awarded the Navy Cross for his gallantry on the night of August 15, ordering hard left rudder that kept his ship from wreaking havoc on LSTs lined up at Beach Green and, although badly injured, rescuing a signalman with a serious broken leg and his engineer officer, who had severe shrapnel wounds. Hans E. Bergner swam to safety and then joined other good swimmers to look for shipmates struggling to get ashore: "It was a horrible night for many of us. Our ship was still burning and, I have been told, smoldering for several days. In the hours afterward I didn't want to look at the LST-282 but somehow I kept doing so."

TWELVE
BURSTING OUT OF THE BRIDGEHEAD

> "Wars aren't won by gentlemen. They are won by men who can be first-class sons of bitches . . . It's as simple as that. No son of a bitch, no commander."
>
> —Lieutenant General Lucian Truscott

On the night of August 15, General Truscott had every reason to be satisfied with the events of the preceding twelve hours. With the exception of the switch of the assault landing from Beach Red to Beach Green, and continuing house-to-house fighting in Fréjus-Saint-Raphaël, all of Dragoon's initial objectives had been achieved, and the 3rd and 36th Divisions were pushing on to the Blue Line. Truscott also noted with pride that the day marked the twenty-seventh anniversary of his commission as an officer in the U.S. Army. He estimated that 6th Corps had broken the power of two enemy divisions, taking some 2,130 of their men prisoner. His Corps's casualties had been remarkably light, 183 killed and wounded in battle and a further 479 non-battle casualties.

Making his way to his forward command post on the beachhead at Sainte-Maxime, Truscott was accompanied by Colonel Jean Petit, his

French liaison officer and an old associate. Stepping ashore, Truscott scooped up a handful of sand and, turning to Petit, asked, "Well, Jean, how does the soil of France feel to an exile?" Petit could not answer; his eyes were filled with tears. Truscott later reflected: "In an offensive battle, the object is to destroy the enemy. Every military leader on the offensive seeks to attack the enemy in flank and rear where he is most vulnerable . . . Every military leader dreams of the battle in which he can trap the enemy without any avenues or means for escape and in which his destruction can be assured. My study of the terrain of eastern France, and of the many possible ways in which the battle might develop, led me to dream of creating such a maneuver."[1] The opening days of Dragoon were to place such an opportunity in his hands.

In the planning stages of Dragoon it had been envisaged that once a bridgehead had been established on the French Riviera, the American and French corps would advance abreast to clear the enemy from the approaches to Toulon and Marseille before leaving the two cities to be taken by the French, an acknowledgment of the courtesies of coalition warfare. However, Allied pressure in northern and southern France in August 1944 had forced OKW into a rapid and radical revision of the strategic situation in both these sectors, which in turn enabled Truscott and Patch to refashion the second stage of the Dragoon campaign.

Army Group G and 19th Army headquarters had both received reports of the Allied air- and seaborne operations in the early hours of August 15, although confusion remained about the precise focus of the attack, largely because of the Allied deception measures undertaken in the buildup to Dragoon. The confusion was compounded after 0800 on the 15th when the FFI cut communications between the two headquarters, forcing General Wiese to rely on intelligence reports originating from OB South-West in Italy. Army Group G fell back on information supplied by the OB West headquarters outside Paris. A third blow was delivered when the communications of General Neuling's 62nd Corps, headquartered at Draguignan, five miles north of the Blue Line, were cut by men of First Airborne Task Force after they had landed in Le Muy six miles to the south.

If they did nothing else, the airborne operations around Le Muy had enabled General Blaskowitz, long a proponent of withdrawal,* to move formations in the western coastal sector away from the Mediterranean littoral on the pretext of preparing for a counterattack. While dissembling, he moved his headquarters to Avignon. At the same time Blaskowitz ordered the 338th Infantry Division, which was headquartered in Arles and in the process of pulling out of its position at the mouth of the Rhône, to stay in place. He then instructed the commander of the 189th Infantry Division, Major General Richard von Schwerin, to form a Kampfgruppe (battle group) to relieve the 62nd Corps and then counterattack the beachhead. By dawn on August 16, Schwerin had scraped together his battle group, consisting of four infantry battalions, and at 0700 moved on Le Muy. Within half an hour it had shouldered aside an outpost of 517th PIB at Les Arcs, on the northern edge of the Blue Line, but stiffer opposition was at hand in the form of 2nd Battalion, 180th Infantry Regiment, which had advanced from the Camel beachhead, supported by a platoon of M10 tank destroyers of the 645th Tank Destroyer Battalion. They halted Schwerin at Les Arcs. As darkness fell, Schwerin extracted his Kampfgruppe, having lost half his men and much of his heavy equipment. By midday on August 17, 36th Division had arrived in force at Le Muy to relieve FABTF.

Army Group G was fast running out of room to maneuver. Communications had collapsed between its commands, and the Luftwaffe was incapable of flying reconnaissance missions over the Dragoon assault area. The appearance and then disappearance of successive proposed German defense lines recalled the Allied collapse in France in May 1940, as did the American air superiority over France in 1944. In 1940 the Luftwaffe had been largely unopposed until the Dunkirk evacuation. The movement by the Germans of reinforcements to the east side of the Rhône, notably the 11th Panzer Division, was hampered by the destruction of nearly all the major bridges, the constant presence in the daylight hours of Allied fighter-bombers and ground-attack aircraft,

* In early August 1944, Blaskowitz had urged a withdrawal of all his forces from southern France and the establishment of a new defensive line hinged on Dijon, south of Paris. However, in the chaos caused by the failed July 20 bomb plot to assassinate Hitler, this proposal was dismissed by OKW as several of the plotters were senior Wehrmacht officers in Paris.

and a resurgent Maquis. To OKW, the German armed forces high command, the general situation in France looked bleak. In Normandy, the 7th Army and 5th Panzer Army faced encirclement and destruction in the Falaise pocket. Patton's U.S. Third Army was thrusting through the Loire Valley and threatening to leapfrog the Seine to the north and south of Paris against scattered opposition. In southern France, the Dragoon landings placed the 1st Army on the Atlantic coast and the 19th Army to the southeast in equal danger of being cut off unless prompt action was taken.

At a meeting with Hitler at his headquarters in Rastenburg, East Prussia, on August 16, OKW offered the Führer a stark choice. He could either withdraw Army Groups B and G from France or risk their annihilation, which would leave the Third Reich's western frontier undefended. OKW fully expected Hitler to embark on his usual "to last man and the last bullet" tirade. Instead, he agreed to OKW's plan, with a significant proviso. The garrisons of a number of fortified ports, including Toulon and Marseille, were ordered to stay in place, to deny them to the Allies. In a decision that has never been satisfactorily explained, two-thirds of France was effectively handed back to the Allies without a shot being fired.

The principal elements of the Führer Directive were as follows: "Because the development of the situation in Army Group B makes it appear possible that the 19th Army . . . might be cut off, I hereby order . . . Army Task Group G to disengage . . . from the enemy and to link up with the southern wing of Army Group B." This caused no little consternation in the 19th Army's headquarters in Avignon because any suggestion of withdrawal had, until that point, been forbidden. When this was added to the fluidity of the situation in the French theater, both north and south, it presented OB West with a seemingly intractable problem. Blaskowitz did not receive the order until August 18, following which, because of the overall communications breakdown, he failed to pass it on the headquarters of the 54th Army Corps on the Atlantic coast, finally attempting to send it by motor messenger.

Now Ultra came back into the equation. At 0940 on August 17, the Kriegsmarine headquarters in southwestern France (*Admiral Atlantik*), which possessed the only functioning communications network in the theater, received the first part of a message from OKW. It was relayed to Blaskowitz some ninety minutes later, informing him that all elements of Army Group G west of the line Orléans-Clermont-Ferrand-Montpellier, with the exception of those already in combat or garrisoning the "fortresses" preying on Hitler's mind, were to withdraw behind a new defensive line on the axis Seine-Yonne-Canal de Bourgogne. At 1730 the second part was dispatched, instructing that, with the exceptions of its forces in Toulon and Marseille, the 19th Army was to move northward to link with Army Group B and establish another defensive line from Sens through Dijon to the Swiss frontier. The eastern elements of 62nd Corps, including the 148th and 157th Divisions, were to withdraw into the French-Italian Alps and join hands with OB South-West to prevent an Allied drive into northern Italy from the Dragoon assault area, cutting off the Wehrmacht forces north of Rome. The latest hasty reshuffling of the Wehrmacht's hand did not reach Blaskowitz until 1100 on August 18. It had already been intercepted and decrypted at Bletchley Park and relayed to senior Allied commanders, including Patch and Truscott, who received the information at about the same time as did the commander of the 19th Army, General Wiese. In the knowledge that a flank attack on the U.S. 6th Corps from across the Italian Alps was highly improbable, the American commanders were now spurred into a more determined pursuit of the reeling German forces in the South of France. In contrast to the Germans, Truscott issued few field orders in the days following the Dragoon landings. He recalled: "I controlled our strategy, for the most part, by oral orders to [the divisional] commanders; thus, my instructions were based, as near as possible, upon personal up-to-date knowledge and information, which was collected by the staff for dissemination to the commanders, and for the record. The system worked well in this campaign."[2]

Late in the afternoon of August 17, Truscott met with Brigadier General Butler, who reported that his brigade-sized Task Force was assembled just north of Le Muy with the exception of two units that were expected to arrive later that night. The two men discussed the plans they had prepared in the Naples Block House for a northwest advance to the Durance River followed by a drive north to the city of Grenoble or, if the opportunity arose, a westward thrust to seize the high ground to the northeast of the town of Montélimar, a choke point on the probable German line of withdrawal up the N-7. French officers, including Henri Zeller, who had been in the area two weeks before the Dragoon landings, had reported that the German presence in the area was unimpressive in contrast to that of the FFI. This was confirmed by the 36th Division's Cavalry Reconnaissance Troop that had penetrated some forty miles north and northeast of Le Muy on August 17 and 18. At this point, however, it was not clear which of the two options discussed by Truscott and Butler—Grenoble or Montélimar—would take precedence.

Moreover, the logistical problems buried at the heart of the Dragoon planning were about to resurface. By August 19, 6th Corps's overall shortage of trucks and fuel limited the support that Patch could provide for any attempt to cut the 19th Army off at Avignon or farther north up the Rhône Valley. Deeper penetrations inland would depend on the rapid capture and rehabilitation of Toulon and Marseille, and strong German resistance was anticipated in these sectors. With this in mind, on August 19, Patch made Aix-en-Provence the western limit of Truscott's advance to accelerate the capture of the two ports. Nevertheless, Patch and Truscott were eager to exploit the rapid withdrawal of the rest of the 19th Army up the Rhône Valley, and it was precisely for an opportunity like this that Task Force Butler had been created, with its motorized infantry battalion, medium tanks, tank destroyers, self-propelled guns, armored cars, light tanks, and trucks. However, TFB was a mobile offensive force whose balance was undermined by a significant shortcoming in the battle that was to come, one of the most important of the campaign, at Montélimar. Would TFB's single motorized infantry battalion be equal to the task it was about to be set?

Task Force Butler set off from Le Muy at dawn on August 18. In spite of the reports from Zeller and his colleagues, Butler lacked up-to-date intelligence on enemy dispositions and whether they were fixed or mobile. Up to this point, he had received no information about liaising with the Resistance from 4-SFU, the Special Forces unit attached to the Seventh Army, which had not yet arrived in the South of France. Accordingly, he prepared for an encounter battle. When his first units moved away over the maquis-covered hills around Le Muy, Butler had no clear idea of what opposition they might meet.

Accordingly, he launched his command over several routes, with small detachments of the 117th Cavalry Reconnaissance Squadron screening his main body in the vanguard and along the flanks and rear, which would enable him to attack or bypass enemy concentrations when they ran up against them.

The first encounter was not long in coming. Barely fifteen miles from Draguignan, the 117th Cavalry's C Troop was fired on from caves near Aups, a Resistance stronghold. One of Butler's tanks silenced the fire with a few well-placed rounds, following which there emerged the unfortunate Lieutenant General Ferdinand Neuling and his 62nd Corps staff. The German general surrendered his custom-made Luger to platoon leader Lieutenant Joseph Syms, who turned it over to his commanding colonel. Meanwhile, Butler's main column, led by the 117th Cavalry's A Troop under Captain Thomas C. Piddington, pushed on north toward Quinson. At about 1330, when they were some forty miles northwest of Draguignan, Piddington's unit reached the Verdon River, south of Quinson. Butler's first-day objective, the Valensole plateau, was accessible by fording the Verdon and climbing a zigzagging road rising several hundred feet. The bridge across the Verdon had unfortunately been downed by the combined efforts of the USAAF and the Resistance in the days immediately before Dragoon. A Troop's task was made easier by the efforts of the local Maquis, who fashioned a ford at the lowest point of the river and then guided the American vehicles across, losing only one in the process.

By crossing the Verdon River, Task Force Butler had moved into the department of the Basses-Alpes (now known as the Alpes-de-Haute-Provence) of which the spa town of Digne, with its prefectural seat, was the most important urban center. The FFI considered it vital that Digne, garrisoned by the Germans with principally administrative troops, should be liberated as quickly as possible. The country surrounding Digne was controlled by George Bonnaire (Commandant "Noel") a communist and head of the local FTP, who had already informed local FFI commanders of his plan of action. Among them was Captain Justin Boeuf ("Decembre") the Resistance commander on the Valensole plateau, who in the early afternoon of August 18 had been informed that the Americans were moving up into the area he controlled. Boeuf roared off on his motorcycle to meet an advance unit of Task Force Butler and then traveled in their jeep to the town of Riez, which had been secured by TFB at around 1800.

At Riez, Boeuf met Butler and argued forcefully that the latter should order a detachment to secure Digne. This carried no political weight with Butler, who was intending to advance up the Durance Valley, but the American could see that the taking of Digne would secure his right flank and also block the only two roads along which the Germans could bring reinforcements from Italy, should they choose to do so. Accordingly, he agreed to dispatch the 117th Cavalry's B Troop, under Captain John Wood, to Digne along a narrow mountain highway winding through forested slopes where a few well-placed heavy guns could threaten Wood's approach to the town. B Troop's right flank was to be shielded by a ragged command of twenty-five Maquisards armed with a bazooka and a mortar. Butler then bivouacked in Riez, having established an outpost line along all the roads running from the north and west into the town. He had advanced fifty miles from Le Muy and his command was now suffering fuel shortages.

At Riez, Butler had been joined by the field representatives of 4-SFU, including Marc Rainaud, the hero of the Brigade des Maures, who had just been decorated by General Patch. They had made their way to the rendezvous with Butler in a hair-raising nine-hour dash during which they passed in and out of enemy-held territory. The unit consisted of two Americans, a British officer, a British NCO and driver, and four Frenchmen. They reported to TFB's G-3, Major Hansen, met General Butler, and were given their assignments by the Task Force's operations officer, Lieutenant Colonel Hodge. Their leader, the American Captain Henry Leger, an OSS man, was attached to Butler's headquarters with orders to liaise with local Maquis and "anything and everything French that might come his way."

Task Force Butler renewed the attack early in the morning on August 19, moving off the Valensole plateau with the 117th's A Troop in the van. TFB crossed to the west bank of the Durance over a partially destroyed bridge and pushed on toward Château-Arnoux. The day's only sizeable action came at Digne, fifteen miles southeast of Sisteron and the objective of Captain Wood's B Troop. The troop crossed the Asse River and pushed on down the Asse Valley, supported by a battalion of FFI fighters, before running into determined

German opposition at Mézel, where the twisting mountain road began its ten-mile ascent to Digne. Wood's force broke through the German block and worked its way upward to the southern outskirts of Digne, which it reached shortly before 1200. It took up positions that overlooked the German headquarters in the Ermitage Hotel while the FFI set up blocks on all roads into Digne. The Germans holed up in the Ermitage Hotel quickly realized that they were in an impossible situation, and Major General Hans Schubert, commanding the 792nd *Verbindungsstab* (Liaison Staff for the Basses Alpes based in Digne) whose communications with Avignon had been cut off since August 15, decided to capitulate, provided that he could surrender to the Americans. Schubert knew that if he surrendered to the Maquis he and his men would most likely be shot on the spot.

However, this was not the end of the fighting at Digne. There were other elements of the German garrison still at large, most of them administrative and logistical troops, and Wood was by no means sure that B Troop was strong enough to prevail. By about 1500, he was bogged down in the southern part of the town. Meanwhile, TFB's main column was moving up the Durance Valley toward Sisteron. A serviceable bridge across the Durance at Oraison was found by Henry Leger, enabling Piddington to move his A Troop up the west bank toward Château-Arnoux. On the way, the Americans joined forces with more Resistance men, who informed Piddington that a force of some 135 Germans was in Château-Arnoux. The Germans had been ordered to march south from Sisteron to relieve the force in Digne, but had been stranded in Château-Arnoux after the Maquis blew the bridges there in the small hours of August 19. The relief force's commanding officer, in mortal fear of a Maquis ambush, refused to march south to find another bridge, which in any event would have driven his men deeper into wooded and hilly country infested with Maquis fighters. He too had been cut off from his headquarters and took the desperate measure of entrusting a message, requesting further orders from his superior, to a local gendarme. If it was not delivered, he threatened to take hostages and put Château-Arnoux to the torch.

The gendarme delivered the message straight to the Maquis, who in turn shared it with Piddington on his arrival. Piddington, apprised of the enemy's strength and position, prepared to attack but before doing so handed the letter to the gendarme with the suggestion that he return to the Germans and ascertain whether they wished to surrender. It was now about 1200, and the enemy, who had retreated behind the locked gates of a local park, were given just over an hour to make up their minds. Their commanding officer emerged from the park, minus his cap, jacket, and sidearm, to meet Piddington at the local gendarmerie, where he surrendered. Shortly afterward he was followed by his men, who stacked their guns in the bright sunshine and were driven into captivity by some of Piddington's trucks, a temporary inconvenience much regretted by the commander of A Troop, which then advanced on Sisteron followed by the main body of Task Force Butler.

Butler, who was now some ten miles from Château-Arnoux, was aware of the reports he had received from Captain Wood about the enemy resistance at Digne. He dispatched a small task force to Digne, commanded by Major James C. Gentle, executive officer of the 143rd Regiment's 2nd Battalion, and consisting of an armored car, a company of eight Shermans, and a company of infantry. Along the way it brushed aside scattered German resistance, and by 1730 was temporarily halted by a firefight seven miles west of Digne. Gentle had been picking up groups of Maquisards on his progress before reaching a German munitions dump, which during the course of another firefight blew up. By 1900, Digne was in American hands and Gentle and the FFI had taken four hundred prisoners.

The Résistants who had fought alongside TFB considered that their work was at an end. The FFI and FTP were organized departmentally and were concerned above all with clearing Germans from their department, occupying the departmental seat and apprehending its Vichy occupants, and then replacing them with temporary representatives of their own choosing, frequently communists or socialists. At the same time the Gaullist provisional government was responsible for installing a new prefect. This political game of musical chairs was inevitably accompanied by much exuberant local rejoicing while many of the former Résistants melted back into civilian life or continued to fight under their old leaders against the withdrawing Germans.

Present at the liberation celebrations at Digne were the British SOE agents, Francis Cammaerts and Xan Fielding, who had a remarkable story to tell. On August 11 both men had been captured at a roadblock by the Gestapo and taken to the jail at Digne. Cammaerts's SOE colleague Christine Granville, who was still at large, reacted to this news swiftly and decisively. She reconnoitered the jail in Digne where the SOE men were held, whistling "Frankie and Johnny," a call sign that Cammaerts quickly answered. She then persuaded his two principal jailers that she was not only the wife of one of their prisoners but also the niece of Field Marshal Montgomery, commander of the British 21st Army Group. Granville, a woman of exceptional bravery and beauty, explained with complete accuracy that the Allies were on their way and, with slightly less accuracy, the war would soon be over. The price for the release of the two SOE men was two million francs and safe passage for the jailers. Granville arranged for the money to be dropped by an aircraft flying from Algiers on the night of August 16. Five days after their arrest, Cammaerts and Fielding were driven out of the prison and freed by their captors. That night one of the messages broadcast by the BBC was: "*Roger est libre. Félicitations à Pauline.*" ("Roger is free. Congratulations to Pauline.") Roger and Pauline were Cammaerts's and Granville's code names.

On August 20, Butler established his command post at Sisteron. He had good reason to be grateful for the help his Task Force had received from the Resistance, and later wrote: "It is only fair to state that without the Maquis our mission would have been much more difficult." Nevertheless, the mindset of a professional soldier like Butler, or a French counterpart like Lieutenant Colonel François Huet, was far removed from that of the rank-and-file Résistant. The historian of the 117th Cavalry noted of this phase of Dragoon: "We are beginning to meet more and more Maquis. The groups we were meeting were better trained, better disciplined, and more heavily armed. Their assistance is invaluable, as they mop up the rough country between the roads up which we advance. Their enthusiasm and sincere desire to be of assistance is most gratifying. Unfortunately the commanding officer of the Task Force [Butler] lacks confidence in them, with the result that they are not being employed as well they might be. The information which they give to us as to enemy movements ahead has, up to this time, proved accurate in composition and timely to within six hours." There is no doubt that Butler was happier dealing with regular military men like Colonel Jean Constans, the FFI regional chief in the Var (R-2). On August 20, Butler also received a visit from a uniformed but disheveled Cammaerts and Granville and a representative of 4-SFU, Captain Ralph Banbury. Butler dismissed Cammaerts's offer of help with the observation that he had "not the slightest interest in private armies." Cammaerts later suggested that, "Perhaps Butler didn't like our faces . . . When you talk about Butler's relations with members of the Resistance, these were nearly all Army men."

While they were at Butler's command post, Cammaerts and Granville heard about Butler's next northward move, to Gap, an Alpine crossroads on the Route Napoléon and the principal town of the Alpes du Sud, which was garrisoned by 1,200 German soldiers. The intrepid pair reached Gap while Piddington's Troop was preparing to attack the town. At about 1600 Piddington's combined arms force had reached a plateau overlooking Gap, which lay in a bowl some 800 feet below. His command consisted of a troop of motorized infantry augmented by five 105mm assault guns and three light tanks, and reinforced by about one hundred Maquisards riding in armored cars, on the tanks and in jeeps. Poised over Gap, Piddington was informed by local citizens that the Germans had withdrawn to a barracks on a small hill near Puymaure, to the north of the town center. He positioned his assault guns, and at 1640 fired some forty rounds into the enemy positions on and around Puymaure, knocking out the barracks' radio tower with the first shot. This was enough for the Gap garrison, who came out with their hands up. By 1630 a surrender had been agreed, with the German commander and his troops began assembling in the town square amid scenes of wild rejoicing by the citizens of Gap. The situation threatened to get out of hand. Female collaborationists were seized and their heads shaved while three Gestapo agents were identified among the surrendering soldiers and were saved from summary execution by Piddington's soldiers. It availed them little; they were shot the next day.

As darkness fell, Piddington and his Maquis allies had to deal with over a thousand enemy prisoners with no way of dispatching them to the rear. The quick-witted Piddington came up with a solution. Among the captured garrison were many Poles, who detested their German masters and could act as guards. Christine Granville, a Pole herself, was called on to address these men in their own language, encourage them to cast aside their uniforms and join the Allies.

Cammaerts recalled: "She asked them—were they willing to fight with us? We could give them some rifles but they had to take their uniforms off because under the Geneva Convention you weren't allowed to fight in a foreign uniform—we have no others to offer you, so you'll have to go forward *torse-nu* [naked to the waist]; and they tore them off, exultant!"

When General Butler heard of this ecstatic outburst, he threatened to have Cammaerts and Granville arrested for interfering with the Gap operation—"You've been buggering my prisoners about!" This marked the end of the two SOE agents' involvement in Allied operations east of the Rhône. Cammaerts was assigned another mission with French Army B. His and Granville's significant roles in the Resistance were coming to an end. Meanwhile, Butler waited for further orders. He anticipated a German counterblow, delivered from Grenoble, which was not long in coming. By the evening of August 20, an enemy force of about one thousand men, armed with heavy machine guns, mortars, and a 90mm field gun, was about twelve miles north of Piddington's forward position at Col Bayard, a mountain pass connecting Gap and La Mure.

The Germans attacked at 1000 the next day but were halted and were forced to withdraw by Piddington's assault guns. They fell back to Grenoble, pursued by a hastily formed American task force of tanks, tank destroyers, and infantry commanded by Major McNeill, the G-3 of 753rd Tank Battalion, which had been rushed up to Col Bayard from Aspres, Butler's new headquarters, in time to meet the German counterblow. Later that day, Piddington's troop and McNeill's task force were relieved by elements of General Dahlquist's 36th Division and hurried west to join the main body of Task Force Butler, which had been assigned a new mission authorized by General Patch on the morning of August 20. The orders reached Butler at 0400 on August 21, and by the end of the day all but a few of Butler's formations were racing west toward the Rhône.

THIRTEEN
MONTÉLIMAR: THE EYE OF THE NEEDLE

> "At dawn the next morning, we again attacked, with F Company in the lead. We were quite successful and they actually reached and cut Highway 7 just north of Montélimar . . . After a while they launched an attack out of the village; the situation stabilized and turned into a fight that raged throughout the day. I can only describe it as intense . . ."
>
> —Lieutenant Colonel James H. Critchfield,
> 2nd Battalion, 141st Infantry

The rapid development of Dragoon had exceeded its planners' wildest expectations. By nightfall on August 15, over 94,000 men and 11,000 vehicles had come ashore in the assault areas and were establishing contact with the airborne forces that had landed earlier in the day. By August 20, Butler's Task Force was driving north to Sisteron, followed by the 36th Division, while the 3rd and 45th Divisions were moving west toward the mouth of the Rhône River and Toulon and Marseille. The capture of the ports would provide General Patch with a sound logistical base from which a sustained drive could be launched north to link arms with Eisenhower's armies. The task of taking the two seaboard cities had been given to French Army Group B and the French 1st and 2nd Corps, and on August 16 the 2nd Corps came ashore and passed through the U.S. 6th Corps on the Marseille road.

The Allies were meeting little resistance as they moved inland, but both Patch and Truscott were eager to make the most of the precipitate German withdrawal and accomplish the destruction of the German 19th Army, particularly if Blaskowitz planned to make a stand at a point farther up the narrow Rhône Valley. However, until Toulon and Marseille could be secured, and with them the steady supply of fuel, vehicles, and ammunition to accomplish this ambitious undertaking, 6th Corps's task remained formidable.

At midday on August 19, Patch instructed Truscott to prepare an infantry division to take Grenoble. Truscott then ordered General Dahlquist, commanding the 36th Division, to execute this order on the following day, anticipating that on the 20th at least one of Dahlquist's regiments would have reached Sisteron. Confident that intelligence of the German withdrawal up the Rhône Valley provided by Ultra was accurate, Truscott also radioed Butler to remain at Sisteron until reinforced by Dahlquist. However, he urged Butler not to waste the opportunity to dispatch patrols to the west to ascertain "the practicability of seizing the high ground north of Montélimar." This small town, on the east bank of the Rhône, fifty miles north of Avignon and sixty miles west of Sisteron, had long been famous for the quality of the confectionery made there. However, there was to be little sweetness about the battle which the instructions to Butler and Dahlquist presaged.

The message concerning Montélimar was not received by Butler, whose radio communications with Truscott since August 17 had been increasingly ragged. The only message that did get through to Butler, on the night of August 19, was that his Task Force's mission remained unchanged. Butler's response was that he would carry out the reconnaissance requested by Truscott on the 20th but that he was running short of fuel and supplies, which restricted his probes in any direction to some forty miles. He further requested firm direction on whether his principal objective was Grenoble to the north, or Montélimar and the Rhône to the west. Butler was also aware that his task force at

Sisteron was in an exposed position, behind enemy lines and with limited backup. Reports were coming in from the FFI and his own spotter aircraft of strong enemy forces at Grenoble and Gap, both of which might halt his northward drive.

Because Butler still considered that Grenoble was his primary objective, he established a strong outpost at the Croix-Haute Pass, forty miles to the north on the principal road to Grenoble, and sent a force northeastward to Gap. His operations officer then flew to 6th Corps headquarters to obtain precise orders as to his next move. On August 20, with his main body concentrated at Sisteron and Gap in Allied hands, Butler found his Task Force spread over a wide area but was still no wiser as to whether he should push north or drive west. Nevertheless, Grenoble was still in Butler's sights as his operations officer returned that evening with news that firm orders would arrive on the 21st.

That evening, Butler had a meeting with Brigadier General Robert I. Stack, the deputy commander of the 36th Division, who had arrived in Sisteron with an advanced echelon of the divisional headquarters and a regimental task force. Stack was unable to put Butler completely into the fast-moving picture but informed him that the 36th Division was moving north preceded by 142nd Infantry, which was about thirty-five miles away in Castellane. In addition, the right flank of 36th Division, up till now shielded by its 141st Regiment, was from August 21 to be covered by the troops of First Airborne Task Force, fresh from their action at Le Muy. This was the good news. The bad news was that divisional movement across the board had been slowed by the shortage of fuel and transport. When both would be more readily available was unclear. Stack brought the meeting to an end by informing Butler that the 143rd Infantry would be tasked with advancing on Grenoble the following morning, and that logic dictated that the city was to be Butler's next objective.

While Butler hung on at Sisteron, American priorities shifted, and late in the evening of the 20th he received instructions to move west to the Rhône Valley with all possible speed at first light on the 21st, the result of a decision taken by Patch and Truscott earlier in the day. Task Force Butler was to take Montélimar and block the withdrawal by the 19th Army, the bulk of which was still south of the town. Truscott was now confident that Allied air superiority over the theater ruled out the possibility of a German counterattack. Dahlquist was to support Butler with the 143rd Regimental Combat Team (minus the battalion already attached to TFB), Corps artillery Long Toms (155mm guns firing a 95lb shell to a range of fourteen miles), and the 36th Division's 155th Battalion. The bulk of 36th Division would follow as rapidly as conditions permitted. As soon as Dahlquist was established in the Montélimar sector, Task Force Butler would be attached to the 36th Division and come under the former's command.

Clarity, of a kind, had arrived, but Butler's situation was far from enviable. He was still unsure of the enemy's strength and dispositions in the immediate area. His Task Force was now dispersed over approximately ninety miles of rough, mountainous terrain. Most of his heavy weapons had been assigned to combined arms forces blocking two major mountain passes—Croix-Haute and Gap—threatened by enemy formations operating from Grenoble. These blocking forces would be unavailable to Butler until they were relieved by lead elements from the 36th Division, an eventuality in turn made imprecise by the fuel shortages of which he was only too well aware. The three divisions of Truscott's corps consumed about 100,000 gallons of fuel a day, but the reserves came to only 11,000 gallons on the beachhead, augmented by some 25,000 gallons of captured stock. Finally, Butler was at the end of a 235-mile supply chain and was expending ammunition, particularly artillery and tank rounds, at an alarming rate. The last consideration ruled out the possibility of sustaining any further offensive operations. The task confronting Butler as he moved toward Montélimar was, to say the least, challenging. He now disposed of two weakened infantry and artillery battalions, a weakened cavalry squadron, and a company of combat engineers. The arrival of 117th Cavalry's A Troop later, on the evening of August 20, improved the situation, but the Task Force was still shorn of much of its armored hitting power.

On the evening of August 20, after receiving orders to move west toward the Rhône, Butler sent patrols from B Troop, and C Troop, 117th Cavalry, to reconnoiter the road along the Drôme Valley from Aspres to Crest, thirteen miles east of the river. The respective troop commanders, Captain John L. Wood and Captain William E. Nugent, reported that they had encountered no Germans, prompting Butler to reflect: "The route lay over a formidable mountain range with a twisting road cut into the side of the cliffs. Movement off the road would have been impossible. Our path could have been blocked in any one of scores of places, but no enemy action developed, nor had demolitions been executed. Whether we had the Maquis to thank for this free open road, I do not know but open it was . . . I was horror-struck at the grade and nature of the road but all elements had made excellent time and not one of the heavy vehicles had succumbed."

Captain Wood and his men reached Crest at about 0900 on the 21st. With the help of guides provided by the Maquis, two platoons of B Troop headed south to Puy-Saint-Martin, and southwest over the Marsanne plain to the outskirts of Montélimar. Between the edge of the plain and the Rhône was a heavily wooded area stretching some three miles north of Montélimar to the village of Savasse, concealing some five hundred lightly armed Maquisards. Beyond the trees, toward the Rhône, the Germans retained a degree of control. Wood was able to observe the approaches to Montélimar and noted that its perimeter was protected by formidable roadblocks.

Wood then reported back to Butler, who had established his headquarters at Marsanne, on the eastern edge of the forest north of Montélimar and about halfway between Montélimar and the Drôme River. Here he waited for the arrival of the 36th Division's 141st Regiment, now released from its flank-guarding duties by FABTF and, employing the "Truscott Trot," heading west at top speed. Ten miles to the north of Marsanne, Captain Nugent's C Troop was approaching the town of Livron, the base for Maquisard attacks on Germans moving north along the N-7. The enemy withdrawal was, at this stage, disorderly rather than determined, and was described by a local priest in disparaging terms: "August 21. German columns continually passing. They have more and more the appearance of hunted beasts. They pass, guns ready, watching the side of the road and windows. Near Ponsan a tank helps them get through, firing on the Resistance . . . They get Frenchmen and place them on the hoods of their cars. This afternoon they took some young people in the rue St.-Rambert and used them as a shield."

The Germans were moving steadily into a landscape ripe for interdiction. To the north of Montélimar was the high ground east of the

Rhône, a ridge running north-south from the town of La Coucourde with a maximum height of about one thousand feet, which slopes down almost to the water's edge, crowding the N-7 and the railway alongside it into a passage less than one thousand yards wide, a feature characterized by Truscott as the "Montélimar Gap." The highest point on the ridge, at about 990 feet and designated Hill 300 by the American military planners, was on the ridge's northern tip. In the center of the ridge was another significant high point known as Hill 294, which was about twenty feet lower. Truscott judged that the seizure and retention of this high ground was the key to blocking the German retreat up the east bank of the Rhône. His eye was also drawn to a parallel ridge northeast of Montélimar that dominates the valley of the Roubion River, flowing into the Rhône, and the secondary roads running seventeen miles north and northeast from Montélimar toward the town of Crest on the north bank of the Drôme River. Truscott considered that this might be another escape route for the 19th Army that could be blocked by the seizure of the lower foothills of the Alps at Crest.

In his memoirs Truscott recalled that the dispositions he was about to make in the Montélimar sector were influenced by his study of the classic double envelopment of the Roman army by the Carthaginian general Hannibal at Cannae in 216 B.C.E. during the Second Punic War. To achieve an equally comprehensive victory at Montélimar, Truscott knew that the engagement would have to pass through three carefully coordinated phases. First he would have to maneuver a force ahead of the retreating Germans to block their main line of retreat north of Montélimar. To achieve this, his own forces would have to seize and hold the high ground to the east of the Rhône. German control of this terrain would allow the enemy to make good his escape. The second requirement was the destruction of all the bridges over the Rhône and those over its tributaries flowing into the river from the east, a task that had been undertaken by the Allied air forces and the French Resistance. This would leave the 19th Army's right flank exposed and isolate the forces to the east and west of the Rhône. The German columns converging on Montélimar would then be channeled north into the jaws of Truscott's trap. Finally, they would be propelled into the Montélimar bottleneck by a division-sized Allied pursuit pressing up from the rear.

By late afternoon on the 21st, Task Force Butler had reached Crest. Spread before it was the Rhône Valley, the arena for a battle that was to last eight days. Michel Stubinski, a soldier with the 143rd Infantry, attached to TFB, described the scene: "We had the most beautiful view of the Rhône Valley." To the west and east of the river were crops fields and rich pasture-land checkerboarding the rising and falling valley floor, which was studded with farmhouses, barns, and outbuildings. Stubinski nevertheless remembered the Italian campaign: "The first thought that entered my mind, and I was sure that the others were all thinking the same thing, was how the Germans were looking down on us at Anzio."

Crest, which lies almost twenty miles northeast of Montélimar, was to form the northeast corner of the so-called Montélimar Battle Square, demarcated in the north by the Drôme, in the west by the Rhône, and to the south by the Roubion. More properly a rectangle whose sides varied from nine to seventeen miles, the ground over which the battle was to be fought was some 250 miles square and contained a mixture of rolling farmland and rocky hill country that rose steeply to a height of approximately two thousand feet. Montélimar, the focus of Allied and German attention, sat on a small flat plain that hugs the northern bank of the Roubion, two miles east of the Rhône. The town was cut by the N-7 that ran north to the Drôme. A minor road, the D-6, ran two miles northeast to the village of Sauzet and then bent east along the northern bank of the Roubion.

Task Force Butler was now probing toward the outskirts of Montélimar. Lieutenant Colonel Joseph G. Felber, the officer responsible for the reconnaissance parties led by Captains Wood and Nugent, and a man with a keen eye for terrain, established a command post near Hill 300 at the Château de Condillac, a medieval castle with eccentric later additions. Felber did not have enough men to secure the ridgeline around Hill 300 but established outposts, roadblocks, and guard-posts, supported by FFI fighters holding Sauzet, less than a mile to the southeast. Also taking position on Hill 300 was the 753rd Tank Battalion, which immediately began firing on the retreating German columns, supported by artillery units.

Butler was now in the forward area and ordered the troops operating on the Drôme, to the north, to pull back to Crest to protect the roads running south to Puy-Saint-Martin. As a precaution, he left a platoon on the north bank of the Drôme to guard his northeastern flank. Now established in his command post (CP) in Marsanne, at 2330 on August 21 he informed Truscott's headquarters that he was in the Montélimar sector and was expecting reinforcement by a regiment of the 36th Division and extra artillery. He was confident that he could take Montélimar on the 22nd but until he received more ammunition his artillery and tank destroyers (TDs) could not halt German traffic flowing along the N-7.

On the morning of the 22nd, while Butler was anxiously waiting for his ammunition, the Germans made their first move. On August 13, with German intelligence identifying the Rhône delta as the probable Allied landing area, the 11th Panzer Division had begun to rumble slowly toward the Rhône Valley. However, its progress, initially by rail and by road, was painful, principally conducted at night because of the Allied air threat and hampered by the destruction of bridges along its route. Ferrying its armor across the Rhône proved difficult for the 11th Panzer, with its reconnaissance battalion, *Panzer Aufklarungs-Abteilung 11* (PzAA11) commanded by Major Karl Bode, in the van. Once across the Rhône, the battalion was sent straight into action on August 22 as part of an ad hoc force consisting of elements of the 71st Luftwaffe Infantry Training Regiment, part of the 4th Luftwaffe Field Corps, commanded by Lieutenant General Erich Petersen.

Bode's reconnaissance battalion was equipped with armored cars, eight-wheeled pakwagens mounting 50mm and 75mm guns that could reverse as fast as they could be driven forward thanks to a "reverse driver" who doubled as the radio operator or loader. The battle group went into action north of Montélimar and took the village of Sauzet, on the D-6, driving its FFI occupants back into the hills to the east. This skirmish, however, was only a feint, as the German battle group swiftly reassembled south of the Roubion, pushed nine miles east before turning north, crossing the river and then moving on to Puy-Saint-Martin, which it took that afternoon before targeting Marsanne, threatening to sever Butler's supply line to Crest and Sisteron. The situation was retrieved by TFB's detachments previously deployed to Croix-Haute and Gap, which had been relieved on August 21 and were now hastening to join Butler. The Gap detachment was traveling south on the afternoon of the 22nd and its commander, grasping the significance of the German advance, threw his tanks and infantry into an attack on Puy. The tanks plastered the road from Puy to Marsanne, and Puy was cleared before darkness fell.

The units from Gap and Croix-Haute had thwarted a determined German probe but Butler, still waiting for fuel and reinforcements from the 36th Division, anticipated a maximum effort from the Germans on the 23rd. Apart from the units from Gap and Croix-Haute, the only reinforcements he had received on the 22nd were two 155mm artillery battalions from 6th Corps. His ammunition reserves were down to about twenty-five rounds per gun, half the optimum ration. But help was on the way. Just before 2200 on the evening of the 22nd, a single battalion of 141st Infantry, running on captured fuel stores, arrived with the regimental commander, Lieutenant Colonel John W. "Jazz" Harmony, who established his command post in Condillac, three miles east of the Rhône and six miles northeast of Montélimar.

For men of the 36th Division, the journey to Montélimar, made at night through narrow, winding, rain-swept country roads that passed in and out of German-held territory, was exhausting and dangerous. Major Marcel F. Pincetl, who was with the Headquarters Company of 1st Battalion, 141st Infantry, recalled a revealing encounter on the night of August 22: "It was night and we were moving forward under blackout conditions. We followed the noise of the tank treads ahead as it was too dark to see. When dawn came we found to our surprise that our jeep had been following a German tank. The tank noticed us also and stopped. We were lightly armed so we turned off the road and the jeep turned over on its side . . . We ran for cover. The tank backed up, the hatch opened, and the gunner took aim. Then one German soldier got out of the tank and walked over to our jeep, took out his knife and cut the rope holding the wheel of cheese that we had liberated, and took it to the tank and left."[1]

The Germans were eager for the cheese but unconcerned about the rattled Americans in their overturned jeep. The contrast between the well-fed Americans and the hungry Germans was striking. Major Richard Nott, the 36th Division's Inspector General, visited several prisoner of war cages in the Var during the hectic days of August 1944. His aide, Tech/4* Glenn C. Raithel, was initially surprised to find that the Germans were "not the least bit arrogant but quite satisfied and content." In combat, nevertheless, they had been fearful of American artillery, which they dubbed "whistling death." One dejected soldier told Raithel, "It's no use. If you live through the strafing by the American planes you have to sweat out the American artillery; if you are lucky enough to get through that deadly fire, the infantry comes up—it's just no use!"

For General Butler, the situation at Montélimar was approaching crisis point. On the morning of August 22, his troops on the heights overlooking the N-7 numbered only a few hundred men and a dozen armored vehicles. Below them moved a growing tide of enemy troops and hundreds of vehicles, many of which were commercial and civilian transport confiscated from the French. Municipal buses were highly prized by the Germans but proved tempting targets for marauding Allied fighters. Forlorn attempts were made to camouflage the motor transport under branches torn from trees, but there was precious little natural cover along the Rhône River Valley, particularly on either side of the highway.

Butler, desperate for reinforcements, was also hampered by the slow approach to Montélimar of Dahlquist's 36th Division. This was Dahlquist's first divisional combat command, and his method in the early stages of the clash at Montélimar was tempered by the Allies' bitter experience in Italy of the unmatched German ability to deliver telling counterpunches. Thus, as more American units began to arrive in the Montélimar sector, Dahlquist remained reluctant to take bold action against the enemy streaming along the N-7 until a viable defensive perimeter had been established to the east of the Rhône to shield the road network behind his forces. This had the inevitable effect of slowing the American buildup on the N-7 and limited the forces attempting to block the highway. In mitigation it has to be said that a simpler form of interdiction, by an overwhelming artillery bombardment from the high ground to the east of the N-7, had been rendered impossible by the lack of fuel and trucks to transport sufficient artillery ammunition to the Battle Square.

---

* Technician, 4th Grade, often addressed as sergeant although technically not an NCO.

Nevertheless, Dahlquist's increasingly indecisive decision-making was testing Truscott's patience. At midday on August 22, Truscott arrived at the 36th Division command post near Aspres, west of Gap, to find Dahlquist absent "up the front somewhere" and out of communication, according to the division's chief of staff, Colonel Stewart T. Vincent. Truscott demanded that the entire formation now pivot westward to the Rhône. The advance to Grenoble was to be entrusted to the 179th Regiment of the 45th Division. On returning to his command post, Truscott wrote Dahlquist a letter emphasizing that, "The primary mission of 36th Infantry Division is to block the Rhône Valley in the Gap immediately north of . . . Montélimar. For this purpose you must be prepared to employ the bulk of your division. If this operation develops as seems probable, all of your division will be none too much in the Rhône Valley area."[2]

Truscott nevertheless acknowledged the logistical problems plaguing 36th Division and had ordered Seventh Army headquarters to send an emergency fuel convoy northward on the afternoon of the 22nd. That night Truscott and Dahlquist sought to bury their differences during a telephone conversation. However, while the commander of the 36th Division temporized, his superior's patience snapped and Dahlquist was bluntly told to forget his transportation problems and get his men to Montélimar even if they had to walk. Chastened, Dahlquist began to reshuffle the cards in his hand. The 143rd Regiment was dispatched to Montélimar through Valence, securing Butler's northern flank, while his task force was shielded in the south by the deployment of the 142nd to Noyon. Priority was now given to the movement of the 141st to Montélimar, and the 45th Division assumed responsibility for the Grenoble sector, leaving Dahlquist to concentrate on the Rhône. However, Truscott was still beset by nagging doubts, and in the small hours of August 23 he telephoned Dahlquist once again to remind him of the crucial importance of halting and then destroying the German forces withdrawing up the N-7.

The Germans were by now keenly aware of the growing danger to the 19th Army posed by Task Force Butler and the reinforcements coming to its aid. General Wiese's first move had been the commitment of the 11th Panzer Division's reconnaissance battalion to probe

Butler's dispositions north of Montélimar on August 22. The rest of the division, minus a force feinting toward Aix, then began blocking the principal roads running from the east to the Rhône. However, TFB's clearing of Puy set the alarm bells ringing for Wiese, who decided to order Wietersheim to bring the entire division north as soon as possible to clear the high ground northeast of Montélimar and secure the N-7 running north to Valence. The commander of the 85th Corps, Lieutenant General Baptiste Kniess, who was in Avignon, was to provide support for the 11th Panzer with the 198th Infantry Division.

The Germans had their own difficulties with which to contend. Kniess, moving north, was struggling to cross the Durance and was unable to dispatch a regiment up to Montélimar. Fuel shortages, clogged roads, and movement by night hampered the progress of 11th Panzer into the Montélimar Battle Square. Wietersheim had divided his units into four Kampfgruppen: Bode's reconnaissance battalion, which had already been thrown into the battle for Montélimar; Lieutenant Colonel Hax's 110th Panzergrenadier Regiment; Major Thieme's Gruppe, containing a battalion of infantry, ten Mk 4 tanks, and a self-propelled artillery battery; and Colonel Wilde's 111th Panzergrenadier Regiment. Thieme's was the first major element of 11th Panzer into the Montélimar Battle Square on August 23. The rest of the division was expected to arrive on the 24th. The men of the 11th Panzer knew that any delay would give the enemy more time to gather strength along their unprotected line of withdrawal.

In the late afternoon of August 22, General Wiese had received a report from the 11th Panzer that men of the U.S. 36th Division had been taken prisoner in the Montélimar sector and that the N-7 was under artillery fire from positions in the foothills northeast of Montélimar between Condillac and Puy-Saint-Martin. The enemy guns were those in Dahlquist's field and self-propelled artillery battalions firing on coordinates supplied by forward observers (FOs) established in positions overlooking the Rhône. The fire missions began to blanket targets to the west, south, and north. Wiese immediately took action, ordering the 11th Panzer to clear the enemy from the Montélimar bottleneck, the route that the 19th Army's Chief of Staff, Lieutenant General Walter Botsch, recognized as the formation's lifeline.

On August 23 Dahlquist assumed overall command in the Montélimar Battle Square and the next day Task Force Butler, now reinforced with fresh units, reverted to divisional control to act as a reserve. Around Montélimar, however, the initial American moves were tentative and ill-coordinated. By noon on the 23rd, the 1st Battalion, 141st Regiment had established itself without opposition on Hill 300. Before darkness fell, the regiment's A Company, supported by eight tank destroyers and three tanks, made its way down the western slope of the ridge to the floodplain below with the aim of establishing a roadblock outside the town of La Coucourde, at the base of the ridge six miles north of Montélimar. However, A Company's infantry and armor were still deploying when night closed in, plunging their defensive preparations into chaos. The crews of the armored vehicles, alerted by the sound of enemy infiltrators, requested and were denied infantry support. The tankers' suspicions were confirmed when at about 0100 on the 24th German infantry armed with hand-held *Panzerfaust* anti-tank weapons and *Hafthohlladung* magnetic mines* destroyed all but two of A Company's armored vehicles. Later in the small hours a second, stronger German force, consisting of infantry and tanks, shouldered aside the roadblock and reopened the N-7.

The 2nd Battalion, 141st Infantry, commanded by Lieutenant Colonel James H. Critchfield, also went into action on August 23. It had arrived in Marsanne, to the northeast of Montélimar on the edge of the forest, and was ordered by Lieutenant Colonel Harmony to seize Montélimar as quickly as possible, reinforced by the 117th Cavalry Reconnaissance Squadron's B Troop, and two companies of the Maquis, with fire support provided the 59th Field Artillery Battalion. The decision to send a single battalion across open ground to attack Montélimar

* The *Panzerfaust*, a hand-held recoilless anti-tank weapon, consisted of a steel tube containing a propelling charge with the tail stem of a shaped-charge bomb inserted in the mouth of the tube. The firer tucked the weapon under his arm, took aim across the top of the bomb and pressed the trigger to fire the charge, which in turn blew the bomb forward while expelling the gases from the rear of the tube to counteract the recoil. The *Hafthohlladung*, dubbed the "*Panzerknacker*" (Tank Breaker) was a magnetically-adhered shaped-charge anti-tank grenade used by Wehrmacht tank-killing squads. With three magnets at the base, each with a pair of poles creating a strong magnetic field across their gap, an infantryman could attach it to an enemy tank no matter the angle of the surface. It could penetrate 140mm of armor.

was a tactical error. It would have been more sensible for the battalion to move into the higher ground overlooking Montélimar to reinforce Task Force Butler. Nevertheless, Critchfield's force concentrated at Sauzet and launched its attack at 1630 without the support of armor, which had failed to arrive.

Less than a mile from Montélimar, the 2nd Battalion's spearhead, F Company, was caught in a heavy firefight with the town's German defenders, who also launched attacks on the company's flanks. The battalion took up a defensive position in a cluster of stone buildings on a low hill and beat off an attack by echeloned panzers and infantry while continuing to take casualties. During the engagement tracer bullets from American and German machine guns set fire to parched undergrowth, sending smoke and flames billowing skyward and covering the battlefield in a dense haze. When night fell, visibility was down to zero. Fighting ceased, enabling Critchfield to bring up supplies.

At dawn Critchfield renewed the attack and succeeded in cutting the N-7 just north of Montélimar. The Germans attempted to smash the roadblock with a series of attacks launched by infantry and Mk 5 tanks that overran Critchfield's position, forcing 2nd Battalion back and threatening to cut it off from Marsanne. Toward midday, an intervention by tanks and infantry led by Critchfield's executive officer, Major Herbert E. Eitt, stabilized the situation, preventing a complete rout.

However, F Company was still isolated from the rest of the battalion and shortly afterward came under attack from two Mk 6 Tiger tanks.* Critchfield provided a vivid account of the ensuing one-sided encounter: "The battle between our medium tanks with 75mm guns and our tank destroyers with the larger 90mm gun did not last long. Hits on the forward armor of the German tanks seemed to be doing no damage; within a few minutes six plainly visible Mk 6 tanks were

* At the time of its introduction in 1942, and for some time after the end of hostilities, the Tiger was the most powerful tank in the world. Slow-moving but well-armored, its 88mm gun, for which it carried ninety-two rounds of ammunition, out-ranged and out-punched all Allied types. It was most effectively used in battalion-sized formations of about thirty vehicles under the control of an army corps headquarters. It was reckoned that it took at least six well-handled Sherman medium tanks to knock out a single, cornered Tiger.

firing on us. I could call up neither artillery nor air support. Within minutes . . . all our tanks and tank destroyers were out of action—most in flames resulting from direct hits by the German 88mm guns on the Mk 6."

At 1500 Critchfield was ordered to abandon the attack and pull out. That night his withdrawal was covered by a sixty-minute barrage from 59th Field Artillery Battalion. The evacuation route for his battalion's wounded had been closed since noon, and the casualties were driven away in a tank destroyer that had its turret blown off and which was towing a disabled truck and a 57mm anti-tank gun. Aboard this improvised ambulance were some fifty men, "swathed in blood-soaked bandages and a handful of Medicos with their white and red helmets gleaming in the moonlight." The rest of 2nd Battalion withdrew to Marsanne, where Critchfield took over temporary command of the 141st Regiment from a wounded Lieutenant Colonel Harmony.

Harmony knew that the key to the battle at Montélimar was the retention of the ridge overlooking the N-7. A determined German attempt to seize the heights had been driven off by the 1st Battalion, 141st Regiment, on August 23, prompting the recall of the regiment's 3rd Battalion from its position north of Montélimar to reinforce the units holding the positions on Hills 300 and 294. Fighting had died away during the night of August 23, but the troops manning forward positions on the ridge could hear the clear sound of German activity below them: motor transport moving along the roads; the rattle of tanks and tank destroyers on the move; and the muffled sounds of men giving orders. The men of the 141st Regiment were holding a porous network of outpost and strongpoints on the heights that could easily be penetrated by enemy infiltrators, and their ears and eyes strained for suspicious sounds and movement. Remaining still for hours on end on hard rocky ground was extremely demanding. Pins and needles and itching scratches and wounds added to the individual soldier's torment. Most men chose to urinate or defecate in their helmets before tossing the contents over the sides of their foxholes.

For inexperienced troops this proved an unforgiving battleground. On August 23, Butler's initial shortage of men had forced him to commit two platoons from A Company, 116th Engineers, to plug a gap in the line along the Roubion held by 143rd Infantry. A Company, accustomed to serving in rear areas, had never been under fire nor in contact with the enemy. The engineers, understandably jittery, started firing on each other in what Butler described as case of "buck fever," inflicting more casualties on themselves than on an invisible enemy. Later, these units became experienced infantrymen, but the night's experience had been a tragic baptism of "friendly" fire.

The Emperor Napoléon Bonaparte was given to enquiring of his generals, "Is he lucky?" By that criterion Dahlquist may not have made the grade. Nevertheless, the increasing intensity of German counterattacks confirmed that he had been right to reinforce his defenses along the line of the Roubion before undertaking the orders given to him by Truscott to interdict the German traffic on the N-7. However, in the small hours of the 25th Dahlquist was guilty of misleading Truscott by assuring him that his troops were "physically on the road," the N-7. While small units of the 36th Division may have been present on the N-7 at various times on the 24th, it was incorrect to imply that they controlled the road and had effectively interdicted the enemy's progress along it. This has led some subsequent commentators to suspect that in the heat of battle Dahlquist's grasp of the precise disposition of his troops was to a greater or lesser extent faulty.

Dahlquist's frayed nerves were also tested on the evening of the 24th when the Germans captured a copy of his operational plans for the following day that gave a detailed description of his forces in the Montélimar sector. Wiese exploited this windfall by forming an ad hoc corps under Wietersheim to deal with menace on his flank once and for all. The improvised force included the 11th Panzer and 198th Infantry Divisions, 63rd Luftwaffe Infantry Training Regiment, 18th Flak (antiaircraft) Regiment, and a railway artillery battalion fielding five heavy-caliber railway guns ranging from 270mm to 380mm. It outnumbered Dahlquist's force in the Battle Square by more than three to one. Kniess, whose 85th Corps had crossed the Durance on the night of August 23, was now some thirty-five miles south of Montélimar and was urged to move his force north as fast as he could to funnel it through the Montélimar Gap.

By August 24, the volume of German traffic on the N-7 had intensified, stretching back for miles. As Dahlquist's artillery ranged up and down the road, the German columns inched forward, bumper to bumper. Armor, artillery and horse-drawn transport crawled through a Bosch-like landscape littered with dead and wounded men, the swollen corpses of horses, and burnt-out and smoldering vehicles. Above the N-7 ranged Allied fighter aircraft flying from Corsica. Republic P-47 Thunderbolts, with their powerful armament of eight .50 machine guns and 2,500 lbs of rockets or bombs were particularly effective. One American eyewitness had a grandstand view from the ridge: "We watched as a formation of big-bodied P-47s, with their huge cowls came sweeping up the valley from the south. We were actually looking down on the planes from above." One Thunderbolt "peeled off and knocked out the lead vehicle. Another hit the vehicle in the rear, forcing the entire column to come to a halt. The formation zoomed back around and made several strafing and bombing runs. They tore the convoy to pieces. We could actually see the cannons flashing and the bullets exploding."[3] Still the German columns pressed on, rolling over American roadblocks, as they encountered them, in a matter of hours. The men of the 36th Division could not muster sufficient armor to go toe-to-toe with the 11th Panzer's Mk 4s, Panthers, and the occasional Tiger supported by swarms of infantry. Once the way was clear, German engineers would push the debris aside and the column would resume its running of the gauntlet northward.

In the late afternoon of the 24th, the Germans managed to seize Hills 300 and 294 while men of the 1st and 3rd Battalions, 141st Infantry, still clung to the lower slopes. Throughout the small hours German patrols infiltrated the American positions, pushing Harmony's men off the ridge just before dawn. Harmony ordered his battalions to reform on Hills 430 and 260, northwest of Sauzet, which look down on the Roubion. With the immediate threat from the ridge removed, the 19th Army could resume its retreat down the N-7. Toward midmorning on August 25, Wiese attempted to drive the two regiments of the 36th Division from the entire area to enable the passage of Kniess's corps. His plan of attack, devised by Wietersheim with Dahlquist's captured plans in his hand, was ambitious but overly complicated and was dependent on the ability of its disparate units to arrive at their assembly areas on time and ready to go into action. However, the chaos reigning in the Montélimar Gap made this almost impossible.

❖

Wietersheim had divided the troops under his command into no fewer than six separate task forces or Kampfgruppen: four were drawn from the 11th Panzer—Gruppen Hax, Wilde, Thieme, and Bode; and two were built around the 198th Division's 305th and 326th Grenadier regiments. The formations from 198th Division, reinforced with armor, were to shoulder the brunt of the effort. The 305th Grenadiers were tasked with attacking northeast of Montélimar, seizing the eastern portion of Hill 430, thus sealing the western end of the Condillac Pass, five miles north of Montélimar, before moving northwest to the N-7. It was to be supported on its eastern shoulder by 326th Grenadiers crossing the Roubion near Bonlieu on the boundary between the 141st and 142nd Infantry and then thrusting north. To the west, Gruppe Hax's two panzergrenadier battalions and two Luftwaffe training regiment battalions, reinforced by artillery and armor, were to clear the ground to the north and northeast of Montélimar, the rest of hill 300 and the western slopes of Hill 430. Gruppe Thieme's panzer battalion, stiffened with armor and the 119th Replacement Battalion, was to mass at Loriol and then drive east along the south bank of the Drôme to Grane, five miles southwest of Crest. Meanwhile, Gruppe Wilde, consisting of a panzer grenadier battalion, an artillery battalion, and handful of tanks, was to relieve Gruppe Thieme on the N-7. Bode's reconnaissance battalion, meanwhile, was to move on Puy-Saint-Martin to cut the American lines of communication. The aim of these maneuvers was the isolation and destruction of the weakened Task Force Butler and the dispersed 36th Division; the acceleration of the German withdrawal up the N-7; and the creation of the time and space to deal with the U.S. 3rd Division, advancing slowly up from the south, which had reached Avignon by about 1400 on August 25.

The Germans, however, had committed the cardinal sin of overelaboration. The planned attacks by the 305th Grenadiers and Bode's reconnaissance battalion never got underway. The only effective German success of the day was achieved by Gruppe Thieme, which brushed aside a weak American cavalry screen north of the Drôme on the road from Grane to Allex, briefly threatening Dahlquist's jealously guarded supply lines. The other Kampfgruppen, launching ill-coordinated attacks later in the day, were checked by determined U.S. infantry and concentrated artillery fire from the high ground to the east. Moreover, in focusing on the envelopment of the Americans around Montélimar, the Germans had taken their eye off Hill 300, the northern slopes of which were retaken by 2nd Battalion, 143rd Infantry in the late afternoon of the 25th. Simultaneously, 1st Battalion, 141st Infantry, supported by armor, struck west out of the Condillac Pass and made for La Coucourde, where by 1900 the N-7 was once again blocked. Until darkness fell, observed American artillery fire prevented the Germans from massing for a counterattack, but Colonel Harmony doubted that the roadblock on the N-7 could be maintained throughout the night of August 25 and 26. He was under mounting enemy pressure along his entire front and was unable to reinforce or resupply the roadblock. He favored an overnight withdrawal and the blowing of a number of adjacent minor bridges, but was overruled by Dahlquist who, mindful of Truscott's express orders, instructed him to maintain the roadblock for as long as possible.

Then the weather intervened. Although it was hot, the waters on the Drôme had risen, threatening German movement northward. It seemed that the 19th Army was trapped against two rivers. All the bridges across the Rhône, providing its western exit route, had been destroyed. While to its north the Drôme had swamped its banks and American artillery fire had wrecked any potential crossing sites in the sector. To the south and east only the 11th Panzer and 198th Divisions stood between the Americans and the German forces withdrawing up the N-7.

Now Wietersheim, frustrated by the failure to drive off the Americans and keep the N-7 open, assembled an ad hoc force to deal with the roadblock at La Coucourde and at midnight led a cavalry charge that by 0100 on the 26th had scattered the American blocking force and driven it back into the Condillac Pass. There were still two of Harmony's rifle companies on the northern section of the Hill 300 ridgeline, but they were unable to intervene. Dahlquist's determination to keep the bulk of his force in reserve or in defensive positions—the 142nd and 143rd Infantry had seen little or no action—had enabled Wietersheim temporarily to wrest back the initiative, but stalemate nevertheless ensued. Like two weary heavyweight boxers circling each other in the closing rounds of a punishing fight, neither side had been able to deliver a knockout blow.

Both sides strove to restore their balance. Truscott, alarmed by Kampfgruppe Thieme's move against Dahlquist's supply lines, ordered 45th Division to move the 157th Infantry Battalion and the 191st Tank Battalion into the northern sector of the Montélimar Square. Wiese, smarting over the failure on August 25, disbanded his ad hoc corps, placing the greater part of its remaining forces under Kniess with renewed orders to clear the Montélimar sector. Now acting as the 19th Army's effective rearguard was the 198th Infantry Division, commanded by Major General Otto Richter, an officer viewed with some suspicion by one of his subordinates, Major Georg Grossjohann, a company commander in the 198th Division's 308th Regiment, who saw his superior as "a man more interested in form than function." As a veteran of the Eastern Front, Grossjohann considered that at Montélimar there "was little room for that." A seasoned old soldier, Grossjohann was happy, in his memoirs, to distribute his disdain in equal measure on comrades and enemies.

Early in the morning of August 27, Grossjohann's highly decorated Oberfeldwebel Christian Braun volunteered to take some American prisoners, using a method he had perfected on the Eastern Front. He cut the telephone wires in the enemy's rear and then waited for a repair party to arrive. Grossjohann recalled that the ruse never failed to work. Within an hour Braun and his men returned with a platoon of American infantrymen, including two lieutenants. They had been taken prisoner while resting up in an isolated house, and it required only a short burst from Braun's *Sturmgewehr* automatic rifle, and a loudly barked order to surrender, to persuade the Americans to emerge. Back at Grossjohann's command post, the two officers declined an offer of wine and cigarettes, possibly because they were reluctant to accept something that could not be shared with their men, and, in Grossjohann's words "proved to be exemplary prisoners." The next day, as Grossjohann and his men prepared to break out of the tightening American grip on the Montélimar sector, his prisoners were offered the chance to return to their own lines. This the officers declined, declaring, "No, sir, we are prisoners now." Grossjohann reflected that all they wanted was speedy transportation to a place of safety, a wish that he regretted he could not fulfil. He also recalled that during attacks by their own "Jabos" (short for *Jagdbombers*, ground-attack aircraft) the Americans had "run around in all directions, but afterward I had them all back on my neck! Only a nation, based upon its tremendous material superiority, and being so sure in the end of the war's outcome in their favor, can afford to go to war with fighters like these. Of course there were different experiences with Americans on other occasions."

In his memoirs Gossjohann was equally critical of the German high command's handling of the withdrawal up the N-7. The effectiveness of the two most battle-tested units in the theater, the 198th Infantry and 11th Panzer Divisions, initially placed on the wrong (western) side of the Rhône was further reduced by the mounting volume of rear-echelon units pouring northward along the highway. He considered that Blaskowitz should have been solely concerned about these units if they were needed to bring supplies up to the fighting line. Otherwise, Grossjohann would have ordered them to get out of the way to enable the combat units to operate freely. The painstakingly slow efforts to transfer the 198th and 11th Panzer Divisions to the east bank of the Rhône served only to compound the original error.

Frustration was now mounting on both sides of the hill. Although he had acknowledged Dahlquist's transportation difficulties on August 22, Truscott's patience with his subordinate was wearing thin. On the morning of the 26th he arrived at Dahlquist's headquarters fully intending to sack him. He considered Dahlquist's situation reports and his attempts to interdict the German withdrawal wholly inadequate. Dahlquist's defense, which he was given five minutes to make, was threefold: he had sometimes been misinformed by subordinates about the precise progress and location of the fighting; German pressure on his supply routes at Crest and Puy had demanded the full attention of his reserve force; and the shortage of fuel, transport, and ammunition had made it impossible to block the N-7 and hold the ridgeline on Hill 300. Truscott, who in his Piper L-4 Grasshopper had now flown over the terrain at Montélimar, took a step back and decided to stay his hand, but remained unhappy with the state of affairs he found at 36th Division's headquarters.

Instead, Truscott decided that Task Force Butler should reimpose a roadblock at La Coucourde before moving over the Drôme and on to

Crest to close all the crossing sites on the river. Butler was then to drive north, bypassing Valence, to seize Lyon, in the process preventing the 4th Luftwaffe Field Corps from crossing to the east bank of the Rhône north of Montélimar.* Truscott was to retain control of the main body of the 157th Infantry (minus the 3rd Battalion, assigned to Dahlquist) to aid Butler in closing the crossing sites on the Drôme. At the same time he urged the commander of the 3rd Infantry Division, Major General O'Daniel, to push up to Montélimar by August 27 to relieve some of Dahlquist's units there.

Unfortunately for Truscott, the fighting on August 27 seesawed back and forth inconclusively. The Germans were pushed off the eastern slopes of Hill 300 but still held on to the rest of the ridge. To the south, 141st Infantry drove off enemy attacks on Hill 430 while the cautious Dahlquist retained 142nd Infantry in defensive positions on the Roubion. To the north, the Americans moved into Grane toward the end of the day and cleared Allex, but were still short of the Loriol-Livron sector on the N-7. Outside the Battle Square, to the south, the 3rd Division was moving slowly forward, hampered by transportation problems as well as German minefields, downed bridges, and felled trees, which ensured that when darkness fell it was still four miles short of Montélimar.

Nevertheless, Wiese was looking over his shoulder at O'Daniel's slow but steady progress and growing increasingly anxious about the slow progress of the withdrawing of 85th Corps. He had anticipated that, with the exception of the rearguard 198th Division, all his forces would have crossed the Drôme by the evening of August 27. However, two Kampfgruppen, Hax and Wilde, were still south of the river and the 338th Division had been committed by Kniess to fruitless attacks on Hill 430 and Condillac. German losses of men and materiel in the Battle Square were remorselessly mounting. The railway at Montélimar was blocked by wrecked engines, and the carnage on the N-7 had reached proportions noted by Audie Murphy as his unit reached the outskirts of Montélimar: "A huge enemy convoy has been caught by our artillery fire. In their haste to escape, the doomed vehicles had

* In fact the 4th Luftwaffe Field Corps was able to pass Montélimar, on the west bank of the Rhône, on August 26, largely undisturbed except by air attack.

been moving two or three abreast. Our artillery zeroed in on them. The destruction surpasses belief. As far as we can see, the road is cluttered with shattered, twisted cars, trucks, and wagons. Many are still burning. Often the bodies of men lie in the flames, and the smell of singed hair and burnt flesh is strong and horrible. Hundreds of horses, evidently stolen from the French farmers, have been caught in the barrage. They look at us with puzzled, unblaming eyes, whinnying softly as their torn flesh waits for life to drain from it. We are used to the sight of dead and wounded men, but these shuddering animals affect us strangely. Perhaps we have been in the field too long to remember that innocence is also caught up in the carnage of war."[4]

As night drew in on the 27th, Wiese ordered Kniess to get 338th Division and Hax and Wilde's Gruppen over the Drôme while 198th Division and rearguard engineers held back the U.S. 3rd and 36th Divisions. Once their comrades had crossed the Drôme, the men of 198th Division were to make the crossing as best they could. While Wiese's assessment of the situation was increasingly gloomy, Truscott radiated confidence. On the basis of some doubtful intelligence, he was now convinced that the greater part of the 85th Corps had been destroyed south of the Drôme and that only three German regiments remained in the Montélimar area. With reports coming in that the French were on the point of clearing Toulon and Marseille (see next chapter) he could see the moment approaching when he could turn his attention to the northward drive and the link-up with the Allies driving south from the Normandy bridgehead.

Truscott's orders for the 28th were as follows: 3rd and 36th Divisions were to mop up the enemy forces between the Drôme and the Roubion; Task Force Butler was to push on to and occupy Loriol and Livron; and elements of 45th Division were to move out from Grenoble (liberated on August 22) and head for Lyon. However, Truscott had seriously overestimated the speed of the German withdrawal and underestimated the strength of enemy forces south of the Drôme. On August 28 the 141st Infantry's advance on Montélimar was thrown back by units of the 198th Division supported by artillery. Butler's attack on Loriol was also checked by German armor and anti-tank fire. The attack on Livron, undertaken by the 157th Infantry, was beaten back by the tanks and infantry of the 110th

Panzergrenadiers, which halted the Americans before they reached the outskirts of the town.

The Germans also also brought heavy pressure to bear on the 2nd and 3rd Battalions, 143rd Infantry, defending Hills 300 and 430 and Condillac. American artillery continued to pound the N-7, but the attempt to block the highway at La Coucourde was abandoned. Forward units of 3rd Division had fought their way into the southern outskirts of Montélimar by the evening of August 28 but were unable to secure the town for another twenty-four hours. However, all this came at cost to the Germans. To the south of Montélimar, the 3rd Division overhauled and captured a column of some 350 German vehicles, taking 500 prisoners. By now, Kniess had succeeded in getting Kampfgruppe Hax and a number of other units across the Drôme, but Kampfgruppe Wilde and the 338th Division remained stranded to the south, blocking Task Force Butler. Sundry other units were still fighting at Loriol and around Hill 300, They were all still in place as darkness fell, while the main body of 198th Division was concentrated a few miles north of Montélimar.

During the night of August 28 Kniess ordered Major General Richter, commander of the 198th Division, to break out of the Battle Square in the early hours of the 29th. Richter split his force into three columns, each built around a grenadier regiment and each moving north along a separate route. For Grossjohann's 308th Regiment, the first stage of the withdrawal, the approximately twenty miles from Montélimar to the Drôme River, after which the Rhône Valley widens, was the most problematic as he had been ordered to move through the woods to the east of the N-7. However, Grossjohann was understandably reluctant to tangle with well-armed Americans in this sector of the Battle Square. Moreover, it seemed less than ideal territory for the tanks he had been promised. At dawn on the 29th, Grossjohann and his men set off, the tanks having failed to arrive. Only part of his battalion was with him as the rest were still skirmishing with the Americans. Grossjohann's route march took him away from the woods and along the eastern bank of the Rhône, where his progress was hidden by high swamp grass and brush. He was unfazed by the failure of the tanks to turn up. To deploy the armor "on narrow mountain roads, through the woods with dense undergrowth on each side, where the enemy could lie in wait behind every bush, was especially dangerous for them."

By late afternoon on the 29th, Grossjohann and his men had crossed the Drôme virtually unscathed. Major General Richter* was not so fortunate, having been taken prisoner by 141st Infantry during the skirmishing that erupted during the German withdrawal. In the closing phase of the fighting at Montélimar, three converging American regiments—the 36th Division's 141st and 143rd and 3rd Division's 7th—captured some 1,500 Germans while sustaining casualties of seventeen killed, sixty wounded, and fifteen missing. The 3rd Division's 15th Infantry, in clearing Montélimar itself, took another 450 prisoners. The mopping up operation undertaken by the 3rd Division's 30th Infantry Regiment, which continued throughout the day, bagged several hundred more. By August 31, the Montélimar Battle Square had been cleared and another two thousand prisoners had been taken.

By August 30, the fighting inside the Battle Square was almost over. Livron and Loriol had been secured while the departing Germans contrived to land some small but carefully weighted counterblows on their pursuers. During the night of the 29th they overran two American roadblocks and captured thirty-five enemy troops. American casualties in the Drôme sector on the 29th were some thirteen killed, sixty-nine wounded, and forty-three missing. Throughout the night of August 29 and 30, small parties of Germans continued to cross the Drôme and slip through the American net. Kampfgruppe Wilde pulled out in the afternoon of the 29th, followed by the remnants of the 338th and 198th Divisions. Not so fortunate was the 338th Division's 757th Grenadiers, which was virtually wiped out while defending the Loriol-Livron crossings.

The battle ended with the clearing by 142nd Infantry of the north side of the Drôme on August 31. During the fighting in the Battle Square, the 19th Army had suffered just over 2,100 combat casualties and a further 8,000 captured on either side of the Rhône. American casualties amounted to just under 1,600. Both sides, and particularly

---

* In his memoirs, Grossjohann records his commanding officer's surrender with barely concealed amusement: "Much later, we laid our hands on an old American newspaper in which his (Richter's) capture was described in detail—when a US soldier tried to get him out from behind a bush, he demanded to be taken prisoner by an officer. Of course, I could not judge if the U.S. Army paper reported truthfully, but that he put such great emphasis on good manners certainly sounded right. After all, this was a man who spent an entire evening toasting his subordinates at his own party."

the Americans, viewed the week-long passage of arms through the distorting lenses of missed opportunities and individual initiative. Wiese later described the withdrawal up the N-7 as "almost a miracle," while Dahlquist bitterly blamed himself for allowing the enemy to escape, confessing that he had "fumbled it badly." This was his first combat command, but his cautious style was compounded by the shortages of ammunition and fuel, themselves determined in the planning stages of the campaign, which prevented his superior, Truscott, from inflicting another Cannae, a battle of annihilation, on the 19th Army. In this context criticism can justifiably be laid at the door of Dragoon's overly pessimistic planners, who had not considered the possibility of an early German withdrawal and had not allowed for the provision of more fuel and mechanized forces. Nevertheless, this oversight did not prevent Dahlquist and his subordinate Butler from both acquitting themselves creditably at Montélimar against numerically superior German forces that made concerted attempts to outflank the American positions in the Battle Square and break through northward.

The principal American failure was that although the leading elements of 6th Corps were already northeast of Montélimar by August 21, they were unable to block the N-7 permanently. They also could not identify a main point of attack, but rather launched a series of piecemeal assaults in different places that had the effect of further weakening their already stretched forces. The Germans' six-pronged assault on August 25 committed the same error. In spite of their capture of Dahlquist's orders for August 24, Wiese, Kniess, and Wietersheim were never able to form a complete picture of the strength and dispositions of the enemy they were facing—hardly surprising given the breakdown in Wehrmacht communications—and consequently failed to exploit a number of local tactical successes. Like the Americans, they failed to focus on key aspects of the battle but instead dissipated their strength. Hindsight suggests that by focusing on the retention of Hill 300 while concentrating the rest of their strength on one of the American flanks, possibly at Crest or Puy, they might have hastened their withdrawal while inflicting a heavy blow on their pursuers.

Nevertheless, the withdrawal up the east bank of the Rhône was dearly bought. The 20 percent casualties sustained by the 19th

Army came principally from front-line combat units. By August 31, for example, the fighting strength of the 198th Division had been reduced to 2,800 while the 338th Division's strength had fallen to 1,800. Both formations had lost the greater of their artillery and quantities of other equipment. At the beginning of September, American military intelligence estimated that the 338th Division was only 20 percent effective while it overestimated the 198th Division as 60 percent effective. However, the 11th Panzer had emerged from the Montélimar withdrawal in relatively good shape, a happy state of affairs that it was not long to maintain. It had sustained some 750 casualties, but at the end of the withdrawal still boasted 12,500 effectives. It had saved most of its artillery, the majority of its heavy tanks and three-quarters of its other transport. American intelligence, with some accuracy, rated its effectiveness at about 75 percent. Its survival as a fighting unit had been secured by the reluctance of the German high command to fully commit it to battle but rather employ it principally as a reserve.

The true testament to the bitter fighting lay in the miles of smoldering, smoke-blackened vehicles, some four thousand of them, littering the N-7 for miles on the road to and from Montélimar. During the battle, the senior commanders on both sides made significant errors: Dahlquist, anticipating heavy German counterblows, failed to get a grip on the battlefield while Truscott erred in his estimation of enemy strength north and south of the Drôme; and Kniess managed to convince himself that he was conducting an orderly withdrawal rather than a barely controlled retreat. It can be said, however, that throughout the Montélimar episode great credit on both sides was due to the fighting qualities of the ordinary soldiers and junior officers, both American and German, in immensely exacting conditions. As an indication of the fog of war that drifts over battlefields big and small one can turn to a passage in the history of the 141st Regiment: "In the fighting around Montélimar, operations were often in a confused state. Near Crest a fleeing Jerry motorcyclist approached a crossroad near the Divisional Command Post. Standing there was one of the faithful Division MPs attempting to keep straight the mobile affairs of the 36th [Division]. Seeing the Jerry speeding toward him in frantic flight, the MP, following the dictates of his habits, helpfully waved him on."

"Jumbo" speaks: General Sir Henry Maitland Wilson, Supreme Commander Allied Forces, Mediterranean, outlines the Dragoon plan to fellow commanders. Pictured from left: General Alexander Patch, French War Minister André Diethelm, General Jean de Lattre de Tassigny, Wilson, and General Jacob Devers.

ABOVE: Lieutenant General Alexander Patch, veteran of the Guadalcanal campaign in the Pacific and commander of the U.S. Seventh Army in the South of France. BELOW: Two tough customers: Major General Lucian Truscott, commander of the U.S. 6th Corps, left, and Major General John "Iron Mike" O'Daniel, commander of the U.S. 3rd Division.

ABOVE: Major General John E. Dahlquist, commander of the U.S. 36th Division, and a soldier who attracted criticism for his handling of the 442nd Regimental Combat Team in the Vosges in the autumn of 1944. BELOW: American and French commanders present a comradely face at the Belfort Lion monument commemorating the Franco-Prussian war of 1870–71, which was sculpted by Frédéric Bartholdi, designer of the Statue of Liberty. Pictured from left: General de Lattre de Tassigny, General Devers, General Béthouart, and General de Monsabert, who succeeded General de Larminat as commander of the French 2nd Corps.

Commander with a conscience: General Johannes Blaskowitz, who led Army Group G.

ABOVE: An American soldier inspects a makeshift German artillery position at Beach Red, Cavalaire Bay, housing a captured French 75mm gun. BELOW: Glider-borne troops near Le Muy, August 15, 1944. In the background are CG-4A gliders of the 1st Airborne Task Force.

ABOVE: An LST (Landing Ship, Tank) loading in Italy at the end of July 1944. It has been adapted to serve as a "baby aircraft carrier" to launch reconnaissance aircraft from its flight deck to spot for the 634th Field Artillery Battalion, 3rd Division. BELOW: An M4A4 Sherman, *Saint Quentin*, serving with Combat Command Sudre, which participated in the liberation of Marseille.

ABOVE: Mk V Spitfires of the French 337 Squadron, which flew from Corsica in the opening phase of Dragoon and were later based in mainland France at the airfield near Luxeuil-les-Bains. Shown at left is a wrecked German Fw-190. BELOW: A Maquis machine gun team in action north of Avignon, August 22, 1944.

Allied air power: A B-26G Marauder medium bomber of the 44th Bomber Squadron, 42nd Bomber Wing, heads for Corsica after attacking bridges near Arles, August 6, 1944. The Marauder had the lowest loss rate of any U.S. Army bomber in Europe.

ABOVE: The main armament of the U.S. Navy cruiser *Philadelphia* bombards the 45th Division's target beaches in the Delta landing area. BELOW: American and British airborne troops snatch a quiet moment near Le Muy on the morning of August 15, 1944.

ABOVE: Resistance hero Marc Rainaud, leader of the Brigade des Maures, is awarded the Silver Star by General Patch on August 18, 1944, for his part in the liberation of Saint-Tropez. BELOW: The murk from smoke pots, deposited by the first landing wave, obscures Alpha Yellow Beach as LCVPs (Landing Craft Vehicles, Personnel) bring in men of the 15th Infantry Regiment in the third wave.

ABOVE: Men of the 15th Infantry on Alpha Yellow await orders to move inland. Behind them is an M4 Sherman Duplex Drive amphibious tank that has been disabled by a mine. BELOW: Happy survivors: German troops taken prisoner at Saint-Tropez march into captivity.

A medical battalion of the 45th Division comes ashore. Behind them is LCI-552 (Landing Craft, Infantry).

Men of the 45th Division forge inland aboard an M10 tank destroyer, August 18, 1944.

ABOVE: An M10 of the 636th Tank Destroyer Battalion labors across the rocky Camel Green beach, dubbed "Quarry Beach" by the 36th Division. In the background is an LST. BELOW: An American soldier inspects a 274mm Schneider railway gun abandoned by the Germans ten miles north of Montélimar.

American troops enter Grenoble, August 20, 1944.

ABOVE: Welcome home: A French half-track races past a wrecked Luftwaffe truck near Sainte-Maxime, August 20, 1944. BELOW: A photograph of Toulon taken from above Fort Faron. The Saint-Mandrier peninsula can be seen on the upper left. Shown at top right is the Cap Sicié peninsula.

The French victory parade in Toulon along the Boulevard de Strasbourg, August 26, 1944.

ABOVE: A Panzerturm bunker with a PzKpfw 2 turret near the entrance to the Vieux Port in Marseille.
BELOW: An M4A2 Sherman of Combat Command Sudre fires at German positions in Marseille's Vieux Port, August 25, 1944.

ABOVE: Algerian troops near Notre-Dame de la Garde basilica, August 28, 1944. BELOW: The long view: A French sailor checks a 75mm gun set up at the top of a boulevard in the center of Marseille.

Desperate measures: The freighter *Cap Corse* scuttled by the Germans at the entrance to the Vieux Port in Marseille.

ABOVE: Via Dolorosa: The burnt-out remains of a German column outside Montélimar, including civilian transport commandeered during the retreat. BELOW: An M10 barrels past dead horses in Montélimar, August 30, 1944.

Resistance fighters take cover from Milice snipers in Lyon.

ABOVE: End of the road: A Mk 5 Panther embedded in the façade of the Hôtel Lion D'Or in Meximieux.
BELOW: Dragoon Accomplished: French and American troops join hands in a photo staged for *Stars and Stripes* in Autun, southwest of Dijon.

A forlorn German is marched into captivity by informally dressed members of the Maquis.

FOURTEEN
PASTIS IN MARSEILLE

> "If you can see an opportunity to capture the city, seize it. I can assure you that, by the day after tomorrow, I'll be drinking a pastis in Marseille."
>
> —General Jean de Monsabert, August 20, 1944

As the Americans and the Germans traded blows up the Rhône Valley, two other battles of equal significance to the Allied war effort were being fought on the Mediterranean coast. The Germans had not abandoned the ports of Toulon and Marseille. On the orders of Adolf Hitler, they were to be turned into fortresses and defended "to the last man." If they could not be held, their harbors were to be utterly destroyed, just as had happened at Brest, Cherbourg, Nantes, and Saint-Malo in the north and Cannes and Nice in the south on August 15. When the order to deny Toulon to the Allies arrived on General Wiese's desk, he handed it on to Lieutenant General Johannes Baessler, commander of the 242nd Infantry Division defending Toulon.

Baessler was a seasoned soldier who had been transferred into what had seemed a quiet sector in the summer of 1943. In 1939 he had been Chief of Staff of the 11th Corps in Poland and then in the Netherlands, Belgium, France, and the Balkans, the years of Blitzkrieg triumph. In February 1942, he was promoted to Major General and assumed command of the 9th Panzer Division. In the following November, he took command of the 14th Panzer Division at Stalingrad, where the division was virtually wiped off the order of battle and he was seriously wounded after just over three weeks in the post. He was flown out of the encirclement and judged medically unfit to return to active service until July 1943, when he took command of the static 242nd Infantry Division headquartered in Hyères. The division consisted of approximately 18,000 men, including 5,500 naval personnel and 2,800 Luftwaffe troops, plus naval and army artillery and antiaircraft guns.

Toulon itself lay in a formidable defensive position. The city had grown up around a massive bay behind which rose the limestone masses of three hills, Monts Caume, Faron, and Coudon, rising to 2,500 feet and dominating the heights above the port. All three had been heavily fortified by the German occupiers. Below them lay the Saint-Mandrier peninsula, arching into the Mediterranean and connected to the port by a causeway—the Isthme des Sablettes—which housed numerous gun emplacements, containing fifty-four artillery pieces and seventeen antiaircraft guns. The most formidable items of ordnance in this sector, controlling the approaches to Toulon, were two turrets, each containing two 340mm guns removed from the French battleship *Provence*. The *Provence* had been sunk by the Royal Navy in the harbor at Mers el Kébir in July 1940, refloated, and moved to Toulon. In November 1942, when the Germans occupied Toulon, the French scuttled the *Provence*, only for her to be raised in July 1943 and her guns removed for coastal defense. The batteries on the Saint-Mandrier peninsula were linked by a maze of tunnels containing electric power plants and well-stocked ammunition depots. Access to substantial water supplies anticipated a prolonged siege by the Allies. However, the majority of the guns could not be trained inland.

The landward approaches to Toulon were dotted with anti-tank obstacles, pillboxes, minefields, and more artillery positions. A strongly defended Toulon might have unhinged the Dragoon timetable but for events beyond the control of its defenders. Several days before Dragoon was launched, the senior naval commander in Toulon died of a heart attack and the defense of the city was taken over by Rear Admiral Heinrich Ruhfus, who attempted, not wholly successfully, to evacuate the civilian population, who were by now anticipating the arrival of the Allies. Ruhfus's subsequent assessment of Toulon's defenses confirmed his suspicions that they were strongest in all the wrong places. They were at their weakest on the landward side with scant attention being paid to the northern and western approaches to the city. Much depended on the speed of the Allied assault on Toulon. The city's defenders manned their posts, while in the heavily mined harbor block-ships waited for orders to sail into position to deny the harbor entrance to Allied shipping.

Meanwhile, Truscott was executing some nimble diplomatic footwork to ensure that the French Army B took Toulon. General Patch was concerned about the time the French were taking to come ashore and feared a delay in the launching of a full-scale attack on the city. Truscott believed that the Germans were not holding the city in any great strength and was confident that his 3rd Infantry Division could take Toulon within forty-eight hours. In a meeting with Patch on August 17, he offered to undertake the operation if Patch wished him to do so. Patch briefly considered the offer, but both men quickly agreed that the diversion of the 3rd Division for this purpose would be a mistake that would have grave political repercussions and would make de Lattre de Tassigny, the commander of French Army B, even more difficult to deal with than he had been thus far. Truscott was to drive on to the west, isolating Toulon and Marseille before leaving them to be taken by the French.

In the run-up to Dragoon, de Lattre had planned for the separate, successive seizures of Toulon and Marseille, but the accelerated landings of the French 2nd Corps, and the withdrawal of German forces up the N-7, encouraged him to modify these plans and contemplate the simultaneous capture of the two ports from the north. The French 1st and 3rd Infantry Divisions had arrived in France on August 16, along with the armored combat commands of the 1st Armored Division, followed two days later by the French 9th Infantry Division. Once ashore, de Lattre divided them into five tactical groups, breaking up the armor of 1st Armored into its constituent combat commands to support the infantry formations. In overall command of 2nd Corps was General Edgard de Larminat, who had joined the French Army as a private in 1914, served at Verdun, and had risen to the rank of captain by the Armistice. After the war he served in the colonial infantry in Morocco, Mauretania, and Indochina. In 1939 he was a lieutenant colonel in the Middle East. He refused to acknowledge the French surrender in 1940 and was imprisoned in Damascus, but escaped to join the Free French in Palestine. He subsequently saw action with the 1st Free French Division in North Africa and Italy.

Two of de Larminat's four subordinates in 2nd Corps shared his colonial military background. General Joseph Magnan commanded the 9th Infantry Division, consisting of Senegalese and Moroccan units and the Groupe de Commandos d'Afrique (African Commando Group). General Joseph de Goislard de Monsabert led the 3rd Infantry Division, consisting principally of Algerian troops. His relations with de Lattre were notoriously prickly. The 1st Free French Division, commanded by General Diego Brosset and formed by the first units to rally to de Gaulle after the fall of France, contained troops from mainland France and its colonial empire. Along with the 3rd Infantry Division, it was the most highly decorated French division of World War II. Brosset himself had fought at Bir Hakeim, in North Africa, and Italy. The 1st Armored Division was led by General Jean Touzet du Vigier, who had served as an infantryman with 9th Cuirassiers in World War I. After the war he had served under de Gaulle, training troops in the newly independent Poland, before being bitten by the armored warfare bug. In 1936 he was assigned to the Joint Tactical Studies Center at Versailles, where he became head of the cavalry section. As commander of the 2nd Armored Cuirassier Regiment in 1940, Touzet du Vigier witnessed the fall of France and later, during the Vichy regime, headed a cavalry department at Versailles while making clandestine contact with the nascent Resistance movement. His superiors chose to turn a blind eye to these activities and transferred him to Tunisia. When the Allies invaded French North Africa in November 1942, Touzet du Vigier joined the Free French.

De Lattre's first task was to overcome the concentration of German troops at Hyères, nine miles east of Toulon, which had a fortified harbor housing a heavy concentration of artillery. The town of Hyères lies some two miles from the sea, from which it is separated by dense pine forests. The capture of Hyères's offshore islands, Le Levant and Port-Cros, has been covered in Chapter 10. A town much favored by the British from the 18th century, Hyères's famous visitors included

Queen Victoria and Robert Louis Stevenson. In World War I it was a popular convalescing center for wounded British servicemen. Now its unwelcome guests were Armenian Ost troops of the 242nd Division. By August 19, the French were relieving the 3rd Division's 7th RCT north of Hyères, suggesting that Patch had successfully encouraged de Lattre to move more quickly. On a trip to the front, Truscott met with General O'Daniel west of Brignoles, twenty miles north of Toulon. There he instructed O'Daniel to remain east of Saint-Maximin, blocking the roads into Toulon until he was passed by Combat Command Sudre, still under Truscott's command and driving southwest to cut the coast road. Shortly afterward, Truscott instructed Brigadier General Sudre to push west to cut the coast road at Aubagne before joining French forces to attack Toulon from the west.

Later that day, Truscott received an order from the Seventh Army that CC Sudre was to move to Flassans, twenty miles north of Toulon, where it was be relieved of its attachment to 6th Corp at 2100. Truscott was resigned to the loss of the combat command but was furious that the order for Sudre to move to Flassans meant that his combat command had to about-face and countermarch for some twenty miles against the flow of 6th Corps's traffic on the N-7. Truscott's protests were unavailing. When he met Patch later that day in the latter's headquarters in Saint-Tropez, he was told that de Lattre had been informed of his discomfiture but was not prepared to accommodate him. De Lattre, it seemed, was convinced that the capture of Toulon was going to be a difficult operation and had demanded the transfer of CC Sudre to his command. There was nothing Patch could do. Coalition unity trumped common sense and Truscott was obliged to execute his orders. The result, according to Truscott, was "Traffic congestion and confusion on that road [the N-7] all through the night and much of the following morning . . . for there was neither time to plan or facilities for, strict control. And then, no sooner had Sudre reached the Flassans locality than he was turned around and sent back again over the same road toward the same objectives that I had proposed to him."[1]

On August 19, the attack on Hyères was launched by a regimental combat team of Brosset's 1st Infantry Division, while Magnan's 9th Infantry advanced along the N-7 from the north, sealing off the town. Allied warships bombarded the port sector south of the town, including the island of Porquerolles, the largest and most westerly of the Isles d'Hyères. The honor of opening the bombardment was given to the French battleship *Lorraine*. By August 21, French forces had seized control of Hyères and German positions to the north and east, including the fort on Mont Coudon. Among the Germans who fell into Allied hands was General Baessler, who had been trapped in his divisional headquarters. Command of the forces defending Toulon then passed to Admiral Ruhfus, who from the evening of August 21 was headquartered in the Saint-Mandrier peninsula with orders from Admiral Dönitz, commander-in-chief of the Kriegsmarine, to defend Toulon "to the last cartridge."

Allied air raids on Toulon had begun on August 18, and a day later a bombardment was launched by ships of Western Naval Task Force, during which the destroyer *Fantasque* and the cruiser *Georges Leygues* were hit by German artillery. However, by August 21 naval gunfire had silenced most of the German batteries. The only regiment of the 242nd Division in the immediate vicinity of Toulon, the 918th Grenadier, had lost two battalions in the fighting at Hyères but was now tasked with establishing a perimeter defense north of Toulon in the foothills of Monts Coudon and Faron, which for centuries had been studded with stone fortresses. Now they stood in the path of three French columns descending on Toulon from the north.

French pressure on Toulon built up from the north and the east. To the east of the city, the French had fought their way through to Forte Sainte-Marguerite in La Garde, on the sea cliffs, by August 24. The senior German officer there, Lieutenant Commander Franz, agreed to surrender, declaring, "There have been too many deaths, too many injuries. I cannot continue." With the French, he devised a face-saving paper trail indicating that he had defended the fort to the best of his ability before walking into captivity with six hundred officers and men in mid-afternoon. By the evening, three more strongholds, Carqueiranne, Colle-Noire, and Gavaresse, had capitulated. At Carqueiranne, the senior naval officer surrendered without a fight.

Progress to the north of Toulon followed a similar pattern. Units of Magnan's 9th Division approached Fort Sainte-Catherine and dispatched a reconnaissance party, led by a Major Gauvin, to negotiate with the German garrison. With the help of his driver, an Alsatian who spoke German, Gauvin informed the fort's defenders that their position was hopeless, and shortly afterward took the surrender of the strongpoint and sixty-five officers and men. Gauvin was less successful with the fort at Artigues, where the commander, a Major Fleischhut, refused to surrender, prompting a three-hour barrage. The way to the sea was open to the French, but the fort at Artigues, now isolated, still held out.

The German grip on the western approaches to Toulon was weakening. At the Hôtel de la Tour in Sanary-sur-Mer, ten miles from the center of the city, a battery commander, Lieutenant Kaiser, agreed to terms of surrender, and with his men handed over their weapons. French troops had now surrounded Toulon and were moving into the heart of the city, leaving holdouts like the fort at Artigues completely cut off. The assault on this strongpoint was renewed on the afternoon of the 25th, cheered on by a watching crowd of French civilians. Losing patience with the recalcitrant Fleischhut, Colonel Raoul Salan,* the commander of the 6th Senegalese Infantry Regiment, who had broken into the fort's communications system, threatened the German commander over the telephone with a massacre by his bloodthirsty troops. In the early evening terms of surrender were agreed over a table groaning with beer and cigarettes. The approaches to the fort were de-mined and its garrison of 488 men, 62 of them wounded, marched out into captivity.

Later that day, as the sun set, the garrison at Malbousquet laid down their arms. At 0700 on the 26th, 150 of their wounded were evacuated and 1,450 officers and men emerged from the citadel. The last man to walk out was the commander of the port of Toulon. German resistance now collapsed like a house of cards but not without the occasional soldierly flourish. At noon on August 26, the commander of the fort at Six-Fours told his men, "Soldiers, we have honored ourselves through

* After the war, the highly decorated Salan served as commander of French forces in Vietnam and, controversially, in Algeria. After retiring in 1961 he helped to organize a failed putsch against de Gaulle, then president of France, and became head of the *Organisation armée secrète* (OAS) which sought to disrupt the Évian peace accords over Algeria. He was arrested, charged with treason, and sentenced in absentia to death. The sentence was commuted to life imprisonment and he was pardoned in 1968. Salan died in 1984.

combat. We have attempted the impossible. Over three months our battery has brought down 102 aircraft. Today, surrounded on all sides, we are now powerless. As your commander, I am obliged to avoid a pointless massacre. You are from this moment forward prisoners. Conduct yourselves with dignity. Heil Hitler!"

Admiral Ruhfus and some 1,800 men were now under siege on the Saint-Mandrier peninsula. On the 27th General Magnan's artillery, supported by Allied warships, began a heavy bombardment of the batteries on the peninsula, calling a halt at 1745 to give the Germans there time to reconsider their position. The surrender, when it came, left Ruhfus with no choice but to call it a day. He still had almost two thousand men under his command but was not prepared to send them to their deaths. Nevertheless, he remained a stickler for military protocol and reluctant to disobey his explicit orders to defend the port to the "last cartridge." A get-out-of-jail-card soon appeared in the form of a German propaganda broadcast announcing that the stout defense of Toulon had enabled the 19th Army to cross the Durance River. While this escape had been engineered by the 198th Division's rearguard rather than the defenders of Toulon, it gave Ruhfus the excuse he needed. He threw in the towel, surrendering shortly before midnight. On the morning of August 28, the French rounded up approximately 17,000 prisoners who also handed in huge quantities of arms and ammunition. French casualties had been high, at 2,700, over twice the German losses. Nevertheless, Toulon had been taken a week earlier than had been anticipated and with less damage to the harbor facilities than had been feared. Within three weeks, warships of the French navy sailed back into Toulon's harbor that had been abandoned to the Germans at the end of 1940. One down and one to go.

Forty miles to the west of Toulon was the great commercial harbor of Marseille, the second-largest city in France. This ancient city, founded by the Greeks around 600 B.C.E., contained two harbors: the rectangular Old Port (Vieux Port) around which the city grew up and which is guarded by two impressive forts; and the huge modern harbor to the northwest. Unlike Toulon, Marseilles is not cradled by mountains but is sheltered to the southeast and northeast by ranges of hills and mountain chains. Like Toulon, Marseilles boasted seemingly formidable defenses: on the outskirts of the city roadblocks and minefields; numerous coastal batteries, minefields, and anti-submarine nets around its offshore islands; and concentrations of antiaircraft artillery in the Old Port and modern harbor. Block-ships were moored in the harbor, waiting to be sunk. Also targeted for destruction by the Germans was the massive transporter bridge connecting the quays in the Old Port, designed in 1905 but unused since the 1930s due to lack of maintenance. In early 1943, the Old Port district itself had been badly damaged by the Germans, and its population forcibly evacuated to camps outside the city, as a reprisal following the explosion of a number of bombs by the Resistance.

Tasked with the defense of the city was the 244th Infantry Division, which had been weakened by the transfer of one of its regiments, two of its regimental headquarters, and two artillery batteries. Its remaining formations consisted principally of Volksdeutsche ethnic Germans from Eastern Europe and some 450 Russian and Italian auxiliaries. In all, Marseille's defenders numbered approximately 13,000, including 2,500 from the Kriegsmarine and 3,900 Luftwaffe personnel. The divisional commander was Lieutenant General Hans Schaefer, another veteran of the Eastern Front, who had been badly wounded near Kharkov in June 1943 and had only returned to active duty in April 1944. Schaefer was not convinced of the effectiveness of the defenses in the port sector and the fortified area of La Ciotat to the southeast of the city and had ordered the Kriegsmarine to deploy most of its troops in an infantry role, deploying them as a second line of defense between Marseille's Saint-Marcel and Saint-Jerome districts, to the east of the city. By August 19, many of the outlying defenses of the city had been abandoned but for patrols.

The French advance on Marseille, spearheaded by Touzet du Vigier's 1st Armored Division, was largely unopposed as the concentration of the major German formations on the coast had left the road network unguarded except for military police units, enabling de Lattre to range his forces around the city, exploiting the relatively open ground to the north on either side of Chaine de l'Étoile (Star Mountains). Inside Marseille, the harbor commander, Captain Zoss, reported that he had completed preparations for the demolition of the modern harbor installations and the Old Port. However, it would be a lengthy business, estimated at between four and six days.

There was another factor inside Marseille that was troubling General Schaefer, the French FFI Resistance. Schaefer, clearly a pessimist, estimated the FFI's possible strength at about 80,000. In fact, debilitated by efficient Wehrmacht and SS "anti-terrorist" measures, it now numbered only some 500 armed activists. However, the Résistants in Marseilles had been massively encouraged by events in Paris in August. As late as August 13, two days before the launching of Dragoon, Pierre Laval, Petain's deputy head of state, had returned to the French capital in the hope of reconvening the Chamber of Deputies to accord him powers as a legitimate head of government who might treat on sovereign terms with the liberating Allies. However, it was clear to the city's civilian population that the days of German occupation were numbered, and armed resistance broke out in the streets. On August 18, the Paris police force had raised the flag of revolt on the Île de la Cité, prompting the left-wing FTP to rally to the cause. By August 20, the German garrison was under such pressure to maintain order in the city that the military governor of Paris, General Dietrich von Choltitz, was obliged to negotiate a truce. In Marseille feelings also ran high, particularly in the small towns on the city's outskirts where support for the Resistance was highest. Attempts by the Germans to establish outposts in these districts were often thwarted by armed insurgents. If anything, the Résistants in Marseille were more effective than their counterparts in Paris, not least in their ability to alarm the apprehensive Schaefer and disrupt his attempts to defend the city.

Another man whose resolve was wavering was the German consul general in Marseille, Freiherr Edgar von Spiegel, a World War I submariner and from 1942 an SS *Oberführer* (colonel), who advised Schaefer to spare the dock facilities at Marseille. Schaefer was reluctant to do this, but delayed giving the go-ahead by some sixteen hours to enable Spiegel to seek permission from OKW to countermand the demolition. Unsurprisingly, OKW did not reply, but Schaefer then approached the harbor commander, Captain Stoss, with an order to spare the Old Port and the road that ringed it, which was also scheduled for destruction. This intervention proved to be crucial to the rehabilitation of the dock facilities at Marseille following the German surrender.

A second intervention, this time on the French side, also had a direct bearing on the fate of the Old Port. De Lattre had ordered Monsabert's

3rd Infantry Division to move into Marseille's northeastern suburbs and hold them. De Monsabert had other ideas. He informed one of his subordinates: "If you see an opportunity [to capture the city] seize it. I can assure you that, by this time tomorrow, I'll be drinking a pastis in Marseille." On the evening of August 20, Monsabert attacked with the 7th Algerian Infantry Regiment, two shock battalions, and the armored units of CC Sudre from the 1st Armored Division. The immediate effect of the arrival of these elements of the French 3rd Division in the eastern outskirts of Marseilles was to spark a popular insurrection and the establishment of a "provisional government" inside the city. At this point, however, the Resistance lacked the strength to wrest control of Marseille from its occupiers. Nor did the Germans have the ability to crush the revolt.

On August 21, the German anti-tank positions in Aubagne, on the eastern edge of Marseille, were overrun after a sharp fight in which the French colonial troops went in at bayonet point. On the same day, Monsabert sent in two battalions of the 7th Algerian Regiment with orders to push into Marseille from the north. The route they chose lay across a mountain range two thousand feet high that brought them down into the La Valentine and Les Olives districts in the city's 11th arrondissement. In Les Olives the colonial troops surprised dozens of German soldiers stripped to the waist and enjoying the sun.

Inside Marseille, FFI forces surrounded the naval hospital and attempted to seize the post office in the Old Port, where they were dispersed by overhead fire from antiaircraft guns. De Lattre was attempting to restrain Monsabert until the arrival of forces released from Toulon while at the same time taking an anxious note of American reports, derived from Ultra, of the 11th Panzer's approach to Avignon. Meanwhile, Monsabert, champing at the bit and convinced that the German forces in Marseille were too weak and disorganized to offer much resistance, gave the commander of the 7th Algerian Regiment, Colonel Abel Chapuis, a free hand to thrust into the heart of the city.

On the morning of the 23rd, Chapuis's men were greeted with cheers, flowers, and kisses from the overjoyed civilian population. Guiding the 7th Algerian Regiment down La Canebière, an impressive boulevard running down to the Old Port, was an army chaplain, Captain Jean Croisa.

Suddenly the column's progress was interrupted by shellfire from the Saint-Jean and Saint-Nicolas forts, which guarded the north and south entrances to the Old Port, and the arrival by car of representatives of the FFI. They told Croisa that they had a plan: they would inform Schaefer that they had captured Spiegel, who was now in their hands. Croisa then telephoned Schaefer and persuaded the general to meet at 1600. The meeting, held behind German lines, was also attended, to Schaefer's considerable astonishment, by General Monsabert. The meeting opened with the discomfited Schaefer raging against Marseille's Resistance fighters, whose actions, he legitimately claimed, had caused the Old Port to become a combat area and thus a target for the German artillery firing from the harbor forts. The meeting closed with both sides demanding an armistice.

Monsabert was allowed to leave and the battle was resumed at 1900. According to de Lattre, the fighting was confused and untidy: "In a few yards, one passed from the enthusiasm of a liberated boulevard into the solitude of a machine-gunned avenue. In a few turns of the track, a tank covered with flowers was either taken by the assault of pretty, smiling girl or fired at by an 88mm shell." By the end of the day, the 7th Algerian Regiment had reached the waterfront. On the 25th, Monsabert's troops captured the cathedral of Notre Dame de la Garde, a massive 19th-century basilica, topped with a gilded statue of the Virgin Mary, which dominates the Old Port. Monsabert had forbidden artillery barrages or air raids on the cathedral. It was to be taken by infantry supported by the tanks of CC Sudre. There were German positions around Notre Dame de la Garde but, as it turned out, none within it. At 0600 on August 25, troops of the 7th Algerian Regiment began to move cautiously up the slope toward the cathedral under heavy German fire.

With the aid of a French soldier, Pierre Chaix-Bryan, who was familiar with the street layout, an indirect route into the cathedral was taken by some Algerian riflemen through a house on rue Cherchell (now rue Jules Moulet).* Inside they found a priest, some Franciscan monks, and seventy-four German soldiers seeking sanctuary from the city's vengeful civilian population. Meanwhile, the fate of the

---

* Today a nearby plaque commemorates the spot.

cathedral hung in the balance. German positions in the harbor were now in the French line of fire from around Notre Dame de la Garde and Schaefer came under increasing pressure to bring his guns to bear on the cathedral. He held firm, and on the morning of the 26th resumed his dialogue with Monsabert, writing: "I take the liberty of informing you that the German [companies] located in the vicinity of the cathedral . . . had been subjec[ted] to repeated mortar and machine gun fire from the church. Up until now, I have rejected all [artillery requests] to shell the structure. However, should this fire continue, I shall be forced, much to my regret, to hold you responsible for the fate of Marseille's sacred shrine."

Predictably, Monsabert took a different view. While thanking Schaefer for sparing Notre Dame de la Garde, he denied that his division had occupied the cathedral and stated that French fire was coming from around it but not from it. The fighting continued. During the afternoon tanks from the 1st Armored Division were maneuvering on the approaches to the cathedral. One of them, *Jeanne d'Arc*, took a direct hit that killed its crew.* A second tank, the *Jourdan*, hit a mine and was disabled, but continued firing from cover. Its wounded commander, a Sergeant Lolliot, climbed out of the tank and attached the *Tricoleur* to the cathedral's railings. In mid-afternoon a section of 1st Company, 7th Algerian Regiment stormed the hill on which the cathedral stood and the *Tricoleur* was hoisted on the bell tower. German fire was still coming in from Fort Saint-Nicolas but the cathedral was unscathed.

While German positions in the north and south of Marseille were being mopped up one by one, Schaefer, increasingly isolated, held on in the Old Port. Its dank underground shelters were crammed with naval personnel, many of them wounded. Smoke from the fighting drifted into the shelters and into a railway tunnel at Cap Janet, in the north of the city, where hundreds of civilians had taken refuge. In a bizarre turn of events they were fed and cared for by German military personnel. On the evening of the 27th, Schaefer wrote another letter to Monsabert in which he confessed: "The situation confronting my forces has changed entirely since our August 23 conversation. The majority of positions have surrendered after an honorable resistance.

* *Jeanne d'Arc* can be seen today, preserved in situ.

In light of the superior forces engaged against us, the continuation of the struggle will have no result beyond the total annihilation of the forces remaining under my command. I therefore request for the evening, at 2130, an armistice that will allow the agreements of honorable surrender conditions for the morning of August 28. In the absence of such agreement, we will fight to the last man."

When the two men met at 0800 the next day, the first item on the agenda was the de-mining of the harbor. Its commander, Captain Stoss, who had drawn up all the demolition plans, had been killed in the fighting for the Old Port, and his plans had been destroyed, possibly by himself. Ongoing demolitions were halted at midday. Only then did German engineers come forward to begin the dismantling of the mines and explosives seeded in the harbor and its approaches. German troops also stood guard over magazines and weapons stores until they could be handed over to the French. The Old Port was now clogged with seventy-five sunken ships and the remains of the transporter bridge, which had been partially demolished on August 22. The Germans had wrecked some 260 cranes, and the merchant ship *Cap Corse* blocked the Old Port entrance between Fort Saint-Nicolas and Fort Saint-Jean. Behind it stretched a vista of oil-blackened water, smashed concrete, and twisted metal. One significant item of machinery, the giant floating crane *Goliath*, had been spared, thanks to the venality of an Austrian harbor official who pocketed 200,000 francs from the Marseille Chamber of Commerce for towing it out of the harbor before the city was retaken by the French.

The Germans had wrought havoc in Marseille, but the total destruction of its modern harbor facilities, vital to the Allies, had been prevented by the prompt action of French anti-scorch teams. They had poured cement into the primer ducts leading to preset demolition charges, and in so doing had prevented the destruction of several quays. The Operation "Caique" team, led by a French engineer, prevented the sabotaging of the pipeline terminal at Port-de-Bouc, vital to the operational plans of the Seventh Army, and also refloated three tankers. Within three weeks of liberation, Liberty ships were able to unload alongside one of Marseille's quays.

The liberation of Marseille was accompanied by wild jubilation. Unlike Paris, it had fallen after an entirely French assault and was only the second French city, after Toulon, to be liberated in this way. On August 29, de Lattre, tearing himself away from the pursuit of Army Group G in the north, participated in the victory parade alongside de Gaulle's ministers for war and the interior, and watched what was for the general "the unforgettable and poignant procession of all the makers of this second victory—the *tirailleurs*, the Moroccan Tabors, troopers, zouaves, and gunners—followed by the motley, fevered, bewildering mass of the FFI, between the two lines of a numberless crowd, frenzied, shouting with joy and enthusiasm, whom the guardians of order held back."

French casualties in the retaking of Marseilles were 1,825 killed and wounded. Some 11,000 Germans surrendered at the end of the fighting, which came about a month earlier than the Allies had calculated, on D+13 rather than D+45. In spite of the thorough job the Germans had made of the demolition of the harbor facilities, Marseille was rapidly restored as a working port by American engineers. On September 15 the first Liberty ship arrived to disgorge its cargo, and by the end of the month Marseille had taken delivery of over 100,000 tons of cargo. By October, Marseille, Toulon,* and other ports in southern France had were receiving over 500,000 tons of cargo a month to feed Eisenhower's broad front drive into Germany.

* At the end of October the Americans handed Toulon back to the French for the landing of civilian supplies.

FIFTEEN
THE DRIVE TO DIJON

"We were aware of the armor fighting in the center of the village. We had no anti-tank weapons with us. We had only rifles. Herb and I went back toward the center of the town, on our side of the east-west street, in search of some weapons. We located a bazooka as well as a rifle grenade launcher with an anti-tank grenade, then we headed back to our position. Someone asked us what we were doing and I, in my smart-mouth way, said we were going 'tiger hunting'."

—PFC Robert A. Schmuhl,
A Company, 179th Infantry
Regiment, 45th Division

On August 25, with the fighting around Montélimar coming to the boil, Lieutenant General Patch was working on the next stage of the campaign in southern France. Ultra-derived intelligence was still playing an important part in shaping the implementation of the Seventh Army's pre-assault plan. A decrypt intercepted on the 25th and received by Patch three days later revealed German plans to regroup around Dijon, some two hundred miles to the north of Montélimar, and to employ the 11th Panzer Division to shield the forces retreating to the east of the Rhône. Truscott's 6th Corps was to maintain the pursuit up the N-7, first to Lyon, France's third city, and then on to Dijon, with French forces covering his left flank. Because de Lattre had yet to complete the retaking of Toulon and Marseille, and the securing of the coastal area around them, French participation in the early stages of this unfolding plan was necessarily going to be limited.

The U.S. 6th Corps's and Seventh Army's eastern flank was to be secured by FABTF from the mouth of the Var, near Nice, and north into the Alps for about sixty miles to the pass at Larche, which connects Barcelonnette, in France, with Cuneo in Italy. Once the clash at Montélimar had concluded, 6th Corps was to drive north and northeast to a line extending from Grenoble to Lyon. As the French disengaged from the Toulon/Marseille sectors, they were to be assigned sectors on the northward advance. On August 28, Patch ordered Truscott to move on Dijon as soon as possible, with Lyon as his first major objective. Meanwhile, the French were to reconnoiter west and southwest of Avignon, simultaneously pushing forces north to support the advance on Lyon. The French were also tasked with supporting Truscott's right flank by pushing east of Lyon before tilting the axis of their advance toward the Rhine River through the Belfort Gap, a plateau lying between the northern rim of the Jura Mountains and the southern edge of the Vosges range, and a significant military highway since Roman times.

De Lattre was unhappy with these orders. If carried out to the letter, they would divide his French Army B into several parts: two to shield the U.S. Seventh Army's eastern and western flanks; and two more on Truscott's flanks on the drive to Lyon. This would leave de Lattre, with his relatively weak logistical support, hard pressed to push through the Belfort Gap. However, he was able to reach a compromise with Patch. The FABTF was to hold the area from the Mediterranean to the Larche Pass. North of Larche, responsibility would devolve on de Lattre. To the west of the Rhône, Patch conceded that a small reconnaissance force would operate in conjunction with FFI forces. De Lattre then agreed to send his reassembled 1st Armored Division up the west bank of the Rhône as soon as possible. To the east of the Rhône, he would guard Truscott's right flank as he pushed north from Grenoble. Once Lyon was taken, de Lattre was to redeploy east of 6th Corps for a drive through the Belfort Gap and on to the Rhine.

By now, Patch envisaged the liberation of Lyon principally as a stage in the Allied progress to the German border rather than as a chance to finish the uncompleted job at Montélimar. However, a soldier with the terrier-like qualities of Truscott was unlikely to ignore another chance to maul a retreating foe. Lyon was a likely candidate for such a confrontation. Located at the confluence of the Rhône and Saône Rivers, Lyon is France's third city and an important road and rail hub. Its seizure would hand the Allies an important logistical and propaganda victory.

Lyon also lay athwart the two most likely German routes of withdrawal: that which ran northeast through Bourg-en-Bresse and Besançon to the Belfort Gap; and an alternative that struck north through the Saône Valley to Dijon. The latter escape route would enable Army Group G to join hands with other forces facing Eisenhower's Expeditionary Force or, by continuing eastward, make for the safety of the Belfort Gap. The first option, Lyon-Besançon, was shorter but featured many defiles, ideal for American and French interdiction, as had happened at Montélimar. The Lyon-Dijon route was easier and faster. Truscott's G-2 section thought that Blaskowitz would take the Lyon-Dijon route, followed by an eastward realignment into the Vosges, where the 19th Army could anchor its southern flank on Belfort and the Swiss border while still joining hands in the north with Army Group B.

Truscott's intelligence men guessed correctly. OB West ordered Army Group G to project its right wing through Dijon to establish a defensive line with the retreating Army Group B from Besançon to the Swiss border. This would screen the approaches to the Belfort Gap while establishing a German salient west of the Vosges. This decision also coincided with Hitler's growing conviction that the Allied eastward drive through northern Europe was beginning to lose momentum. He likened it to the force of "a wave according to the laws of nature, the more it expands . . . the more it runs on into ever vaster regions."* OB West had also correctly estimated that the Allies' advance across a broad front would inevitably bring with it serious supply problems. Armed with this information, Hitler saw a chance of turning the tables on the Allies with an armored counteroffensive launched

* This observation confirms the folly of Barbarossa, which Hitler seems to have conveniently forgotten.

from the Vosges.* At a conference on September 1, he described the area west of the Vosges as a strategically vital sector from which such an operation could be mounted against the southern flank of Patton's U.S. Third Army, which was straining at the leash to cross the Rhine in the area of Worms. For very different reasons, Blaskowitz urged the holding of the salient to facilitate the extraction of the German 64th Corps withdrawing from the Atlantic coast.

Blaskowitz and Wiese, with Montélimar still weighing on their minds, were understandably fearful that the Seventh Army might attempt another envelopment north of Lyon. Their alarm had been stoked by mistaken intelligence that American forces had already bypassed Lyon to the east. More accurate but no less worrisome was the fact that since August 24 an FFI uprising was underway in Lyon. On that day, workers and FTP guerillas in the city's Villeurbanne quarter rose up against the occupiers. As in the Vercors, the action was gallant but premature. Thousands of German troops were now streaming through the city, and General Wiese could ill afford the possibility of losing an escape route over bridges spanning the Rhône. He moved quickly to quash the uprising.

Unlike Wiese, the Lyon insurgents had to wrestle with a dilemma. Was Lyon to be liberated wholly by an internal insurrection or should its citizens wait for an Allied intervention? Communist and leftist Resistance factions, supported by FTP fighters, saw the insurrection as a means of seizing power before the arrival of the Allies, presenting them with a fait accompli. De Gaulle, with the backing of the FFI and de Lattre de Tassigny, strained every sinew to establish order behind authorities that recognized the General's provisional government. The regional chief of R-1, Alban Vistel, was an FFI man while one of his subordinates, Henri Provisor, responsible for Lyon to the west of the Rhône, was with the FTP and an advocate of an uprising within the city.

Another subordinate, Marcel Descour, responsible for Resistance activities to the east of the Rhône, was a former regular in the French

* Hitler's high command regarded his proposal with deep scepticism. Field Marshal Model, from August 17 Commander in Chief West, observed, "There seems to be a belief that it is still possible to mount attacks here. Were my situation estimates not submitted to the Führer? . . . I simply cannot keep commanding in this way."

Army, in contact with U.S. 6th Corps and an advocate of waiting for Allied troops to arrive. Vistel sat on the fence but could not help but be impressed by the fervor of the Résistants in Lyon. On August 24 the prison at Montluc* in the city's 3rd arrondissement, a grim place of torture that had once held de Lattre and the Resistance hero Jean Moulin, was liberated by General Marie-Pierre Koenig, defender of Bir Hakeim and from June 1944 commander of the FFI. Koenig had entered the prison in a stolen German staff car while posing as a Gestapo officer and had persuaded the prison's governor to free his prisoners on the orders of the head of the Gestapo in Lyon, the notorious Klaus Barbie.**

By the end of August, Lyon was surrounded by thousands of FFI fighters. Nevertheless, it was now abundantly clear to all the factions within the Resistance that any uprising should be coordinated with the Allied advance into the city. For his part, Truscott was most reluctant to become entangled in a house-to-house battle for Lyon when precise German intentions remained unclear. Moreover, he was still preoccupied with shuttling scant fuel supplies to Dahlquist at Montélimar. Aware that both he and de Lattre would be hard-pressed to release substantial combat units for the advance to the north, Truscott ordered General Eagles, the commander of the 45th Division, to reconnoiter from Grenoble to Lyon. On August 28, the 45th Division's 179th Regiment moved north, joined by the 157th Regiment, then stationed in the area Crest/Livron. If a situation arose in which it was deemed necessary to move into Lyon, Truscott judged that the task could be accomplished by the 36th Division, freed from the fighting at Montélimar by September 1 and now advancing up the Rhône. Truscott aimed to bypass Lyon and had his eyes eyes fixed on Bourg-en-Bresse, thirty-five miles to the northeast. The combative Truscott calculated

* Montluc was a former French military prison used by the Gestapo after November 1942 as a prison, interrogation center, and internment camp for those in transit to concentration camps. In mid-August 1944 prisoners were taken from Montluc to an airfield at Bron where 109 of them, including 72 Jews, were executed in the so-called "Charnel House of Bron."

** Barbie, the "Butcher of Lyon" had been responsible for the torture and death of many Résistants, including Jean Moulin. After the war he assisted American intelligence with information about French Communists. The United States resisted all attempts to bring Barbie to trial before helping him to flee to Bolivia.

that the swift capture of Bourg might offer another chance to trap and destroy the retreating enemy.

Truscott was now in possession of a wealth of intelligence supplied by the Seventh Army's G-2 and attached OSS agents. One of the latter, Captain Justin Greene of the Strategic Services Section, had been attached to the 36th Division since the landings of August 15. Once Grenoble had been liberated, Greene assembled a number of French agents who had been working for the OSS and tasked them with obtaining information from the Rhône to the Alps. Two of them were members of Penny Farthing, the network controlled by Henry Hyde. They were infiltrated into Lyon where they obtained the complete German plan for the defense of the city, which was passed on to a delighted General Dahlquist as his division approached its outskirts.

On August 29, Generals Patch, Devers, and Wilson had met with de Lattre at Saint-Tropez. The history of the Seventh Army records that when the subject of an insurrection in Lyon was raised. "General de Gaulle's military representative warned against 'premature action.' On August 30, the FFI at Lyon was given orders to be ready to establish contact with the Allied columns, which were rapidly closing on the city's suburbs. The enemy was to be harassed but not actively engaged. An all-out attack was to take place only in cooperation with troops of the American and French armies."

In Lyon, Blaskowitz's overriding mission was that of pushing his units as rapidly as possible into and through the city before it was engulfed by chaos. The 4th Luftwaffe Field Corps, which had escaped largely unscathed up the west bank of the Rhône, was responsible for the restoration of order and holding the passage through the city open throughout the night of August 31, by which time all of Blaskowitz's units were expected have passed through. Anticipating that the Americans would move on Bourg-en-Bresse, Blaskowitz ordered the 11th Panzer Division to destroy all the bridges over the Rhône and Ain rivers east of Lyon. The Lyon to Bourg highway was as important to him as it was to Truscott, as it would provide flank protection for Wiese's 19th Army. These tactical considerations were to lead to the last serious clashes in this theater around the town of Meximieux, ten miles northeast of Lyon and fifty miles west of the Swiss border.

Today, Meximieux is a pleasant little town that bears few of the scars of war. But in early September 1944 it was the scene of small-scale but fierce fighting during the closing stages of Truscott's northward drive. With no apparent German resistance in the area to the immediate northeast of Lyon, the 45th Division's 179th Infantry Regimental Combat Team, commanded by Colonel Henry Meyer, was ordered to occupy Meximieux and support the 157th and 180th Regiments' northward push to Bourg. The Germans had started to withdraw from Meximieux on August 23 with the aim of forming a new defensive line in the Vosges mountains. Posters printed by the town's Committee of Liberation began to appear in Meximieux, urging the local population to hit back at the occupiers. The next day some sixty FFI fighters attacked a small German outpost at Meximieux, taking its occupants prisoner. As the tempo of the German withdrawal increased, abandoned positions were taken over by Maquisards waiting for the Americans to arrive.

On August 25 Meximieux was bombed by American aircraft. Excitement mounted and church bells were rung to herald the approach of Allied forces. *Tricoleurs* appeared in windows and toasts were exchanged in the town's cafés. On August 31, a single U.S. Army jeep roared into Meximieux and was swamped by joyous locals, one of whom noted: "An American jeep pops out from the road to Charnoz with four men on board . . . The American scouts are surrounded by the crowd . . . Solid and smiling, they are perfectly reassuring. They announced the arrival of the American contingent, then they make a tour of the town and disappear."

The jeep was soon followed by Meyer's regimental combat team, preceded by a small boy waving the Stars and Stripes. The RCT drove through the town and took the road north to Chalamont, where it was strafed by two German aircraft. The flags and posters in Meximieux were quickly taken down. The next American unit to arrive was the understrength 1st Battalion, 179th Regiment, commanded by Lieutenant Colonel Michael Davison. The battalion headquarters was established in the local railway station and defensive positions were thrown up around the town. Anticipating that any enemy attack was almost certain to be launched from the west, Meyer neglected to place a guard on the Chazey Bridge over the Ain River to the east of the town. During the night of the 31st, German infiltrators took the bridge from a Maquisard patrol, who had mistaken them for Americans, and blew it up in the small hours. Five miles to the west of Meximieux, where F Company was manning a roadblock with one hundred FFI fighters, the Germans took the position by surprise, capturing three hundred men.

Colonel Meyer was unaware of these developments. Early the next day, all seemed quiet at Meximieux and Valbonne, five miles to the southwest. He recalled, "I found there was no news, everything was going as scheduled, so I mounted the jeep and in high spirits took up off north to watch the action of the [2nd] Battalion which was 'up front' [manning a roadblock at Valbonne]." Meyer's quiet start to the day was then rudely interrupted by the sound of gunfire to the south, which he initially dismissed as a skirmish between the 1st Battalion and a stray German unit. This was followed by more alarming news. He was told by his executive officer, Colonel Preston Murphy, that "there was a distant threat of tanks to the southwest." Then the communications net dropped.

The German attack about to descend on Meximieux was made by a Kampfgruppe consisting of elements of the 15th Panzer Regiment, 209th Panzer Regiment, and 111th Panzergrenadier Regiment of the 11th Panzer Division. At about 0900 on September 1, the Kampfgruppe attacked from the northeast and southwest. The first American position to come under threat was Davison's CP at the railway station, which was attacked by infantry supported by tanks. One of them, a Mk 5 Panther,* was destroyed by 155mm artillery fire, discouraging its three companions from pressing home the attack. They held back at a distance of eight hundred yards, lingering like vultures, before Davison's men, aided by the FFI, drove the German infantry back after a fierce firefight.

By 1000, Murphy, now temporarily in command at Meximieux, realized that he had a real battle on his hands rather than a brush with

---

* The Mk 5 Panther main battle tank, the German answer to the Red Army's T-34, entered production in November 1942 and first went into action at Kursk in the summer of 1943. After teething problems had been ironed out, it became a formidable weapon, equipping one of each panzer regiment's two battalions. Its principal characteristics, unchanged in three versions, were its 75mm L/70 gun, sloped glacis, wide tracks, and interleaved suspension.

German stragglers. He had to deal with the Mk 4 and Mk 5 Panthers of the counterpunching 11th Panzer Division. From his headquarters in a former convent, he ordered the 2nd Battalion back to Meximieux and requested armored and anti-tank reinforcement from 45th Division's headquarters at Voiron. Throughout the morning German probes from the east and west had been turned back but the perimeter of his defenses was buckling. Wounded Americans and Maquisards were arriving at the convent, where they were treated in the basement by American and French doctors. The FFI outpost at Pérouges, on the northwestern outskirts of Meximieux, which had been reinforced with two tank destroyers, was also under attack. The tank destroyers were abandoned. One had run out of fuel and the other's turret had jammed. The Germans drained the gas from the TD with the jammed turret, filled up its still-operational companion and drove it around Meximieux.

Colonel Murphy, who was still waiting for word from the 2nd Battalion, Colonel Meyer, and 45th Division's General Eagles, decided to pull his perimeter defenses back into Meximieux. The Maquisards were now fighting alongside their American allies in a pitched urban battle, a rare if not unique event in the war in France. Colonel Davison deployed his two tank destroyers back-to-back in the town's main street, the rue de Genève, covering the two principal roads into Meximieux. The Germans put in their main effort in the early afternoon, when six tanks rolled into the town from the south with infantry perched on their turrets. Heavy American fire forced the infantry to leap off while the tanks ground down the main street toward the *Hôtel de Ville* (City Hall), toppling its tower with a single round. Davison takes up the story: "The first tank, knocked out by the M-10 (tank destroyer) burst into flames and ran into the lobby of the [Hôtel] Lion D'Or. Then the second was hit. The third and fourth got into high gear and charged the tank destroyer, scraping the paint as it went. But the other tank destroyer knocked it out. Number 4 tank went by the TD; Number 5 not sure. Meanwhile the tank destroyer was reloaded and hit Number 4 and D Company hit Number 5 with a mortar, and blew it to hell."

The smoldering hulks of Wietersheim's tanks bore testimony to the bitter fighting around Meximieux. The American artillery also played a significant role in blunting the 11th Panzer's backhand blow. The Morning Report of the 189th Field Artillery noted: "At approximately 1100 a strong force of enemy tanks and infantry attacked roadblocks northeast, north, northwest, southwest and south of the Battery A position, thus forming almost a complete ring around a wide area on three sides of Meximieux, and at some points coming between the battery position and the infantry. The battery kept on firing until afternoon when a message was dropped from a liaison plane saying that enemy tanks were approaching little more than one thousand yards away. The four guns of Battery A fired 223 rounds of HE [high-explosive] and twenty rounds of smoke in meeting the attack. After the attack had begun, ammunition at the battery position was running low. The battery ammunition train . . . was dispatched down to the only available highway, even though it was doubtful if the road was still in the possession of our troops. The train got through. On the return trip, the train had to cross the bridge at Loyettes, which was under heavy enemy rocket fire. An officer at the bridge stopped the convoy, inquired the destination, and upon learning that Battery A was near Meximieux told the drivers there was nothing but enemy troops in that area since the enemy breakthrough. The train moved on regardless and safely ran the gauntlet of enemy fire back to Battery A with much-needed ammunition, arriving at a time when the enemy was closest. It was a trying time for Battery A but every man responded superbly."

By late afternoon on September 1, the 11th Panzer began to pull back, having been ordered by Wiese to form a defensive ring around Bourg. Wiese had correctly deduced that the Americans had decided not to push into Lyon but rather to strike northeast. A token force of infantry and two tanks stayed behind on the Ain to keep the Americans occupied. During the evening the Germans used the tank destroyer they had appropriated on September 1 in an attack on the 19th-century château to the north of Meximieux that was held by a combined force of Americans and FFI fighters. Hand-to-hand fighting also raged around the convent. An FFI commander whose nom de guerre was Captain Clin reported: "The Maquis lads were at all the doors, all the windows. The order was to hold until reinforcements arrived, but not to waste ammunition. An enemy detachment climbed over the walls, slid into the courtyard and deployed in ditches. After heavy firing, the barrage stopped all of a sudden. The Germans let us know through prisoners of war that they demanded our surrender. They advised the 'terrorists' [the FFI] not to obey their chiefs because they are all sleazy foreigners (*métèques*). Maybe they believed it, but they were quickly interrupted by a loud 'merde.' Gunfire sprayed from all the windows. One of our patrols sneaked into the courtyard and moved up within a yard of the Germans, whose chief was knocked out by one of our lads. Ten minutes later we had chased off all our assailants. A second attempt to climb over the wall was stopped cold by our machine guns. We sent out a strong reconnaissance detachment. We got word back; the Germans were withdrawing."

In the fight for Meximieux, FFI casualties were thirty-nine killed and forty wounded. The Americans suffered eleven killed, thirty wounded, and fifty taken prisoner, plus two M10 tank destroyers, two M8 armored cars, and a number of vehicles. The Germans lost eighty-five men killed, forty-one captured, twelve tanks, three self-propelled guns, and several vehicles. To this day the memory of the battle at Meximieux is kept alive. Colonels Murphy and Davison were made honorary citizens of the town. Davison, who in 1972 became the commander of US forces in NATO and subsequently the commandant at West Point, has a square in the town named in his honor.

On the morning of September 2, there was no sign of the Germans in Lyon, although they had left their customary calling card in the destruction of all but one of the bridges over the Rhône and most of those over the Saône. Toward midday an advanced patrol of the 142nd Regiment, 36th Division, reached the center of Lyon guided by Tony Brooks ("Alphonse") one of SOE's most effective agents and founder of the "Pimento" sabotage organization that had paralyzed German railway movements in southern France immediately after D-Day. The next day Lyon teemed with Maquis fighters and Allied Jedburgh units. Among them was the American OSS officer Major Alfred Cox, who was with the Special Operations Center (SPOC) and had parachuted into France a few days earlier to coordinate Resistance activity. In Lyon there was still a lingering danger from Milice* snipers, and Cox recalled: "It would be interesting to record something of the mad hysteria that sprang up

* Vichy paramilitaries.

in Lyon. The Milice were hunted down and killed with mad displays of hate. The actual battle casualties consisted of one or two Maquis and one or two civilians, but for the next two or three days, simply pointing a finger at a person and yelling 'Milice' was enough to have him torn limb from limb . . . The FFI as quickly as possible regained some semblance of control, and the sporadic firing gradually died away."[1]

While the French celebrated the liberation of Lyon, Truscott still nursed hopes of catching Wiese's forces withdrawing to the north, screened by the 11th Panzer and a regiment of 338th Division. Truscott instructed the 36th Division to sidestep Lyon to the northeast and the 45th Division to prepare for an attack on Bourg while the 117th Cavalry Squadron probed to the east and west of the town. However, by now the Germans had largely regained their balance. On September 2, as the 45th Division's 157th and 180th Regiments moved on Bourg from the south and east, they ran into stiff opposition. Searching for a chink in the German lines, Truscott ordered the 117th Cavalry to reconnoiter from Meximieux toward Mâcon, some thirty miles north of Lyon and fifteen miles west of Bourg. At about 1730 on the evening of September 2, B Troop had penetrated to the small town of Marboz, situated on a secondary road ten miles north of Bourg. The troop was initially pushed out of the town by a German counterattack but by nightfall had reestablished themselves in Marboz. B Troop, fielding only light armored cars and trucks, was now vulnerable to a German counterthrust, but Truscott was determined to exploit the chance to unhinge the security force shielding the German flank. He ordered the 117th Cavalry to advance seven miles west of Marboz to occupy Montreval on the N-75, the highway running northwest from Bourg, and the 11th Panzer's principal supply route.

A platoon from B Troop reached the eastern outskirts of Montreval but was swiftly sent packing by the town's German garrison. Meanwhile the 117th Cavalry's commander, Lieutenant Colonel Charles J. Hodge, was struggling to concentrate his widely scattered forces in the Montreval area. A Troop and a forward squadron command arrived on the night of the 2nd, but an effective concentration demanded the presence of E Troop's artillery, C Troop's assault guns, and the light tanks of F Company. When these forces failed to arrive, Hodge decided to attack with just two reconnaissance troops. The attack went in shortly after dawn on September 3, and by 0930 the town had been secured. However, Hodge's men now found themselves in an exposed position, clinging to a low ridge surrounded by rolling farmland without the numbers to defend the position against a concerted enemy attack. Anticipating the usual German riposte, they took up position in the eastern sector of Montreval.

The German counterblow arrived some ninety minutes later, delivered by the 11th Panzer's Reconnaissance Battalion, which had been pulled out of Bourg and reinforced with a battery of self-propelled artillery, six medium tanks, and a company of engineers. By 1330, Hodge's perimeter was under extreme pressure. The chance of reinforcement was denied by a massive traffic snarl-up along 45th Division's line of advance. Attempts at a breakout were snuffed out by German tank and artillery fire. With the number of wounded rising and ammunition reserves falling, the men in Montreval surrendered shortly before 1700. At about the same time, some of the hoped-for reinforcements approached Montreval but by now were too late to affect the outcome. In the battle for Montreval, 126 Americans were captured, including 31 wounded, and 20 jeeps, 15 M8 armored cars, and ten M5A1 light tanks were destroyed. Twelve of the most seriously injured were left behind in the town when it was finally evacuated by the Germans. For the moment, the German escape route remained intact.

In *Command Missions*, Truscott noted that the reverse at Montreval was the result of "almost the only mistake this gallant 117th Cavalry Squadron made during this entire campaign. I had ordered Colonel Hodge to gain the rear of the 11th Panzer Division, which was opposing the 45th Infantry Division at Bourg, and he had done so. This detachment had obviously grown somewhat careless, because when the 11th Panzer Division withdrew during the night, these two companies were surprised and overrun and most of one and a half companies were captured. It was a sad blow to me even though many of those men rejoined us within the next few weeks. It is a testimonial to the 'Cavalry Spirit' and to the attitude of the American soldiers that this blow only spurred the squadron on to greater efforts." This does scant justice to the situation on the ground on September 2 and 3. In effect, Truscott had asked too much of the 117th Cavalry Squadron and had failed to reinforce it with armor. It is possible that he and his staff had not gauged the strength of German opposition in the area, although it is revealing that in a postwar statement Wietersheim observed that at this stage in the war his division habitually went into action with only about 50–60 percent of its available strength because of the complete dominance of Allied air and artillery power. Therein lay the remarkable staying power of the Ghost Division when it was for long periods playing defense. Nevertheless, this enforced posture and Truscott's persistence ultimately condemned Wietersheim's division to near destruction in a protracted war of attrition.

The only German formation to be destroyed in this phase of the withdrawal was 4th Luftwaffe Field Corps's rearguard that was overhauled twenty miles north of Lyon by the French Combat Command Kientz, an element of Touzet du Vigier's 1st Armored Division, reinforced by the 2nd Algerian Spahis. Some two thousand Germans were taken prisoner. The Allies' rapid advance was continuing to outpace the calculations of the Dragoon planners and pose awkward logistical problems for Truscott and his staff. On September 1 all 6th Corps's supply dumps lay south of the Durance River, although the Army was planning to open a supply base at Montélimar within a few days. The distance between the three US divisions and their fuel, ammunition, and supply points meant that resupply hauls of four hundred miles were commonplace. The trucks hauling these essentials around the clock could not be used for troop movements. For those movements northeast of Lyon, three provisional truck companies, one for each division, were allocated for troop movements. This juggling of stretched resources had also to take into account the requirements of the French formations, which now outnumbered those of the Americans.

On September 3 de Lattre announced, without prior consultation, the formation of two French corps-level commands, 1st and 2nd, commanded respectively by Lieutenant General Émile Béthouart and General de Monsabert. De Monsabert was also to exercise overall control of the French 1st Armored and 1st Infantry Divisions west of the Rhône and Saône and moving on Dijon. Béthouart's 1st Corps was to operate on the U.S. 6th Corps's right while the French 2nd Corps was to advance north toward Dijon before swinging east toward Strasbourg. Truscott's northeast drive was to be supported by 1st Corps while its

2nd Moroccan Division assumed responsibility for the northern sector of the Franco-Italian front. Control of the southern sector was to be retained by the FABTF and 1st SSF. In effect de Lattre had now established himself as an army-level commander, controlling two corps on the way to the formation of the French 1st Army.

Patch had no alternative but to accept the fait accompli and amend his own orders. On September 4 the French 2nd Corps was ordered to advance on the southern shoulder of the Belfort Gap while the U.S. 6th Corps was to make for the northern shoulder. Meanwhile, Blaskowitz, mindful of Hitler's fanciful notions of launching a counterattack from the Belfort Gap, was preoccupied with stitching together from his dwindling resources a force to defend its approaches in a bridgehead around the city of Dijon while simultaneously accelerating a junction with Army Group B. Blaskowitz now considered that the principal threat to Army Group G, most of whose withdrawing columns had not yet merged, came from Patton's U.S. Third Army, which had crossed the Meuse at Verdun and Commercy, to the north.

The few units immediately available to Blaskowitz included SS police security formations, Ost battalions, the Autun artillery school, and two engineer companies. His most urgent task was to reinforce the bridgehead around Dijon with capable combat units to allow him to pass the remaining units of Army Group G through the bridgehead. To buy time for the trailing elements of 64th Corps, it became necessary to slow down the withdrawal of the 19th Army, placing it at considerable risk. On September 3, a new commander, Lieutenant General Otto Lasch arrived at 64th Corps, his predecessor, General Karl Sachs, an "Aryanized" Jew, having been dismissed at Hitler's insistence. The change of command made little or no difference to the increasingly disorganized withdrawal as the corps's combat and mobile units were pulled out and pushed toward Dijon while its big march groups were deprived of their screen.

Major General Botho Elster, commanding the corps's rearmost group, considered himself to be in an impossible situation. He had been deprived of the 159th Infantry Division, which took with it most of the group's transport, weapons, and ammunition. His protestations at staff conferences went unheard, and on September 10 he and 19,200 of his men surrendered at Issoudun to Major General Robert

C. Macon, commander of the U.S. 83rd Infantry Division. At the time Elster justified his surrender by pointing to the damage inflicted on his command by the FFI, with whom he had already opened negotiations, but it is more likely that he had been overcome by defeatism.

In spite of Elster's capitulation, by mid-September some 60,000 troops who had begun the withdrawal from the southwest had found safety inside the Dijon bridgehead. Moreover, on September 4 contact had been made with Army Group B, strengthening Blaskowitz's northern flank. As the situation stabilized, Blaskowitz established his headquarters in Gérardmer, in the Hautes Vosges near the German border. In part, his task at the height of the crisis had been made easier by the Allies' fuel crisis that had obliged Eisenhower to make some difficult decisions. The speed of the Allied advance had confounded its high command. Patton was so far ahead of his planned objectives and timetable that he was relying on a Michelin road map. The Allies had arrived at a point which, when planning the invasion of northwest Europe, they had not expected to reach until May 1945. Supply was now the factor dictating Eisenhower's options in the allocation of resources. The Allied air campaign in the run-up to Overlord had been so successful in destroying the French railway system that when the Allies broke out of the Normandy bridgehead the means to sustain their eastward advance could be provided only by truck and road, and this was not enough to meet the daily divisional requirement of seven hundred tons of ammunition, equipment, and rations. As Eisenhower later observed, "the life blood of supply was running perilously thin through the forward extremities of the Army." For the moment, he could maintain momentum only by giving scarce resources to one commander and withholding them from another. Patton, stranded on the German border, was the loser. Field Marshal Montgomery was given the go-ahead for the penultimate Allied airborne operation of the war, Operation "Market Garden," launched on September 17.

A week earlier, on September 10, the spearheads of Patch's Seventh Army and Patton's Third Army met north of Dijon. By September 14, about half of the 19th Army had found refuge in southern Alsace, where it stood ready to defend the approaches to Germany's West Wall. On the same day, the Allied command structure underwent a fundamental change. The Mediterranean chain of command gave way to the European chain of command. General Devers assumed command of the 6th Army Group, reporting to Eisenhower and SHAEF, not Wilson and AFHQ. Patch retained command of the Seventh Army but the French units that had previously reported to him now reported to de Lattre.

The race for the Belfort Gap petered out. It was not an objective favored by Eisenhower, and among his major concerns were the current exhaustion of the troops after the campaign in southern France, the shortage of fuel and the onset of autumn. By mid-October, Truscott reflected: "Operations made slow progress during the first two weeks in October. Rain was almost incessant and vastly increased the hardships of moving and fighting. Cold caused acute discomfort, and the losses and exertions of preceding weeks were having their effect. All units were under strength, and officers and men were in need of rest. North of the Moselle, rugged foothills covered with dense forests made operations most arduous. Thick woods required greater concentration of troops to wipe out the enemy, while the Corps was extended on such a wide front that any concentration was difficult." It was a long way from the sun-drenched lavender fields of Provence to the gripping fogs and damps of the Vosges, but the journey had been worthwhile.

SIXTEEN
THE CHAMPAGNE CAMPAIGN

> "I'll never forget that day as long as I live; the people were really joyful, tears were running down their faces, the girls were kissing everybody . . . even the johnny-come-latelies driving the tank destroyers . . . people were throwing flowers at us . . . just the way it's supposed to be."
>
> —Colonel Harry R. Pritchard,
> A Company, 509th Parachute Battalion

With Truscott chasing the Germans up the Rhône Valley, and Toulon and Marseille invested by the French, General Patch had good cause for satisfaction with the pace and progress of Dragoon. Hitler had sacrificed the 242nd and 244th Divisions in the defense of the two major ports, but two German divisions remained at large on the board: Lieutenant General Karl Pflaum's 157th Division, north of Grenoble; and Lieutenant General Otto Fretter-Pico's 148th Division, near Nice. Both of these formations could be reinforced from Italy through the Alpine passes, but a series of Ultra intercepts had provided a strong indication that they were more likely to withdraw than mount a counterattack in southeastern France.

One Ultra intercept, deciphered and forwarded to Patch on August 20 was an order from OKW to Fretter-Pico to move toward the Italian frontier. When it came to Fretter-Pico's eastern flank, the message was clear: "148 Division to defend area around Grasse [thirty miles northwest of Nice in the foothills of the Alpes-Maritimes] as long as possible without running risk of annihilation. Then to withdraw with main forces via Nice, Breil, Cuneo to take over new sector with left boundary coast at Menton, right boundary Embrun, Chianale-Varaita valley. If situation allows, groups to be pulled back fighting into Tinée and Var valleys as far as Larche-Condamine to bar a possible Allied outflanking thrust across Maddalena [Larche] pass . . . At 0900 August 19, leaving rearguards in contact with Allies, main body of 148th Division to withdraw from evening 19th onward first to east bank of the Var sector. In no circumstances to let Allies push them back by outflanking movement to the north." Late in the evening of August 20, further intercepts indicated that the principal task of the 148th Division was to defend a possible withdrawal route from Grasse to Cannes, while the 157th Division, when pressed, was to pull back along a line Briançon-Chambéry-Aix-les-Bains in the Hautes Alpes.

While the Germans were preparing to withdraw to the east, the French had proven reluctant to provide the Americans with a right flank guard, which would push them awkwardly against the Alps. Devers, attentive to the codes of coalition warfare, had suggested to Patch that the First Airborne Task Force could be given this role and assume responsibility for the Allies' eastern flank.

In a postwar interview, Devers recalled his role in the decision: "At this point [August 18] the French general, de Lattre, came in and said the job of guarding the right flank wasn't becoming to his successes and what he wanted to do was to go up the other side of the Rhône. I happened to come into the headquarters right then and I suggested to Patch, or his chief of staff . . . 'Let him go. Let him go up the other side. I'll take care of that flank over there because we can keep the airborne [FABTF] to protect it.' In other words . . . the airborne group under Frederick took over the job that had been originally assigned to the French. I didn't wire back for authority to do this. That's the way you lose battles. I got them to do what they did . . . Patch issued the order after I had told him I'd take the full responsibility."[1]

Frederick was informed of his new role on August 19. As the British 2nd Brigade, which had participated in the Le Muy landings, was about to leave the theater, it was replaced by the First Special Service Force, the "Black Devils" commanded by Frederick in the Italian campaign, which had been held in reserve since the opening days of Dragoon after their operation against the offshore islands. The FABTF was to establish and hold a defensive flank running south from the hilltop town of Fayence to La Napoule on the Mediterranean. In this context, a "line" was not the equivalent of the trenches on the Western Front in World War I. The terrain running down to the sea from Fayence is hilly, dotted with villages perchés, and cross-hatched with numerous minor roads. Some garrisons in this sector, held by determined German troops, were prepared to hold out for days; others, manned by Ost troops, were more likely to surrender before a shot was fired.

At the northern end of Frederick's line, the garrison at Fayence surrendered to a Jedburgh team, "Sceptre," which had dropped into the Le Muy sector on August 14 and had made contact with Geoffrey Jones during the airborne landings. To the northwest of Fayence was the hilltop village of Callian, which had been reached on D+2 by patrols of the 2nd Battalion, 141st Regiment, 36th Division. It was now taken by a task force assembled by the battalion's executive officer, Major Herbert Eitt, enabling the FABTF to move into the positions held by the 141st Regiment on the N-85, the Route Napoléon, all the way to Digne in the Basses-Alpes.

Frederick, now responsible for protecting the Seventh Army's eastern flank, moved his headquarters to the Hôtel Courier in Saint-Raphaël. On the edge of town, at Valescure, were Geoffrey Jones and an OSS colleague Alan Stuyvesant, now working with a Gaullist intelligence network run by Pierre Escot that had excellent contacts in Cannes and Nice. Escot was rapidly taken into the intelligence set-up operated by Frederick's G-2. Frederick now had in his sights the town of Grasse, the perfume entrepôt on the Cannes-Castellane road, the N-85, where the FFI anticipated that the Germans would make a stand. They were not given a chance. Grasse was surrounded by two regiments of FABTF on the morning of August 24 and its garrison surrendered.

It was in Grasse that a remarkable American expatriate, Isabel Pell, introduced herself to the FABTF. According to the Force's Colonel Bryant Evans, who got to know her well: "The French referred to her as 'The Girl with the Blond Lock' because I seem to remember she had a blond streak in her hair. She had been wild in New York and it was said that her family was paying her 25,000 dollars a year to stay out of the country. I also have a recollection that she held the record for the fastest automobile trip between Grasse and Paris." A handsome, fearless lesbian, Pell had played a key role with the FFI, storing weapons and ammunition dropped by the British and Americans at her farm at Puget-Théniers.* Pell also had a distant family connection to Geoffrey Jones, who recalled: "She protected quite a few people who were hiding out from the Gestapo. On one occasion the Nazis raided her farm, and although she had four people down in the cellar at the time, she swore that there was no one there. In my opinion, things like take more guts than shooting a gun off in battle."[2]

Jones saw Pell as a striking relic of the Roaring Twenties, with a flapper-style haircut and mannish clothes. In spite of her years in Provence, she spoke atrocious French but was adored by the local community. She helped Jones recruit a team of female operatives and gained the confidence of General Frederick who, unconcerned with her heavy drinking and occasionally wilful manner, employed her as a liaison officer, advising the Americans on locals they could trust and those they should avoid. Captain Joseph W. Welsh, the FABTF's Civil Affairs Officer,** remembered: "Everyone loved Isabel. The men at headquarters thought she was crazy, but they all liked her immensely. She was outspoken, didn't really care about authority. Even though she respected and liked Frederick, she disagreed with him quite strongly."

After the taking of Grasse, Frederick drove his men on, although the transport and fuel shortages that had bedeviled the 36th, 45th, and 3rd Divisions threatened to slow the FABTF's eastward progress. However, the airborne troops had their own logistical solution, reminiscent

---

* In November 1944 a square in Puget-Théniers was named after Pell. In 1958, she dropped dead in New York from a heart attack.

** Civil Affairs operations concerned themselves with ensuring the safety and well-being of the civilian population immediately before and after liberation.

of medieval armies on the march. In a letter home, Lieutenant Dick Spencer summed up their freewheeling approach to campaigning: "Almost overnight the parachutists 'mechanized' themselves. The column was cluttered with carts and bicycles, with and without tires. The Jerry convoys had taken a shellacking; it seemed that all their vehicles in southern France had a white [Allied] star painted on the sides and on the top; and adorned with makeshift American flags and bright pieces of silk, nylon, and rayon . . . and surmounted with ten or fifteen parachutists." The buccaneering 517th Parachute Infantry Regiment earned the soubriquet "Colonel Graves and his 5,000 Thieves." Anything that wasn't nailed down was fair game. One of their raiding parties returned from a quartermaster's stores in Marseille with cases of Good Conduct medals, stolen in error. Never a man to look a gift horse in the mouth, Colonel Graves came up with a solution, telling the culprits, "Well, what the hell, give one to everybody who hasn't got a venereal disease."

The FABTF was moving eastward on a sixty-mile front with one foot in the mountains and the other on the coast. It had limited artillery assets, and fire support was supplied by the U.S. Navy. Rear Admiral Morton Deyo's Right Flank Force was tasked with suppressing German coastal batteries and was advised by the army not to hesitate to fire into populated areas if the enemy was there and shelling American troops. In the early afternoon of August 22, the cruiser *Brooklyn* shifted its fire from enemy artillery to troop concentrations and later armored vehicles and, as the day wore on, a railway gun lurking in a tunnel. On the morning of the 23rd the *Brooklyn*, working in concert with a spotter plane, bombarded enemy gun emplacements and trench systems. Liaising with a P-51 Mustang, the cruiser *Tuscaloosa* destroyed a four-gun battery with just sixteen rounds and scored a direct hit on another battery.

On the afternoon of the 24th, the FABTF's 509th Parachute Infantry Battalion entered Cannes. The Germans had already pulled out, leaving behind them a thorough seeding of mines on the resort's outskirts. A local resident, Jean-Paul Carbonel, drove out to greet the 509th on his motorcycle: "We reached the bridge at the Siagne, which had been blown . . . The Americans were on the other side and since there was less than fifty centimeters of water in the Siagne, an

American tank [a tank destroyer from a battalion attached to 509th] crossed the river and wanted to climb up the other side. A man who must have been the owner of the field shouted to them [the crew] that there were mines, but they refused to listen. The tank advanced, so we quickly moved back and a mine exploded and cut the treads on the front left-hand side. Later we found the pieces of an anti-tank mine [a Teller mine] in the sand. The tank behind it sent out a cable and they pulled the tank out of the way. At that moment, some Americans came with metal detectors and they removed all the mines. Afterward the whole column crossed and climbed into the N-7 and they followed us into Bocca [a western suburb of Cannes]."[3]

The German garrison in Cannes, commanded by a Colonel Schneider, had orders to destroy the city before evacuating it. Schneider ignored his instructions and completed the withdrawal by the early morning of the 24th, leaving the city intact, its inhabitants rejoicing, and the FFI parading as liberators. The 509th arrived in time to participate in the celebrations before moving on to the next target, Nice. Once again, Geoffrey Jones, now fully integrated into Frederick's G-2,* played an important part in the initial stages of the operation. On August 27, with the German evacuation of Nice well underway, an enemy staff car was ambushed in the city and a blood-soaked knapsack crammed with papers was retrieved. When the package was presented to Frederick, it was immediately clear that he had in his hands a copy of General Fretter-Pico's field order of the day. Jones later described the incident: "We made an astonishing discovery: these 'papers' were the just written plans for the German forces on the eastern flank to withdraw for the next three days to fortified positions on the Italian frontier—and the Field Order and maps to carry them out! Working all night by candlelight, we translated/processed a complete report that by early morning was ready for me to wake up the General [Patch] who immediately gave me his L.S. [spotter] aircraft and had me flown to his headquarters."[4] The field order concluded with a warning indicative

* Jones and Escot eventually assembled a team of over 120 male and female volunteers from local and refugee Résistants who worked as translators, couriers, counter-intelligence agents, radio operators, and mounted ski and maritime patrols, supplying the FABTF with a regular stream of accurate information on enemy dispositions and intentions.

of the German state of mind in the closing stages of Dragoon. "Watch out—terrorists [the FFI] are everywhere . . . Do not go singly, only armed and in groups . . . Steer clear of the terrorist-infested city of Nice." Frederick never openly acknowledged the importance of this document, but this did not bother Jones, who recalled: "He never gave anyone a pat on the back. You knew you were doing your job if he continued to let you serve him."[5]

Nice was to be the next location of Frederick's headquarters, and this decision plunged the commander of the FABTF into the midst of the intense factional infighting that accompanied the liberation of the city. The Resistance in Nice, the administrative center of the department, was controlled by the FTP while on its outskirts and in the mountains behind it the FFI were the dominant force. In addition, Dragoon's success had prompted a sudden last-minute increase in the numbers of so-called Résistants, ironically dubbed "11th Hour Patriots," which added to the prevailing sense of disorder and indiscipline in the city. Jones, who had been climbing a steep learning curve since arriving in France at the beginning of August, was keenly aware that Nice was a potential powder keg. He later observed: "To be brutally frank, there was very little Resistance . . . in southern France before the invasion because of the independent French nature. It was a motley group down there and I don't think they ever got together. The only Resistance people that we really had were the FTPs . . . These were organized and the FFI were not. And now the non-Communists were refusing to sit back and let the Communists grab power." At the time and later, Frederick was supremely indifferent to the nuances of French Liberation politics: "I was so busy fighting a campaign that I just didn't know who the hell was a Communist and who wasn't. I know that there were many false accusations and that some of them were made for personal reasons. If you didn't like someone, you'd call him a Communist. Some people ran up big bills at the grocery store and then when we came in they'd denounce the owner as a collaborator in order to take him out and get him hanged. Naturally this caused a tremendous amount of ill will."

Nice had been liberated, intact but unruly, on August 28. By September 5 sufficient order had been restored to enable Frederick to move his headquarters there from Grasse and to bring a temporary halt to the internecine warfare within the Resistance forces. On

September 12, the FABTF was detached from the Seventh Army, placed directly under the command of Truscott's 6th Corps,* and tasked with sealing off the enemy's escape routes from southern France. The line Frederick was to hold, and which remained unchanged until March 1945, focused on three entry points into the Italian theater: on the coast, beyond neutral Monaco as far as Menton; the Trende Pass, thirty miles to the north in the Alpes-Martimes; and to the northwest through the Larche Pass that connects Barcelonnette, in France, to Cuneo, in Italy.

As the Americans advanced eastward, German resistance stiffened. Lieutenant General Karl Pflaum, the commander of the 157th Division, observed after the war: "The protection of the passes at the French-Italian mountain frontier was especially important for the German troops in Italy. An advance by American troops over the passes into Italy in the rear of the German front could mean its destruction. Apparently they [OKW] preferred weakening the 19th Army to paralyzing the Italian front . . . From the very beginning it could be supposed that the American forces would attempt an advance into Italy from southern France over the Alpine passes. It was very tempting, indeed, highly possible and promising." Although beset by a high desertion rate, the 148th Division also conducted an orderly withdrawal to the Italian border, skillfully choosing resistance points at which to slow the advancing Americans. The divisional commander Fretter-Pico was awarded the Knight's Cross for his role in the retreat, which was described in arguably over-generous terms in the propaganda that accompanied the award: "Therefore, and because of his good knowledge of the enemy positions, Lieutenant General Fretter-Pico decided under his own responsibility to retreat slowly and in several steps, so that the entire movement to the Var lasted about one week. Because the division commander visited his troops down to the level of the company command posts daily in the heaviest enemy artillery and mortar fire, and was thus able to picture the situation as it really was . . . the difficult operation succeeded smoothly and according to plan. It not only succeeded in enabling the division to pull back without any loss of weapons and equipment, in other words in full combat strength [sic] but also in transporting back all the supplies."[6]

* Truscott was shortly to be promoted to the rank of Lieutenant General.

While Frederick's men were pushing the 157th and 148th Divisions back to the Italian border, the Kriegsmarine was embarking on a last desperate throw of the dice in the coastal waters off Menton. The only weapons available to it were the midget submarines and assault boats deployed by *K-Verbände* (*Kleinkampfverbände*, small combat teams). The midget submarines, or *Marder* (Pine Martens) were three-ton vessels consisting of two torpedoes stacked one on top of the other. The upper torpedo had its warhead removed to allow the installation of a small steering compartment in which the Marder's pilot was seated beneath a perspex dome, much like a fighter pilot in his cockpit. Fitted with a dive tank and compressed air pump, the vessel could submerge to a depth of one hundred feet, which severely limited its endurance. In combat it operated just below the surface, its electric motor giving it a maximum surface speed of about six knots on the surface and five knots submerged, with the perspex dome peeping above the waves and allowing the pilot to maneuver toward his target. Marders had been used in August 1944, with limited success and heavy losses, off the Normandy beaches, where they sank a Liberty ship, a barrage balloon vessel, a landing craft, a minesweeper, and a destroyer. They also damaged a cruiser and an obsolete French battleship, the *Courbet*, employed as a block-ship.

The first twelve Marders to arrive in Menton were those of 1/K-Flotilla commanded by *Oberleutnant zur see* (Lieutenant First Grade) Peter Berger. At 0600 on September 5 they set off to attack American warships just off the coast. They were spotted by the minesweeper USS *Incredible*, whose skipper Bob Ekland, noted, "Twelve human torpedoes attempted to pass through our formation, presumably on their way to the cruisers because none hit any of the minesweepers. They cruise with the torpedo under the water and with just the head of the pilot in a glass dome above water. We all fired at them and I'm sure my ship hit at least two of them."[7]

At 0812 the French destroyer *Le Malin* ("The Malign One") a veteran of the Torch and Salerno landings, spotted a suspicious object in the water, prompting the destroyer USS *Ludlow* to depth-charge the target. This prompted a lively hunt for more of the tell-tale perspex domes, which kept popping up like whack-a-moles in an arcade game. At 0836 *Le Malin* opened fire on a dome, and twenty minutes later the *Ludlow* engaged another. *Le Malin* rescued one of the pilots while another Marder was sunk. The domes, glinting in the sunlight, made excellent targets. The captured pilots were happy to explain the workings of the Marder to their captors and from whence they had come, a launching site to the east of Monaco. One of them claimed that he had made three runs at *Le Malin* and had finally fired his torpedo at the *Ludlow* before a burst from one of her 20mm antiaircraft guns had forced him to take to the water. When told by his captors that Brussels had been taken by the Allies [on September 3] he refused to believe them, insisting that Germany would win the war.

Of the five Marders that approached the Allied ships on September 5, four were lost. Four days later the Kriegsmarine threw in a bigger attack, by fourteen Marders and six assault boats armed with depth charges. The latter were either radio-controlled or steered by crews who abandoned ship at the last moment. Ten of the Kriegsmarine flotilla were destroyed by American destroyers and PT boats. The Germans persisted with Marder and explosive-laden motorboat attacks throughout September, albeit on a steadily diminishing scale. On the evening of September 29, the American destroyer *Gleaves*, patrolling off San Stefano, was ambushed by three groups of explosive boats and fought a high-speed running battle with them, destroying one with depth charges and seeing another self-destruct. The next day the *Gleaves* returned to the scene of the skirmish to search for wreckage and survivors. She found two survivors and one intact boat, the first to fall into Allied hands. The boat was retrieved and later disarmed by an American bomb disposal unit. Unlike the captured Marder pilot, both the Kriegsmarine men rescued by the *Gleaves* freely admitted that Germany had lost the war.

Dragoon, over which so many Allied arguments had raged, was now a fast-receding memory. At the end of November, First Airborne Task Force was deactivated. In a farewell letter, Frederick congratulated his men: "You may take pride in your accomplishments knowing that you performed difficult missions well. I am proud of having commanded a force of superior combat soldiers whose aggressive, offensive spirit brought defeat to the enemy throughout a long series of engagements. I wish to each of you good luck and hope that in all your future assignments you achieve the same success that has marked your operations in southern France."

The speed and scale of Operation Dragoon mark it out as one of the most significant Allied victories in the West in the summer of 1944. In a campaign lasting little more than a month it had liberated nearly two-thirds of France. The planners' cautious predictions had been confounded. It had been estimated that the Seventh Army would not reach the Rhône Valley until mid-October and Lyon until mid-November. There can be no doubt that in July 1944 the diversion of Wehrmacht attention and strength from southern France to Normandy fatally undermined the defense of the Riviera and its hinterland. But the fact that the operation was such a signal success owes much to the strategic insight and persistence of General George C. Marshall and his planners in Washington, who retained faith in the operation during its long gestation when faced throughout with Churchill's stubborn advocacy of operations in Italy and the Balkans.

The FFI could also take great credit for the role it played in Dragoon. It was no match for the Wehrmacht in open battle, but it had significantly undermined the occupation forces' ability to effectively block the Allies' northward drive, particularly around the pivotal point of Grenoble. This operational failure led to the interdiction of Army Group G on the road to and from Montélimar, a disaster Blaskowitz had feared but for which he could not provide an adequate response. The battle at Montélimar was to be the key engagement of the campaign.

Counterfactual arguments have been advanced, notably by John Keegan, that the campaign in southern France was strategically advantageous to Hitler, who readily abandoned the theater while leaving the bulk of the Allied forces in Italy lodged against the strong defenses of the Gothic Line, at a safe distance from the industries of northern Italy and the Alpine approaches to the borders of the Reich. Keegan argued that the Führer remained obsessed with the Balkans, which was also an overriding and misguided British priority, while Dragoon had funneled the Allies' amphibious, naval, and air reserves into an operationally vacant zone. By the same token, it could be argued that the continuing disposition of U.S. Seventh Army in Italy and Army Group G in southern France, combined with an Allied lodgement north of the Loire, could have led to a German flank attack on the Allies mounted in the autumn of 1944 by elements of Blaskowitz's Army Group reinforced by formations from Germany—in effect an earlier version of the Battle of the

Bulge. Hitler had already planned such an operation in September 1944, with the aim of cutting off the U.S. Third Army, but the speed with which Dijon fell limited the counterblow to a series of ill-coordinated attacks in Lorraine. In the final count, it is clear that the prosecution of the Dragoon plan remained clearly in line with Eisenhower's strategy of a broad advance into Germany on all fronts, a hard position to maintain when dealing with prima donnas like Patton and Montgomery, and a thankless burden that the supreme commander bore with great tact and skill. It also underlines America's colossal industrial and war-making reach and power at one of the crucial turning points of the 20th century.

What was undeniable was the severe handling during Dragoon of Army Group G, which ended the campaign a shadow of its former self. In a month of fighting it had lost over half of its fighting strength. By mid-September, it had sustained over 130,000 casualties, 7,000 of which were killed, 20,000 wounded, and 105,000 captured. These figures do not include those for the formations left behind to defend the Atlantic "fortresses," some 25,000 men. The Army Group's combat units had been shredded, with most of its infantry divisions reduced to three thousand or fewer effectives. The 11th Panzer Division had only twelve tanks and two assault guns left. In comparison, Allied casualties were less severe. The U.S. 6th Corps sustained 4,500 battle casualties and French Army B a similar number, depending on whether one takes into account FFI casualties. Both sides, tired but battle-tested, faced a grueling autumnal slugging match in the Vosges.

In a subsequent tribute, the Seventh Army acknowledged the FABTF's role in the campaign in southern France: "These successes, in driving a strong enemy force from a large section of France in which he had every advantage of observation, terrain and organized defense, were won at high cost to the First Airborne Task Force. Virtually one-third of its personnel were either killed or wounded. However, the damage inflicted on the enemy far exceeded our losses. Approximately 4,000 of the enemy were captured and unknown numbers were killed and wounded. The German 148th Infantry Division was completely decimated and the 34th Division, which was rushed to its rescue, was badly mauled. The aggressive spirit manifested by the officers and men of First Airborne Task Force has added another glorious page to the history of the American Army."

APPENDIX

ORDERS OF BATTLE

U.S. Seventh Army	Lieutenant General Patch
6th Corps	Major General Truscott
3rd Infantry Division	Major General O'Daniel
7th Infantry Regiment	
15th Infantry Regiment	
30th Infantry Regiment	
Division artillery (9th, 10th, 39th, 41st FAB)	
756th Tank Battalion (attached)	
601st Tank Destroyer Battalion (attached)	
36th Division	Major General Dahlquist
141st Infantry Regiment	
142nd Infantry Regiment	
143rd Infantry Regiment	
Division artillery (131st, 132nd, 133rd, 155th FAB)	
753rd Tank Battalion (attached)	
636th Tank Destroyer Battalion (attached)	
45th Infantry Division	Major General Eagles
157th Infantry Regiment	
179th Infantry Regiment	
180th Infantry Regiment	
Divisional artillery (158th, 160th, 171st, 189th FAB)	

APPENDIX

Unit	Commander
1st Airborne Task Force	Brigadier General Frederick
517th Parachute Regimental Combat Team	
2nd (British) Parachute Brigade	
509th Parachute Battalion	
551st Parachute Regiment	
Task Force Butler	Brigadier General Butler
117th Cavalry Reconnaissance Squadron	
143rd Infantry Regiment	
59th Armored Field Artillery Battalion	
753rd Tank Battalion	
Co. C 636th Tank Destroyer Battalion	
Co. F 344th Engineers	
FAB: Field Artillery Battalion	
Army B	General de Lattre de Tassigny
2nd Army Corps	General Touzet du Vigier
1st Armored Division	
2nd RC (Regiment cuirassiers)	
2nd RCA (Regiment of Algerian Cavalry)	
5th RCA	
1st BZ (Battalion of Zouaves)	
68th RAA (Regiment of African Artillery)	
1st DMI (Infantry Division)	General Brosset
1st Infantry Brigade	
2nd Infantry Brigade	
4th Infantry Brigade	
1st Artillery Regiment	
(combat attachments)	
1st RFM (Marine Regiment)	
3rd Infantry Division	General de Monsabert
3rd RTA (Regiment of Algerian Infantry)	
7th RTA	
4th RTA	
67th RAA	
(combat attachments)	
3rd RSAR (Regiment of Algerian native reconnaissance cavalry)	
Shock Battalion	
9th Colonial Infantry Division	General Magnan
4th RTS (Regiment of Senegalese Infantry)	
6th RTS	

13th RTS
RACM (Regiment of Moroccan Artillery)
6th RTS
13th RTS
(combat attachments)
RICM (Regiment of Moroccan Infantry)
RCCC (Colonial Tank Regiment)
Groupe de commandos d'Afrique (African Commando Group)

Allied Air Forces
Mediterranean Allied Tactical Air Force
12th Tactical Air Command
Mediterranean Allied Coastal Air Force
Provisional Troop Carrier Air Division

Allied Naval Forces
Task Force 84 "Alpha Force"
Task Force 85 "Delta Force"
Task Force 87 "Camel Force"
Task Force 86 "Sitka Force"
Task Force 88 Carrier Force
TG (Task Group) 88.1
TG (Task Group) 88.2
TG (Task Group) 80.6 Anti-submarine and Convoy Control Group

German Land Forces, Provençal Coast, August 1944

Armeeoberkommando 19 (AOK 19)	General Wiese
62nd Army Corps	General Neuling
242nd Infantry Division	
GR 917	
GR 918	
GR 765	
AR 242	
148th Infantry Division	
GR 8	
GR 239	
AR 8	
85th Army Corps	General Kniess
244th Infantry Division	
GR 932	
GR 933	
GR 934	
AR 244	

338th Infantry Division
GR 757
GR 758
GR 759
AR 338

Heersgebiet Südfrankreich (Army area, South of France) General Niehoff
VS 747
VS 761
VS 497
VS 800
VS 994
VS 792
VS 555

GR: Grenadier Regiment
AR: Artillery Regiment
VS: Verbindungsstab (Liaison Staff)

SELECTED BIBLIOGRAPHY

Adelman, Robert and George Walton. *The Champagne Campaign*. Boston: Little, Brown & Co., 1969.

———. *The Devil's Brigade*. Philadelphia: Chilton, 1966.

Brooke, Field Marshal Lord Alan. *War Diaries: 1939–1945*. Berkeley: University of California Press, 2001.

Ashdown, Paddy. *The Cruel Victory: The French Resistance, D-Day and the Battle for the Vercors 1944*. New York: HarperCollins, 2014.

Bennett, Ralph *Ultra and the Mediterranean Strategy*. London: Hamish Hamilton, 1989.

Brager, Bruce *The Texas 36th Division: A History*. Woodway, Texas: Eakin Press, 2002.

Bimberg, Edward. *The Moroccan Goums: Tribal Warriors in a Modern War*. Westport, Conn.: Greenwood Press, 1999.

Blumenthal, Henry. *Illusion and Reality in Franco-American Diplomacy, 1914–1945*. Baton Rouge: Louisiana State Univ Press, 1986.

Clark, General Mark W. *Calculated Risk*. New York: Harper & Bros., 1950.

Clarke, Jeffrey J. and Robert Ross Smith. *Riviera to the Rhine: U.S. Army in World War II*. Washington, D.C.: Center of Military History, United States Army, 1991.

Clayton, Anthony. *Three Marshals of France: Leadership After Trauma*. Lincoln, Neb.: Potomac Books, 1992.

Connole, Dennis A. *A "Yankee" in the "Texas Army."* London: Brassey's, 2008.

De Gaulle, Charles. *The Complete War Memoirs of Charles de Gaulle, 1940–1946*. New York: Simon & Schuster, 1964.

Fairbanks Jr., Douglas. *The Salad Days*. New York: Doubleday, 1988.

Funk, Arthur Layton *Hidden Ally: French Resistance, Special Operations, and the Landings in Southern France, 1944*. Santa Barbara, Calif.: Praeger, 1992.

SELECT BIBLIOGRAPHY

Gassend, Jean-Loup. *Operation Dragoon: Autopsy of a Battle: The Allied Liberation of the French Riviera August–September 1944.* Atglen, Penn.: Schiffer Publishing, 2013.

Gildea, Robert. *Marianne In Chains: Daily Life in the Heart of France During the German Occupation.* New York: Metropolitan Books, 2002.

Giziowski, Richard. *The Enigma of General Blaskowitz.* New York: Hippocrene Books, 1996.

Grossjohann, Georg. *Five Years, Four Fronts: A German Officer's World War II Combat Memoir.* London: Aegis, 1999.

Guinness, Alec. *Blessings in Disguise.* New York: Knopf, 1985.

Hansen, Randall. *Disobeying Hitler: German Resistance After Valkyrie.* Oxford, U.K.: Oxford University Press, 2014.

Hewitt, H. Kent. *The Memoirs of Admiral H. Kent Hewitt.* Newport, R.I.: Naval War College Press, 2004.

Howard, Michael. *The Mediterranean Strategy in the Second World War.* London: Greenhill Books, 1990.

Jenkins, Roy. *Churchill: A Biography.* New York: Farrar, Straus & Giroux, 2001.

Jenkins, Ray. *A Pacifist at War: The Life Of Francis Cammaerts.* London: Hutchinson, 2009.

Kaufmann, J. E. and H. W. Kaufmann. *The American GI in Europe in World War II.* Mechanicsburg, Penn.: Stackpole, 2009.

Kedward, R. *In Search of the Maquis: Rural Resistance in Southern France, 1942–1944.* Wotton-under-Edge, U.K.: Clarendon Press, 1993.

Lewis, Norman. *Naples '44.* New York: Pantheon Books, 1978.

Ludewig, Joachim *Rückzug: The German Retreat from France, 1944.* Lexington: University Press of Kentucky, 2012.

Masson, Madeleine. *Christine: SOE Agent & Churchill's Favourite Spy.* London: Little, Brown, 1975.

Mazower, Mark. *Hitler's Empire: How the Nazis Ruled Europe.* New York: Penguin, 2008.

Moreno, John A. "The Death of Admiral Moon." In *Assault on Normandy: First-Person Accounts from the Sea Services*, edited by Paul Stillwell. Annapolis, Md.: Naval Institute Press, 1994.

Morison, Samuel Eliot. *History of United States Naval Operations in World War II: The Invasion of France and Germany 1944–1945.* Boston: Little, Brown & Co., 1957.

Murphy, Audie *To Hell and Back.* New York: Henry Holt and Company, 1949.

Porch, Douglas. *The Path to Victory: The Mediterranean Theater in World War II.* New York: Farrar, Straus & Giroux, 2004.

Sussna, Stephen *Defeat and Triumph: The Story of a Controversial Allied Invasion and French Rebirth.* Philadelphia: Xlibris, 2008.

Sweets, John F. *Choices in Vichy France: The French Under Nazi Occupation*, Oxford, U.K.: Oxford University Press, 1986.

Taggart, Donald G. *History of the Third Infantry Division in World War II*. Washington, D.C.: Infantry Journal Press, 1947.

Tomblin, Barbara Brooks *With Utmost Spirit: Allied Naval Operations in the Mediterranean 1942–1945*. Lexington: University Press of Kentucky, 2004.

Trevor-Roper, Hugh, ed. *Hitler's War Directives, 1939–1945*. London: Sidgwick & Jackson, 1964.

Truscott, Lucian. *Command Missions: A Personal Story*. Novato, Calif.: Presidio Press, 1990.

Volpe, Maj. Michael T. *Task Force Butler: A Case Study in the Employment of an Ad Hoc Unit in the Combat Operations during Operation Dragoon, 1–30 August 1944*. Fort Leavenworth, Kansas, 2007.

Weigley, Russell F. *The American Way of War: A History of United States Military Strategy and Policy*. Basingstoke, U.K.: Macmillan, 1973.

Willmott, H. P. *June 1944*. Poole, U.K.: Blandford Press, 1984.

Whiting, Charles *America's Forgotten Army: The Story of the U.S. Seventh*. Cambridge, Mass.: Da Capo, 1999.

Wyant, William K. *Sandy Patch: A Biography of Lt. Gen. Alexander M. Patch*. Santa Barbara, Calif.: Praeger, 1991.

Zaloga, Steven. *Operation Dragoon: France's Other D-Day*. Oxford, U.K.: Osprey, 2009.

ENDNOTES

The author and publisher have made every effort to contact the copyright holders of the material reproduced in this book, and wish to apologize to those that they have been unable to trace. Grateful acknowledgment is made to the following for the passages reproduced on the pages given below.

TWO: THE STRANDED WHALE

1 Lt. Gen. Lucian K. Truscott, *Command Missions: A Personal Story* (New York: E.P. Dutton, 1954).
2 Ibid.
3 Ibid.
4 Ibid.
5 Ibid.
6 Nigel Nicolson, *Alex: The Life of Field Marshal Earl Alexander of Tunis* (London: Weidenfeld and Nicolson, 1973).
7 Truscott, *Command Missions.*
8 Field Marshal Lord Alanbrooke, *War Diaries 1939–1945* (London: Weidenfeld and Nicolson, 2001).

THREE: THE TUG OF WAR

1 Alanbrooke, *War Diaries.*

FOUR: FROM ANVIL TO DRAGOON

1 Truscott, *Command Missions.*
2 Robert H. Adelman and Colonel George Walton, *The Champagne Campaign: The Spectacular Airborne Invasion That Turned the Tide in Southern France in 1944* (London: Leslie Frewin, 1973).

ENDNOTES

FIVE: THE OTHER SIDE OF THE HILL

1 Mark Mazower, *Hitler's Empire, Nazi Rule in Occupied Europe* (London: Allen Lane, 2008).
2 Georg Grossjohann, *Five Years, Four Fronts* (Bedford, Penn.: The Aberjona Press, 1999).
3 Jean-Loup Gassend, *Operation Dragoon: Autopsy of a Battle, The Allied Liberation of the French Riviera, August–September, 1944* (Atglen, Penn.: Schiffer, 2013).
4 Arthur Layton Funk, *The French Resistance, Special Operations and the Landings in Southern France, 1944* (Westport, Conn.: Greenwood Press, 1992).
5 Gassend, *Operation Dragoon: Autopsy of a Battle.*

SIX: READY TO ROLL

1 Stephen Sussna, *Defeat and Triumph: The Story of a Controversial Allied Invasion and French Rebirth* (Philadelphia: Xlibris, 2008).

SEVEN: PLANNING THE LANDINGS

1 Truscott, *Command Missions.*
2 Ibid.
3 Georg Grossjohann (trans. Ulrich Abele), *Five Years, Four Fronts* (London: Aegis 1999).
4 Gassend, *Operation Dragoon: Autopsy of a Battle.*

EIGHT: CHESS GAME OF THE GODS

1 Alanbrooke, *War Diaries.*
2 Truscott, *Command Missions.*
3 J. E. and H. W. Kaufmann, *The American GI in Europe in World War II, The Battle of France* (Mechanicsburg, Penn.: Stackpole Books, 2010).
4 Truscott, *Command Missions.*

NINE: LE MUY FOLLIES

1 Adelman and Walton, *The Champagne Campaign.*
2 Ibid.
3 Gassend, *Operation Dragoon: Autopsy of a Battle.*
4 Adelman and Walton, *The Champagne Campaign.*
5 Gassend, *Operation Dragoon: Autopsy of a Battle.*
6 Ibid.
7 Ibid.
8 Max Arthur, *Men of the Red Beret: Airborne Forces 1940–1990* (London: Hutchinson, 1990).
9 Ibid.
10 Gassend, *Operation Dragoon: Autopsy of a Battle.*
11 Ibid.

12 Adelman and Walton, *The Champagne Campaign.*
13 Ibid.

ELEVEN: THE ASSAULT

1 Truscott, *Command Missions.*
2 Kaufmann and Kaufmann, *The American GI in Europe.*
3 Gassend, *Operation Dragoon.*
4 The 36th Division Archive, Austin, Texas.
5 Kaufmann and Kaufmann, *The American GI in Europe.*
6 Ibid.
7 The 36th Division Archive, Austin, Texas.
8 Kaufmann and Kaufmann, *The American GI in Europe.*
9 Truscott, *Command Missions.*
10 Barbara Brooks Tomblin, *With Utmost Spirit: Allied Naval Operations in the Mediterranean 1942–1945* (Lexington: University Press of Kentucky, 2004).
11 Sussna, *Defeat and Triumph.*
12 Ibid.

TWELVE: BURSTING OUT OF THE BRIDGEHEAD

1 Truscott, *Command Missions.*
2 Ibid.

THIRTEEN: MONTÉLIMAR—THE EYE OF THE NEEDLE

1 Dennis A. Connole, *A "Yankee" in the "Texas Army"* (London: Brassey's, 2008).
2 Truscott, *Command Missions.*
3 Connole, *A "Yankee" in the "Texas Army."*
4 Audie Murphy, *To Hell and Back* (New York: Henry Holt, 2002).

FOURTEEN: PASTIS IN MARSEILLE

1 Truscott, *Command Missions.*

FIFTEEN: THE DRIVE TO DIJON

1 Funk, *The French Resistance.*

SIXTEEN: THE CHAMPAGNE CAMPAIGN

1 Truscott, *Command Missions.*
2 Adelman and Walton, *The Champagne Campaign.*
3 Ibid.
4 Gassend, *Operation Dragoon: Autopsy of a Battle.*
5 Adelman and Walton, *The Champagne Campaign.*
6 Ibid.
7 Tomblin, *With Utmost Spirit.*

INDEX

INDEX

INDEX

INDEX

INDEX

INDEX

INDEX